GEORGE D. VALENTINE

GEORGE D. VALENTINE

A 19TH CENTURY PHOTOGRAPHER IN NEW ZEALAND

KEN HALL

CRAIG
POTTON
PUBLISHING

To Yvonne, Esme and Alberta

First published in 2004 by Craig Potton Publishing
98 Vickerman Street, PO Box 555, Nelson, New Zealand
www.craigpotton.co.nz

Editing: Jane Parkin
Design: Robbie Burton

ISBN 1-877333-12-3
Printed in China through Colorcraft Ltd., Hong Kong

ACKNOWLEDGEMENTS

I sincerely thank all who have helped towards this book and exhibition. Of especial pleasure has been contact with George Valentine's descendants and extended clan in Scotland, England, the United States and Canada, in particular Margaret Fraser, Bunty Watt, Emma Birnie, Ann Patterson, Jean Williams, Sydney Scroggie, Richard Birnie, Muriel Watt, Gordon Valentine and Lorraine Cameron. Encouragement from the late John Valentine is also gratefully acknowledged.

Other invaluable sources of assistance from outside of New Zealand include Roger Taylor, Frances Dimond, Robert N. Smart, Dr Norman Reid, Cilla Jackson, J.B. Ramage, Iain Flett, Dr Alistair J. Durie, Malcolm MacBain, John Bohn, Peter Stubbs, Filmer Lee, Dawn Adiletta, Wendy Chmielewski and Chris Densmore. In New Zealand, my greatest debt is to the late Noleen Hood, for first sharing with me her exquisite album of George Valentine's photographs. Among the many others who have helped I am especially obliged to Gillian Hood, Stuart Broughton, William Main, Mark Strange, R.F. Keam and Neil Roberts. With these, I have also appreciated input and encouragement from John Turner, Ken Downie, John Sullivan, Joan McCracken, Peter Ireland, Annette Facer, Linda Tyler, Roger Blackley, Gordon Maitland, the late Kuru Waaka, Dr Paul Tapsell, Ian Rockel, Patrick McGrath, Tuaari Tuanuku Kuiti Amor, Cherie Meecham, Don Stafford, Philip Andrews, Dr Roger Neich, Maurice Watson, Brian Batchelor, Barbara Smith, Rev Dr J.B. Chambers, J.C. Chamley, Peter Merrick, Joan Woodward, Paul Smith, Murray Hedwig, Mike Bradstock, Rod and Pam Miller, Glenn Busch, Jennifer Hay, Lois Ion, Terry Ryan, Kawiti Tukuru, Ateremu McNeill, Craig Potton, Robbie Burton, Phillippa Duffy and Jane Parkin. I plead pardon from those I have inadvertently missed.

Valued financial assistance in the early stages of this project came through Historical Branch, Department of Internal Affairs in 1994, the Queen Elizabeth II Arts Council in 1993 and the New Zealand 1990 Commission. Thanks to the individuals and institutions who have given permission for photographs to be reproduced and to colleagues at Christchurch Art Gallery Te Puna o Waiwhetu for their very positive support.

Special thanks to Yvonne for all of her enabling support and encouragement.

EXHIBITION TOURING DATES AND VENUES

Christchurch Art Gallery Te Puna o Waiwhetu	2 April – 27 June 2004
Hocken Library, Dunedin	3 September – 24 October 2004
Rotorua Museum of Art and History Te Whare Taonga o Te Arawa	10 December 2004 – 6 March 2005
National Library Gallery, Wellington	8 April – 4 July 2005
Auckland Museum Te Papa Whakahiku	2005

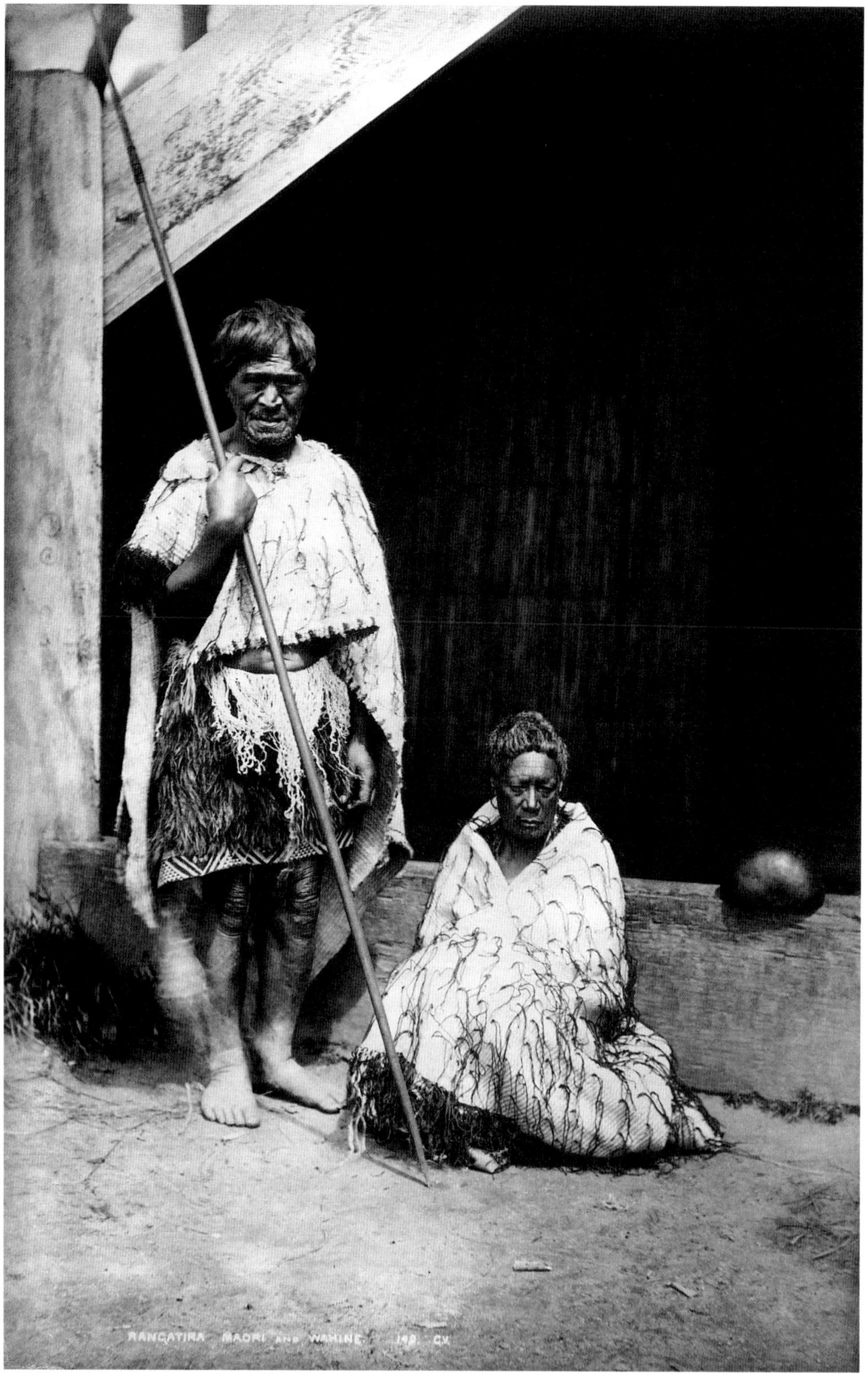

'Rangatira Maori and Wahine', c.1886–87

CONTENTS

INTRODUCTION 8

CHAPTER 1 ~ A PHOTOGRAPHER'S JOURNEY 12

CHAPTER 2 ~ GEORGE D. VALENTINE IN SCOTLAND 14

CHAPTER 3 ~ ANTIPODES 20

CHAPTER 4 ~ HOT LAKES 24

CHAPTER 5 ~ THE PINK AND WHITE TERRACES 36

CHAPTER 6 ~ ACCLAIM 48

CHAPTER 7 ~ ERUPTION 58

CHAPTER 8 ~ AFTERMATH 63

CHAPTER 9 ~ THE SOUTH SEA ISLANDS 82

CHAPTER 10 ~ THERMAL REGION 90

CHAPTER 11 ~ WAITOMO 98

CHAPTER 12 ~ LAST DAYS 103

EPILOGUE 108

ENDNOTES 113

MĀORI GLOSSARY 121

BIBLIOGRAPHY 122

CATALOGUE OF PHOTOGRAPHS BY GEORGE D. VALENTINE 125

PHOTOGRAPH AND ILLUSTRATION SOURCES 128

INDEX 131

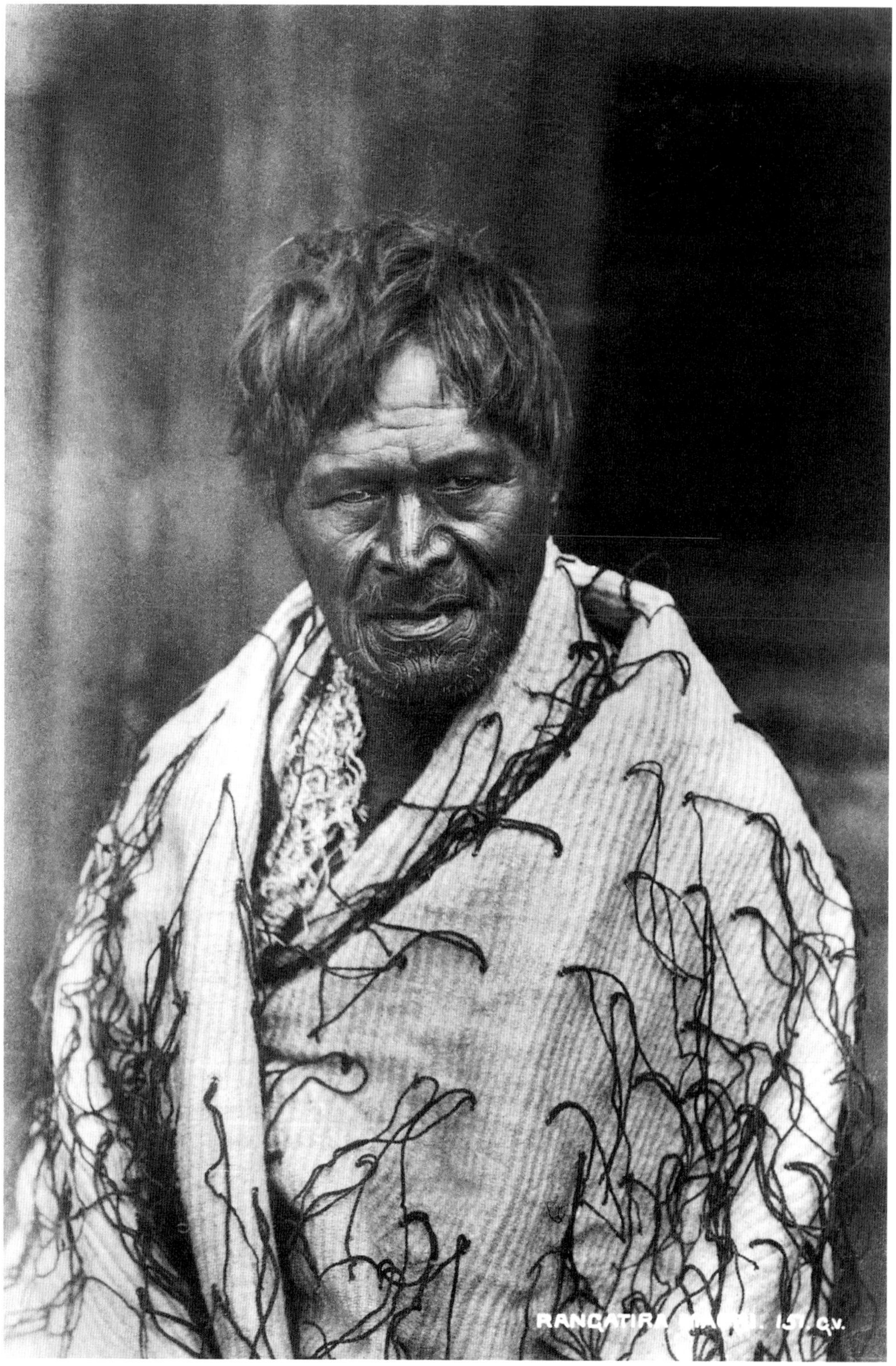

'Rangatira Maori', c.1886–87

Introduction

In his own day, George D. Valentine (1852–1890) was a very well-known photographer. In more recent times his work has come to the attention of a small but devoted band of admirers. William Main in his *History of Photography* article of 1982 prophetically described Valentine as 'an exile whom generations of New Zealanders will come to appreciate more and more as his work begins to become more widely known'.[1] To a small extent this expectation progressed in 1986 through an exhibition marking the centenary of the eruption of Tarawera. In a comprehensive collection of photographs and paintings from before and after the momentous event, George Valentine was recognised as outstanding among photographers of the Thermal Region. Notable others included Daniel Mundy, Charles Spencer, Alfred Burton, Josiah Martin, Charles Pulman and William Collie, with the latter considered Valentine's 'nearest rival in retaining some of the beauty of the Terraces'. Valentine's work was acknowledged also for demonstrating 'a unique combination of classic composition and sharp detail, so that both the whole and the components are interesting'.[2]

Two of Valentine's works from Rotomahana were featured in the 1995 exhibition 'Light from the Dark Room, A Celebration of Scottish Photography', by the National Galleries of Scotland.[3] Here Valentine was described as a 'notable Scottish photographer' – a reasonable proprietary claim, considering that his first 32 years were spent in Dundee and just his final six in New Zealand. New Zealand, however, is where George Valentine found his own means of expression, and where for the first time he could devote himself to the image-bearing potential of an extraordinary landscape. In the Thermal Region and New Zealand bush he created classic, iconic works, and set a high standard for others to follow. The subject matter he sought – silica terraces, thermal geysers, caves or post-eruption landscapes – supplied the work with its own strange and intrinsic beauty, but it is clear that Valentine's engagement with it was strong. Regularly his photographs extend beyond the merely topographical into works which are convincing as consciously artistic, expressive statements – results which were possible only through his enormous facility with the medium. That his approach was strongly intuitive was noted by one of his contemporaries, who once asked Valentine 'what time he had ever given to a particular picture, and he said that he could not tell. He never made a note of his exposures and never troubled to remember them; all he was sure of was "that it was the *correct* time".[4]

With this intuitive approach – and through his appreciation of the variety and scale of nature – Valentine seems to have imparted to many of his works a timeless, spiritual quality. Here a knowledge of his story gives weight to a notion widely accepted in his day, that consumption sufferers (through heightened awareness of their own mortality) increased in spiritual qualities, causing their creative efforts also to flourish in this direction.[5] If such an assessment is difficult to allow, it must at least be possible to accept that George Valentine's circumstances had some effect upon the character of his work, which is so often exceptionally beautiful.

In both significance and impact, Valentine's work was unmistakably altered by Tarawera's eruption. Overnight, categorisation was changed from the scenic or picturesque into historical or documentary. Post-eruption work also fits both categories. Even without a knowledge of what is being depicted, these are some of Valentine's finest images. Accompanied by a knowledge of the event and the historical loss, as well as of his own story, they are even more commanding. Though little known, 'Mnts. Tarawera and Ruawahia from Te Ariki. 129' – the image of Alfred Warbrick's whale-boat and standing boatman above the buried village of Te Ariki – is one of nineteenth-century photography's most potent images.

This book – and the accompanying exhibition – started when I first saw an album of Valentine's photographic albumen prints in 1985. I was touched by the beauty and quality of his work, which seemed to me to rival that of international photographic history's most well-regarded names. Early discussion with William Main (who had been my own photography tutor) confirmed that the person signing his work 'G.V.' was a photographer of significance. I wanted to see more, and a scouring of public collections in New Zealand was to follow. Thus for the first time since Valentine's lifetime a body of his work came together, and pieces of information about his life began to suggest a story requiring its own telling. I was confirmed in the feeling that an assessment of his photography purely in terms of artistic quality, technique, composition or style was insufficient. For me it was equally important to understand the world in which the works were taken, and to place them in a context – one which the photographer himself would have understood. Thus, by connecting photographs with the very real drama of places and events, both personal and public, insights could be gained into what was happening behind the camera and how these works were perceived in their own time.

George Valentine's post-eruption photographs are powerful, framing vast tracts of earth which have been levelled, split apart, heaved aside. Contemporary reportage greatly increases appreciation of such images – especially so the survivors' accounts from the terrible night at Te Wairoa, under Tarawera's increasing shadow. A comparison of photographs of the village from before and after the event offers evidence of the ordeal. In the pre-eruption shot, hotel proprietor Joseph McRae stands confidently in front of his establishment in the company of local Māori chief Aporo Te Wharekaniwha, and surrounded by onlookers. Post-eruption scenes record the same building tottering and dishevelled, surrounded by devastation, with trees and other landmarks stripped of familiarity; or, from the back, with McRae standing amidst the ruins, the building and its contents a crumpling, battered heap.

Understanding this background also increases our admiration for the photographer. We think of his travelling, in his delicate state of health, across steaming, unstable landscapes in a quest to capture the destruction and loss. Or of his photographing the hidden recesses of the Waitomo Caves ('newly discovered' by Europeans) just a few months before his death.

Following George Valentine's story has been a privilege. It has also been a journey, from the vicarious pleasures of an extraordinary nineteenth-century travel experience – and its unexpected end – to a window into our colonial history, the recurring themes of which hold more lasting significance than those justifiably attached to Rotomahana and the Pink and White Terraces.

George D. Valentine's few years in New Zealand were the first in which he was able to focus his talents upon the single-minded pursuit of landscape photography. This book is a tribute to the life and work of a gifted and exceptional photographer.

Ken Hall
2004

TECHNICAL NOTE ON THE PHOTOGRAPHS

George Valentine's photographic output from New Zealand and the Pacific was less than 320 images. Of these, almost 200 have been found, many of these extant as single copies. Often works are in poor condition, with images barely visible. Original glass-plate negatives have never been found. For this book, the copying of a high proportion of the works was expertly done by Mark Strange, at that time with the Museum of New Zealand Te Papa Tongarewa. High-quality prints were produced from 8" x 10" negatives, taken from the album which gave this book its beginning, as well as from a pair of albums in the Alexander Turnbull Library Collection. With these and other photographs used for the book, those faded by time were printed to resemble more closely their original quality. Where appropriate, minor retouching of spots was applied. The book's duotone printing aims to reproduce nineteenth-century albumen print colour and tone. Fifty-six of George Valentine's photographs are included in this book, most of which are being published for the first time.

CHAPTER I

A PHOTOGRAPHER'S JOURNEY

George D. Valentine was relieved to be on land, even if it was at the bottom of the world, or at least the very opposite end of it from his home in Scotland. Five days through a storm from Melbourne had been rough. Now at The Bluff, at the base of the South Island of New Zealand, the steamer discharged its cargo, and the pale, somewhat weary young traveller prepared himself for the last leg of the journey. Next evening, 23 October 1882, the S.S. *Ringarooma* with its 51 passengers left for Dunedin, the colony's largest and most prosperous settlement. Twelve and a half hours up the coast through a strong westerly gale brought the steamer into Port Chalmers at dawn.[1]

The visit was part of a world trip, on which the 30-year-old photographer hoped a change of air might bring improvement to declining health. Despite his youth, he carried an impressive reputation. In the solidly Scottish Dunedin he was greeted as a 'noted home photographer and art critic'.[2] At a photographic society meeting in the city his 'very favourable opinion' on a member's work was also highly regarded, coming as it did from the co-director of one of the largest, most successful photographic enterprises in Britain. Works by the celebrated 'James Valentine & Sons' were to be found on 'almost every drawing-room table' in Scotland.[3] With a production rate of 3,000 prints of 'scenic views' per day, the firm's reputation extended also to America, where they had recently been described as 'gentlemen whose reputation as eminent landscape photographers is world-wide'.[4]

Avoiding the cruelty of Scotland's winter months, George Valentine lingered in the Antipodes long enough to make various stops over the next two months, and appears to have been joined at some point by his wife and young family. After Dunedin he spent a short time in Sydney. In December he travelled to Auckland, where he stayed three days before returning to Dunedin for a further two weeks. Then, on 29 December 1882, with business links established and a general improvement to health, he and his family left New Zealand for the voyage home.[5]

Back in Dundee, Valentine was greeted warmly by family and friends, who were encouraged by the store of health with which he had apparently returned. Those from within his photographic circle of friends looked forward to 'the benefits of his keen observation during his extensive tour'.[6] Valentine himself was pleased to return to the management of a thriving portrait studio.

All of this was to be shattered, and his life rewritten, when at the end of 1883 he and his family were forced to make a permanent departure from Scotland. In his new home in New Zealand, George Valentine would find much to engage his eye and skills. But beyond his exceptional success in capturing the colony's finest natural wonders, events beyond his control would cause his timing to have been immaculate and his reluctant exile to bring surprising recompense.

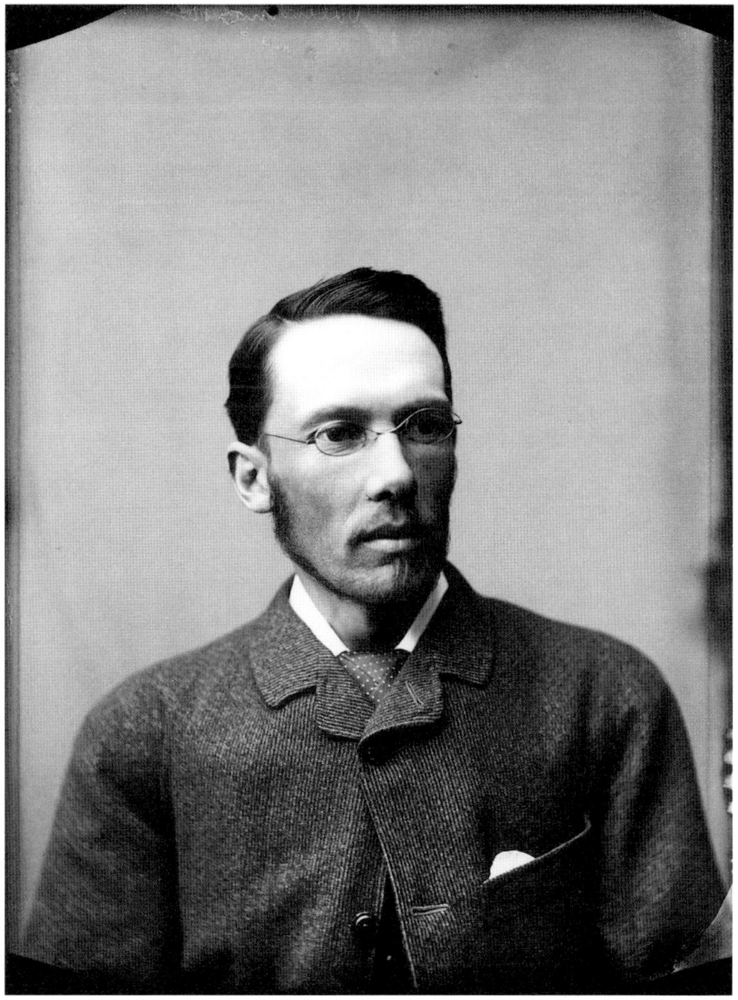

George Valentine, by William Tyree, c.1884–85

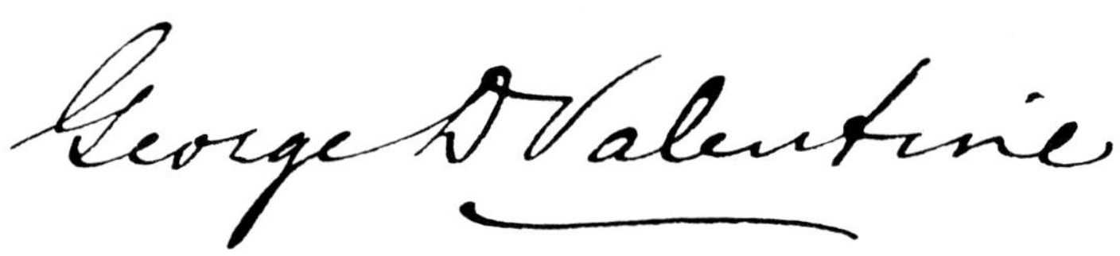

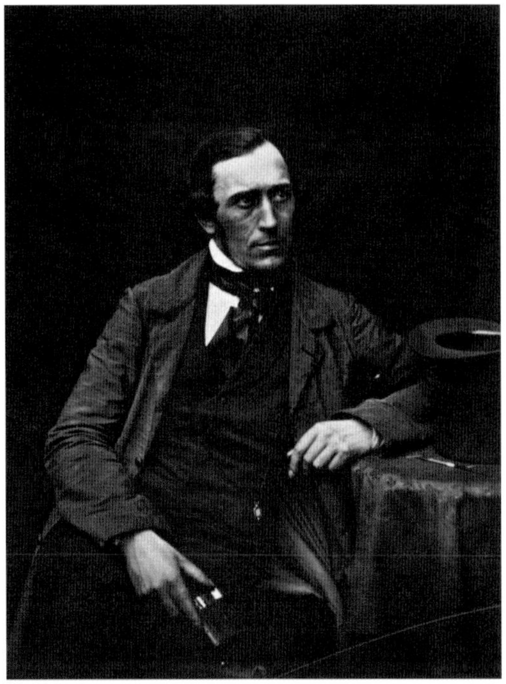

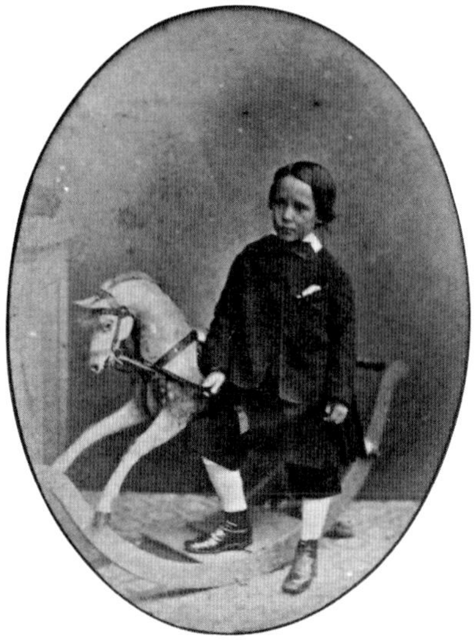

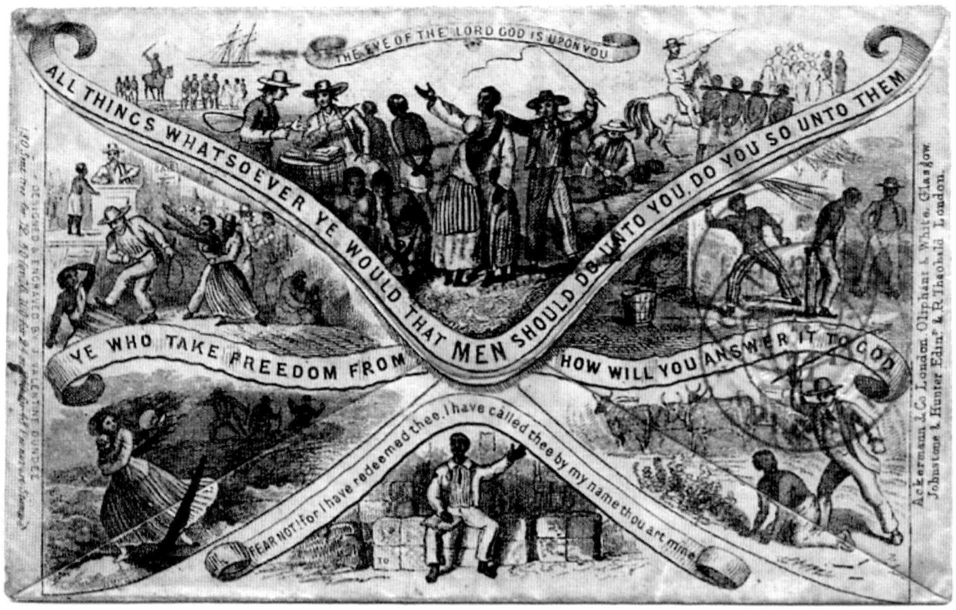

Top left: James Valentine, by Thomas Rodger (attrib.), c.1854
Top right: George Valentine, by James Valentine, c.1856
Left: 'Uncle Tom' Anti-Slavery envelope, by James Valentine, 1854

CHAPTER 2

GEORGE D. VALENTINE IN SCOTLAND

George Dobson Valentine was born on 3 June 1852, the eighth child to the household, in an interesting time and to interesting parents.[1] His father, James Valentine (1815–1879), was an engraver, pioneer photographer and social reformer, who from 1851 to 1854 used his engraving skills to design and publish illustrated envelopes promoting such causes as temperance, the abolition of slavery, 'Universal Brotherhood' and the 'Ocean Penny Post'. Fostering his interest in these causes was a friendship with American social activist Elihu Burritt, a fellow Congregationalist whose trans-Atlantic campaigns Valentine also promoted through engraved notices and pledges of support.[2] George's mother, Rachel Valentine, is also recorded as 'a great worker for the Anti-Slavery Movement' and had been in communication with Harriet Beecher Stowe in 1853.[3] Stowe came to Britain and visited Dundee in 1853 following the 1852 publication of her highly influential *Uncle Tom's Cabin*. One of James Valentine's anti-slavery envelope designs includes images based on illustrations from the novel, and was endorsed by its author; another depicts Britannia sheltering an African slave, while across the sea another slave is mercilessly beaten.[4]

In 1851, the year before George's birth, James Valentine had opened his first 'Photographic Portrait Rooms' in Dundee, so founding a company which would become one of the largest photographic publishing enterprises in the world. In addition to George, two of James's other sons were to become photographers. The eldest, John, became involved with photography in the late 1850s, but in 1863 was forced through ill-health to leave Scotland, settling in the Sandwich Islands (Hawaii) and dying in California in 1867.[5] His second son, William, entered photography in the early 1860s, beginning with a period of study in chemistry at London University, then training under Francis Frith at Reigate, which was no doubt valuable for learning more about the 'view-trade'.[6]

Dundee's close proximity to the major tourist destinations assisted the Valentine company in its success. Visitors with Sir Walter Scott's *The Lady of the Lake* in one hand and a guidebook to the Trossachs in the other all required mementoes of Scotland's wild and romantic places.[7] James Valentine's decision to branch commercially into landscape photography coincided with a commemorative album he made for Queen Victoria in 1864.[8] The Queen's pleasure at his efforts led to annual royal commissions, which included views of locations from Victoria and Albert's 'Great Expeditions', mementoes

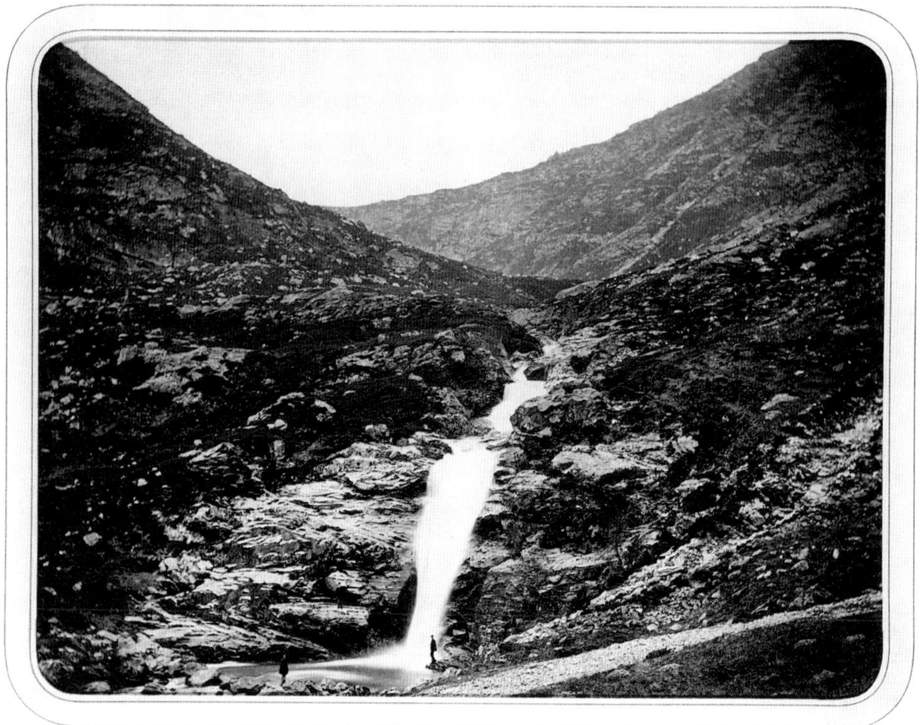

'Falls of Unich', by James Valentine, 1864

of favoured retreats at Balmoral and the Glassalt Shiele, and portraits of Royal family members. In 1868, after four years of royal service, James Valentine was awarded the title 'Photographer to Her Majesty at Dundee in Ordinary'.[9]

Working to expand his register of Scottish scenery, James Valentine travelled regularly throughout the summer months. For the development of his wet-collodion process glass-plate negatives, an ingenious portable darkroom was constructed from a four-wheeled barouche carriage, described by the photographer in 1867 as having 'everything so arranged that only a few minutes' preparation is necessary before commencing my work'.[10] Results from these journeys were sold as 'view cartes', cabinet prints, stereographs or larger albumen prints for albums. As the firm grew and administrative demands increased, William Valentine was conferred primary responsibility for adding to the register of views.

George Valentine joined the firm around the late 1860s and is recorded as having 'chiefly applied himself to local portraiture'.[11] Although the portrait studio became George's responsibility, he also made the occasional foray into landscape photography, evidence of which is revealed in a letter to his brother Easton sometime in the late 1870s from a photographic journey near St. Fillans in Perthshire.[12] With the involvement of three highly skilled cameramen, James Valentine & Sons soon became one of the 'big three' in British photographic publishing, next to George Washington Wilson's in Aberdeen and Francis Frith's in Reigate. In 1878, in a move towards greater efficiency for sales and orders, the Valentine company began numbering, titling and adding the 'J.V.' signature to images. By the end of that year, their rapidly expanding catalogue had 1,713 images of castles, lochs, waterfalls and glens available for an appreciative tourist public.

George Valentine married Williamina Arnot Stirling Smith on 4 November 1876 at nearby Stonehaven. A carte-de-visite of Mina from around this time captures her engaging charm – family lore records her as having been 'the prettiest girl in Stonehaven'.[13] In Dundee, George and Mina lived at the highly respectable address of 2 Johnswood Terrace, where they also kept in employment a domestic servant and a nurse.[14] Their first child, Margaret Rachel, died as an infant of 'teething and hydrocephalus' early in 1879.[15] A second daughter, Mary Smith Valentine, was born later that year, a week before the death of George's father James Valentine. In 1880 a son, James, was born. By this time, George and his brother were equal partners in the business.

The portrait studio must have been a profitable concern, with the 1881 census listing George Valentine as providing employment for 12 men, 16 girls and three boys. A pair of carte-de-visite portraits in one of Queen Victoria's albums, taken in 1880, show that his work also found a

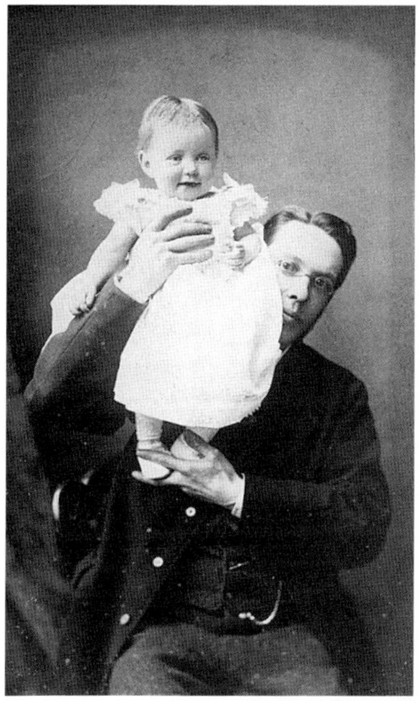 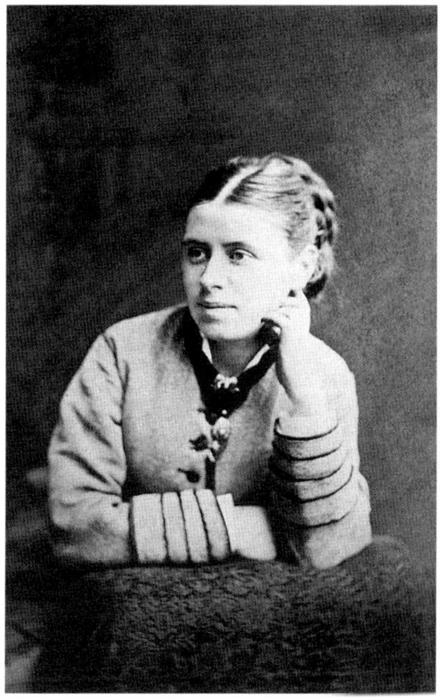 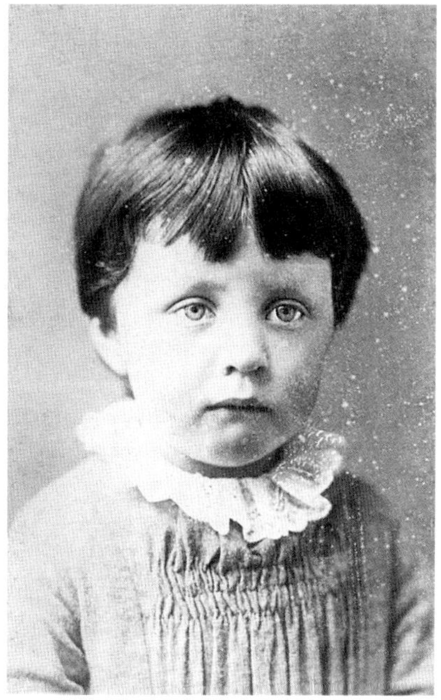 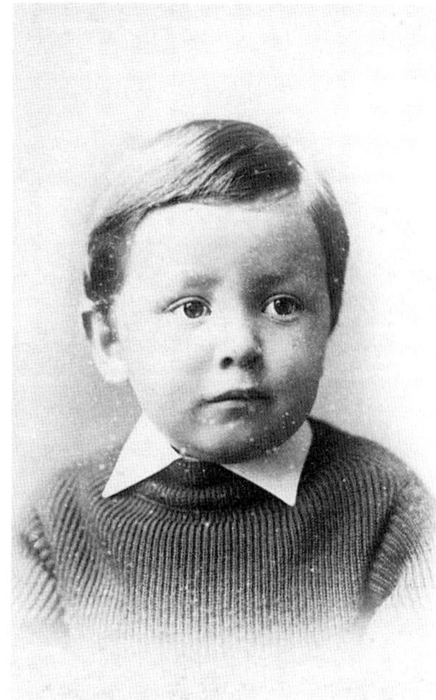

Left to right: George and Margaret Rachel Valentine, c.1878; Williamina Arnot Stirling Smith, c.1876; Mary Smith Valentine, c.1882–83; James Valentine, c.1882–83

royal audience, the photographs being of Mrs Grant and her daughter Victoria, the wife and daughter of Balmoral's Head Keeper.[16]

In 1880 George Valentine became founding vice-president of the Dundee and East of Scotland Photographic Association. Open to both professionals and amateurs (with 'lady members also welcome'), the association was one which encouraged members in all aspects of photography, and advances both technical and artistic.[17] Regular competitions, photographic outings and discussions were also included, along with visiting speakers, among them Eadweard Muybridge – famous for his 'studies in motion' – whose visit was being planned for mid-1882. George is recorded as being always at the fore in 'Exhibitions, Out-door Meetings, or anything calculated to promote the good of the Society'.[18]

In *The Photographic News* of 1882 the Valentine operation was featured in detail and the opinion given that the Valentine brothers had proven themselves 'in every way equal to the task of carrying out their father's designs'. It was noted that 40 employees were engaged all year round, with 3,000 prints a day 'not an unusual number to produce'. Albumen prints were exposed under glass-plate negatives and sunlight; here ('at any rate in dull weather') as many as 700 frames could be found on the printing tables. William was credited with being 'responsible for the negatives' of views of Scotland, and with having created

> ... the most delightful scenes that have ever been taken of that delightful country. Every phase of Scottish scenery is here. A cluster of dark granite boulders, strewn with brown seaweed, and beaten by angry waves, whose white foam is tritely characteristic of their spent wrath; a placid loch, with stately craft floating calmly on its surface; a solitary lighthouse of silver grey, riding from a clump of black rocks, and surrounded by turbulent waves flecked with white – a very painting; lichen-grown crags, sweet forest glades,

> delicate fern gardens, bowery foliage – in a word, nature in every shape and mood is here represented.

George's domain was also acknowledged in the observation that 'The Messrs. Valentine also enjoy high reputation as portraitists, and it is, indeed, into the portion of the establishment devoted to portraiture that we are first led. A hall tastefully furnished leads to the reception-room, whence again a corridor takes us through the dressing-rooms to the studio.' An open, glowing 'gas cinder' fire in the reception area connected to a heating system that piped hot water throughout the building, including to the glass-roofed portrait studio where snowfall would quickly be melted by the room's nicely warmed atmosphere. It was also noted that the firm had the only steam-powered print burnisher in the world, and that silver residue from washing prints was ingeniously collected and sold by the firm – £30 worth in the previous year. It was indeed an impressive operation, two pages of fine-print description leaving the writer regretting that 'we feel we have done but scanty justice to this magnificent establishment'.[19]

Under the Valentine brothers' capable management, the firm had an assured future and was set for every good prospect. George Valentine, however, had been experiencing less than perfect health, suffering pain, bouts of exhaustion, sometimes a fever and a cough. Following a doctor's examination, the 30-year-old photographer received the awful news that he had the dreaded pulmonary phthisis or consumption – tuberculosis of the lungs.[20]

The implications of such a diagnosis – this was a disease responsible for one in every seven deaths – were impossible to ignore.[21] In its early stages, George's best course of action was to leave Dundee and its cold, grey winters, and to seek clean air, sunshine and open space elsewhere. A world trip to warmer climes (including New Zealand) in 1882–1883 at first seemed to sidestep the need for emigration through the improvements gained. Back in Scotland, he made an attempt to resume life as normal, with running the portrait studio, photographic society meetings and outings and likely the occasional visit to the Scottish countryside to add to the 'Valentine & Sons' register of views. By the onset of winter, however, George was compelled once again to take serious stock of his health. His doctor's advice was to leave Scotland and this time to make a permanent departure for New Zealand, which was fresh in his experience and had a climate thought to be 'highly favourable to people of consumptive tendencies'.[22]

It was to be a sudden farewell to everything that was familiar: home, friends and relations; the thriving family business; and old Dundee with its docks, factories and grey stone buildings built to last. If this was a total personal upheaval, it was also his only hope against an inevitable decline. George Dobson Valentine saw his last view of Scotland on 25 November 1883, sailing alone for New Zealand, with his wife and children soon to follow.[23]

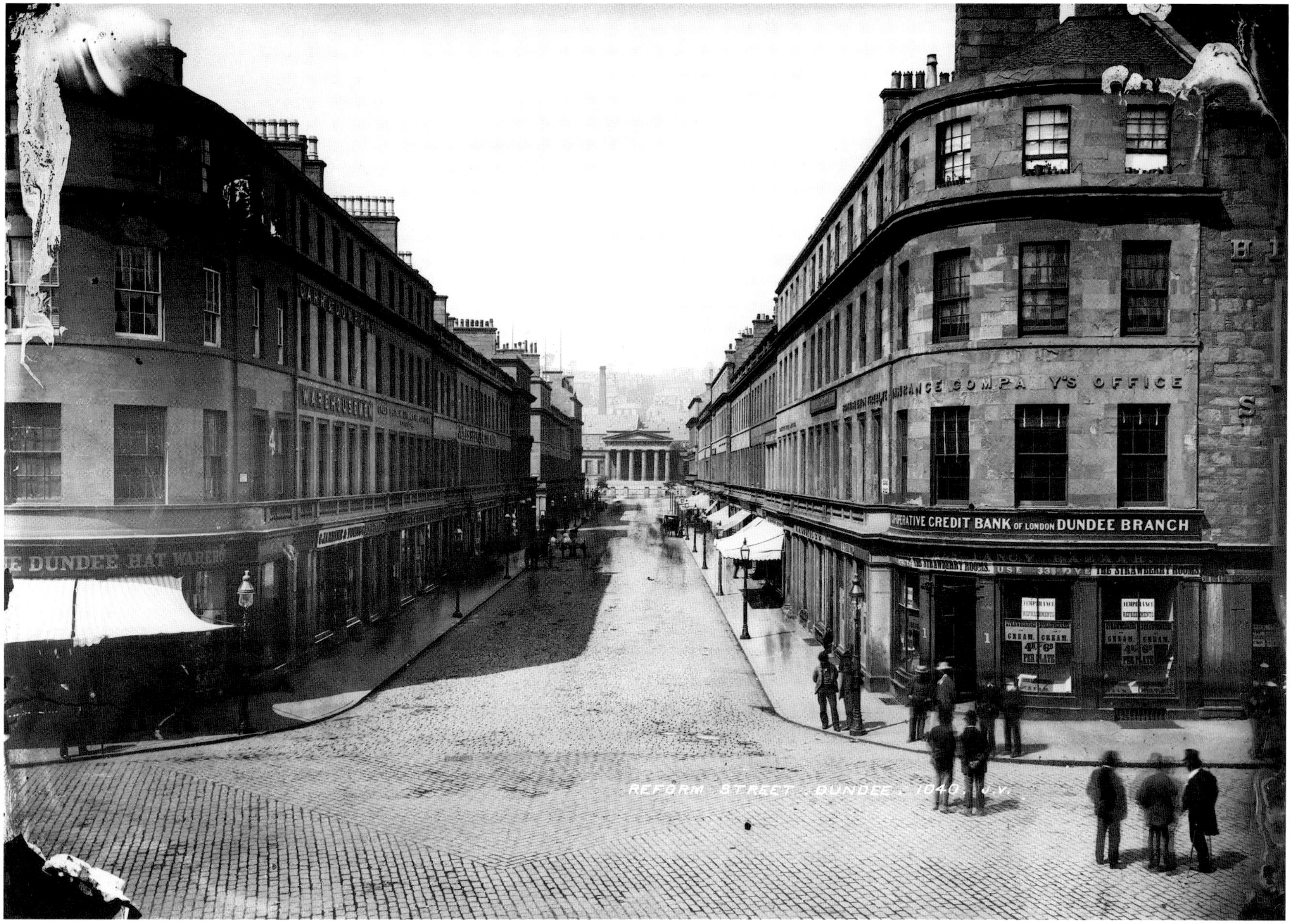

'Reform Street, Dundee', c.1875–78

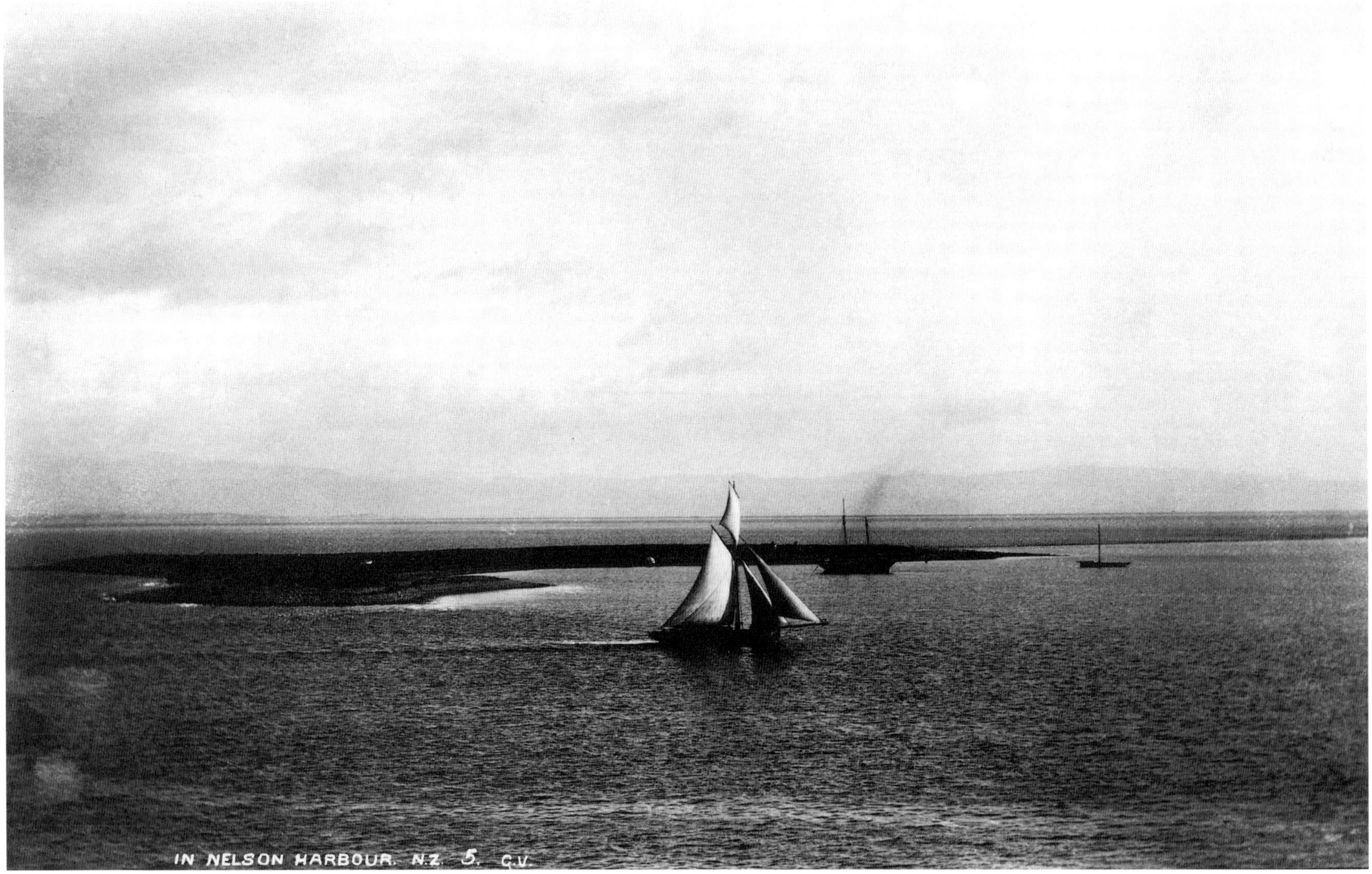

'In Nelson Harbour, N.Z.', 1884

CHAPTER 3

ANTIPODES

George Valentine reached Auckland late in January 1884 and was joined in the following month by Mina, James and Mary.[1] Soon afterwards the Valentines left for Nelson, a flourishing settlement at the northern end of the South Island. Here they found the ideal environment for George's prescription of rest and being out of doors as much as possible, with horse riding, beaches, fresh sea air and a sunny climate all making their contribution. Rented accommodation was found in a wooden house overlooking the sea, away from the main part of the town. 'Walmer House', with its view across the harbour, had been home to the late Nelson pilot and harbourmaster, Captain James Cross, before his death in 1882.[2] James Cross was the first European to step ashore in Nelson in 1842 and had been hailed as the natural harbour's 'discoverer', with help from a local Māori who knew it to be suitable to the needs of the arriving colonists.

By 1884 the immigrants had truly outnumbered the indigenous Māori inhabitants by more than 12 to one, with Europeans born in the colony about to exceed the number of those born on British soil. Long had the Treaty of Waitangi giving Māori the full rights of British citizens been cast aside – in the minds of many, they were 'a dying race' and heading for extinction.[3] Indeed, numbers of Māori were still heavily in decline, even as the total population in the previous decade doubled, with Europeans now at over half a million and immigration still a strong tide.[4]

While hardly reconciled to their own new-found settler status, the Valentines received some compensation through friendships old and new, including with the Patties of Riwaka (a pioneering family from the same part of Scotland), local merchant grocer M.M. Webster and his family, and contacts through the Scottish Congregational movement.[5] Of wider interest is George Valentine's friendship with local photographer William Tyree, a son-in-law to the late Captain Cross and someone with whom Valentine had much in common. The 'Tyree Brothers' operation specialised in both portraiture and landscapes, with William running the portrait studio while his brother Frederick worked at building up a large collection of 'scenic images'.[6]

George Valentine's own photography in New Zealand began in his immediate surroundings with a small set of views of the town and its harbour.[7] Following this came the decision to publish using his own 'G.V.' signature, given first to a small series of sea, ships and sails – images which seem

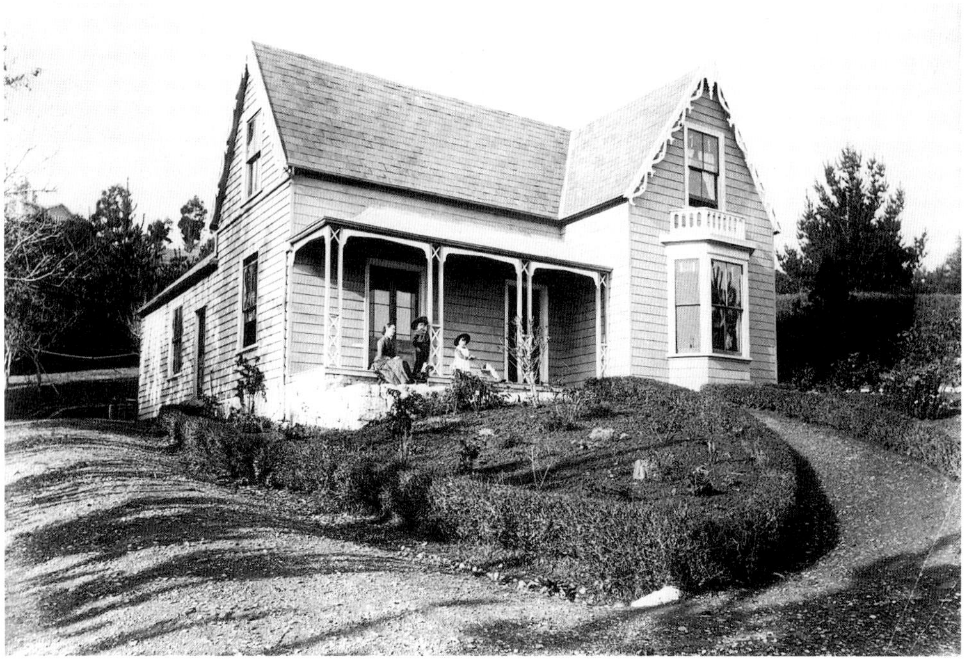

'House of G.D. Valentine in New Zealand', 'Walmer House', Mary Ann Street, Nelson, c.1884–85

quietly symbolic of arrival and isolation.

A letter written by George at the end of that first year to a favourite aunt in Scotland reveals much of his state of mind, shedding light also upon some of the trials of colonial life, including the common difficulty of holding onto one's 'domestic help':

> Walmer House, Nelson 7 November 1884
> My dear Aunt,
>
> Just a few lines to arrive about Xmas so as to wish you all the best wishes of the season – it will be strange for us here to be spending Xmas in very hot weather and so far from all that we hold dear. Our thoughts will be with you all, as I have no doubt yours will be with us ... Now as to news I am afraid it will have to be the old story of egotism or nothing, for really there is nothing to be seen or heard here that would be of the slightest interest to any of you.
>
> Several weeks ago I had a very pleasant run up to Auckland for a week to visit my friends the Chapmans (one of the daughters who is at home on a visit was staying with Willie's folks). While in Auckland, I was spending the evening at a friend's house when a lady called, and on hearing I was in the house, she said her visit was to hear about me. She said a friend of hers asked her to come and hear from my friends when I was to be found, as she must see me before I left Auckland. This friend turned out to be Mrs. Whitelaw or you will know her better as Grace Hutton – as she only lived a short way off she was sent for and came at once. I have no recollection of her whatever but she says that very likely I was only an infant when she used to come about the house. She was greatly delighted to see me and amused us all very much by every now and again exclaiming eh you're like your Mother or Father as the fancy seemed to strike her ...
>
> I went with her to see her husband who is very ill a case evidently of consumption (I have heard last week that he is much worse and that their youngest child is dead). [He has] a family of twelve and dependent on his salary. He is an accountant in the Bank of New Zealand with £700 a year, but that of course will be no provision for them. Mrs. Whitelaw is a very bright happy being and I am sure poor thing she has enough to depress her ... Mrs. Whitelaw exclaimed when she saw me, you don't look very ill! as my friend Mr. Knox said in comparison with her husband I looked the very picture of health. I am very sorry for them, dear me what a world of sorrow – there seems hardly room for much joy.
>
> You will all be delighted to hear that my health continues to improve steadily. This is putting us all in a brighter and more hopeful frame of mind and I think if the improvement only continues that through time we may

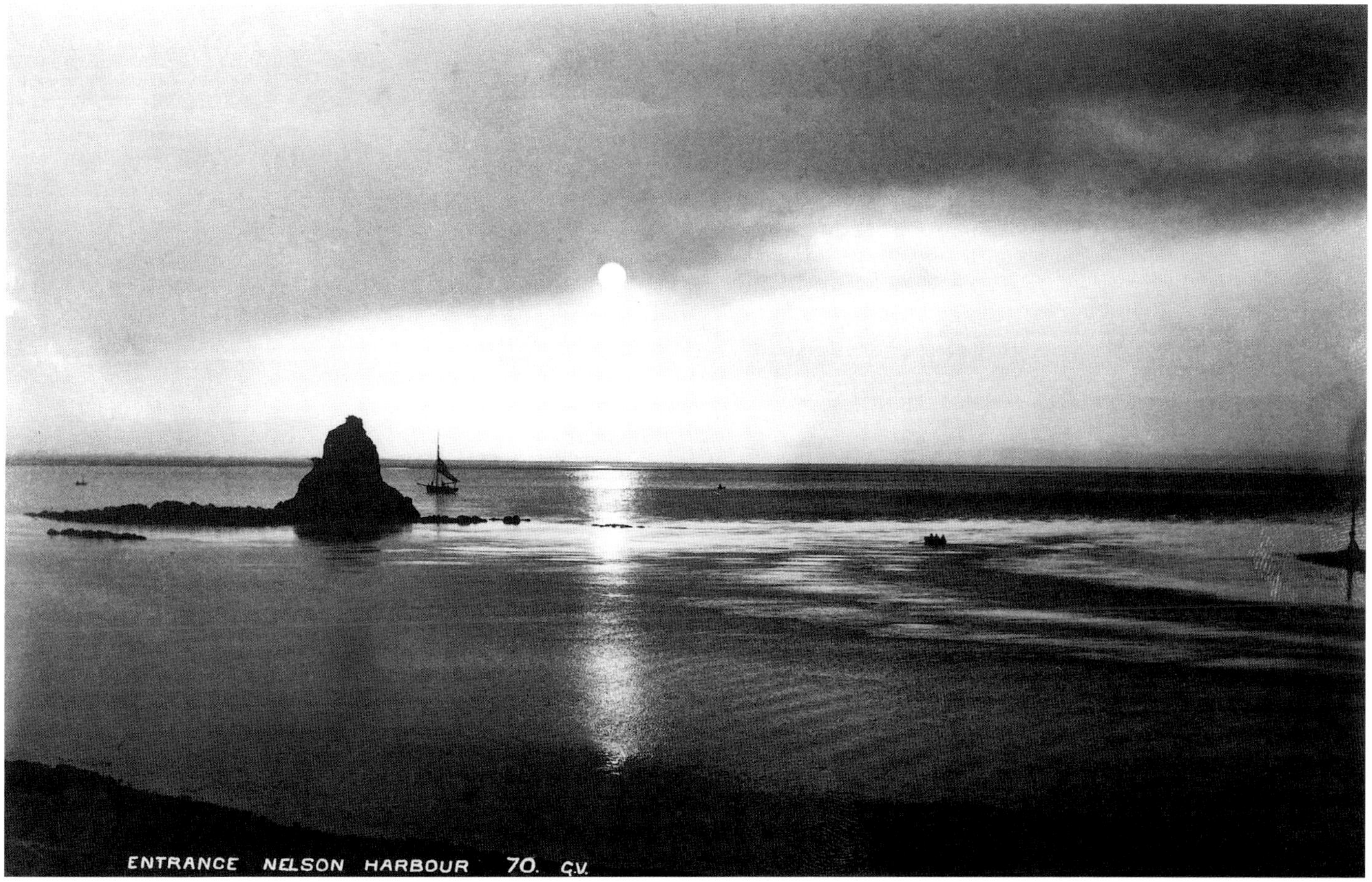

'Entrance Nelson Harbour', 1885

begin to feel less banished (that's not a very proper term – tell the maister to skip this bit) and take more kindly to colonial life ...

Mr. Pattie was down to tea last night. I am going over to his place end of this month, when he and I are to have a holiday! Don't laugh, for I have been working so need holidays like other folk – its the fashion here. I have sown three rows of peas and two of lettuce – my horse got mixed up with the peas sticks and ate the peas, and the hens eat the lettuce, so I have come to the conclusion that gardening is not my forte ... Our servant lassie is going away to see her sister and not coming back, and as we have not got another I have taken the work in hand, only I don't think I will please the mistress, and as I have no sister to go and see handy, I will go and see Mr. Pattie. Now I think I have conclusively proved the urgent need I have of a holiday, and if you are not satisfied, I am, and as I have another letter to write tonight I will have to ask you to be good enough to let this rubbish pass muster for a letter and take the will for the deed ...

Now with very kindest regards to all in which Mina joins, I am, Your affectionate nephew, George D. Valentine.[8]

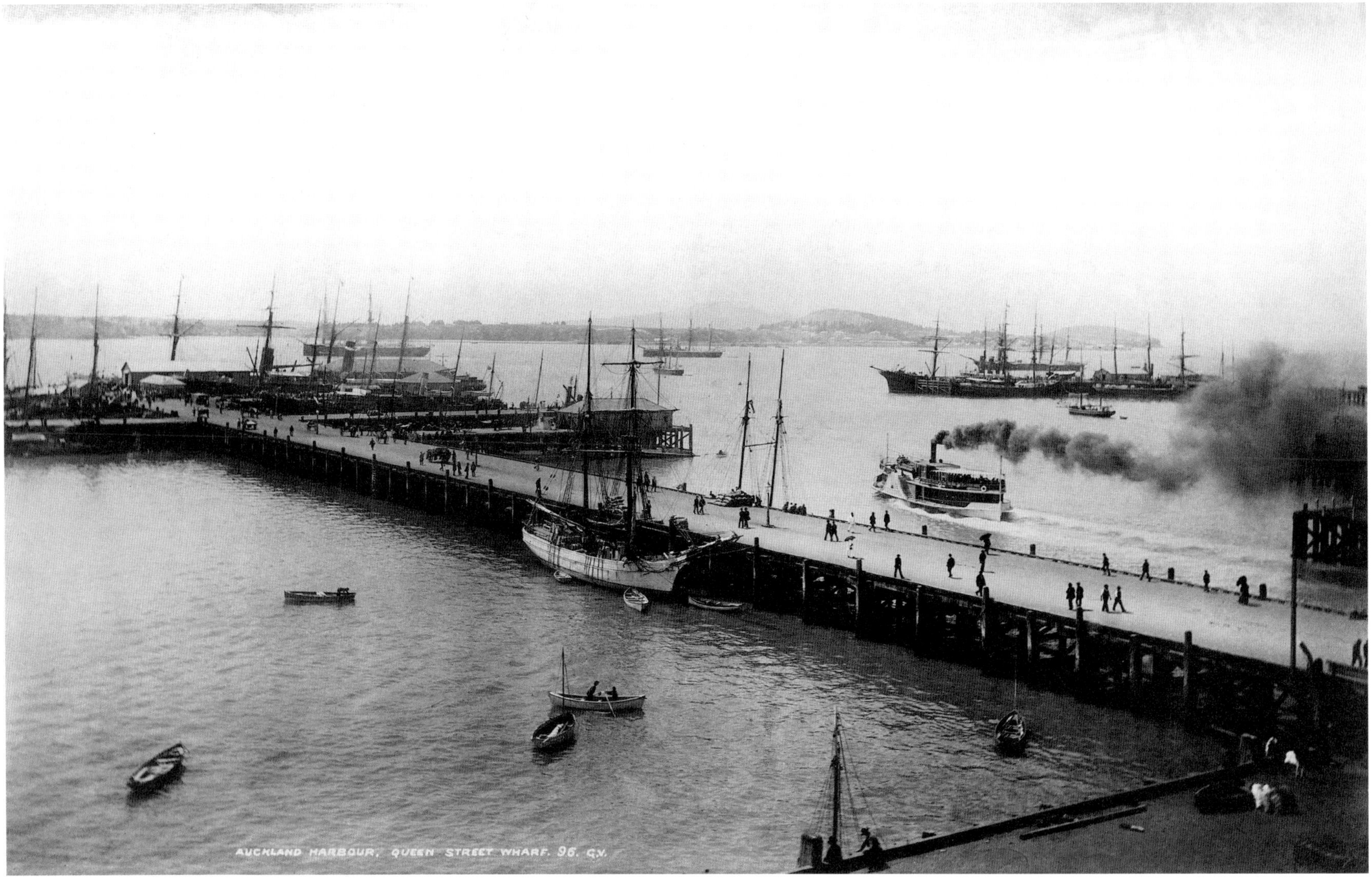

'Auckland Harbour, Queen Street Wharf', c.1885–86

CHAPTER 4

HOT LAKES

As 1885 began, George Valentine prepared himself for a more ambitious, working photographic journey, through an invitation from Auckland bookseller Charles R. Chapman, whom Valentine had visited on his recent trip to Auckland. The intended destination was the North Island's Hot Lakes, or Rotomahana District, a destination for which Chapman's late father, George T. Chapman, had published two guidebooks.[1] Valentine's principal task would be to match his talents to capturing the Pink and White Terraces – Ōtūkapuarangi and Te Tarata – world-renowned geothermal attractions hailed by many as the 'Eighth Wonder of the World' and responsible for a great influx of tourist traffic to the colony.

The Terraces were two shining natural staircases spreading fan-like beneath a hot spring and a geyser on opposite shores of Rotomahana, a small lake in the heart of the Thermal Region. Constantly bubbling silica-charged waters had through countless years of geothermal ebb and flow erupted and cascaded to construct these celebrated formations. Generations of Te Arawa Tūhourangi had used their hot-water basins for luxurious bathing. From the early 1880s, they had become New Zealand's principal tourist attractions, with British Royalty, Royal Geological Society experts and famous authors, poets and artists among those to have experienced their glories. In a deluge of published applause, even the most well-travelled had declared them to be nature's finest wonders. American adventure writer Thomas W. Knox had likened the glistening Terraces to 'a collection of all the precious stones in the world'.[2] Another American visitor, the self-styled poet Frank Cowan, had devoted 24 pages of passionate prose poetry to the Terraces, hailing them as 'The Taj dissolved indeed ...'[3]

On a two-day steamer journey from Nelson, George Valentine reached Auckland on 7 January 1885.[4] With Chapman, the plan was formed to spend an ambitious ten days at Rotomahana so that the wonders of the lake might be captured in a way never done before.[5] In the papers, however, Valentine and Chapman read of recent troubles experienced there by the artist Charles Blomfield – obstacles which could affect their own intended journey.

The Auckland artist and his eight-year-old daughter Mary were camping at the lake for six weeks over the summer, for the purpose of arresting Rotomahana's beauty upon canvas. Normally the Tūhourangi tribe who owned the lake

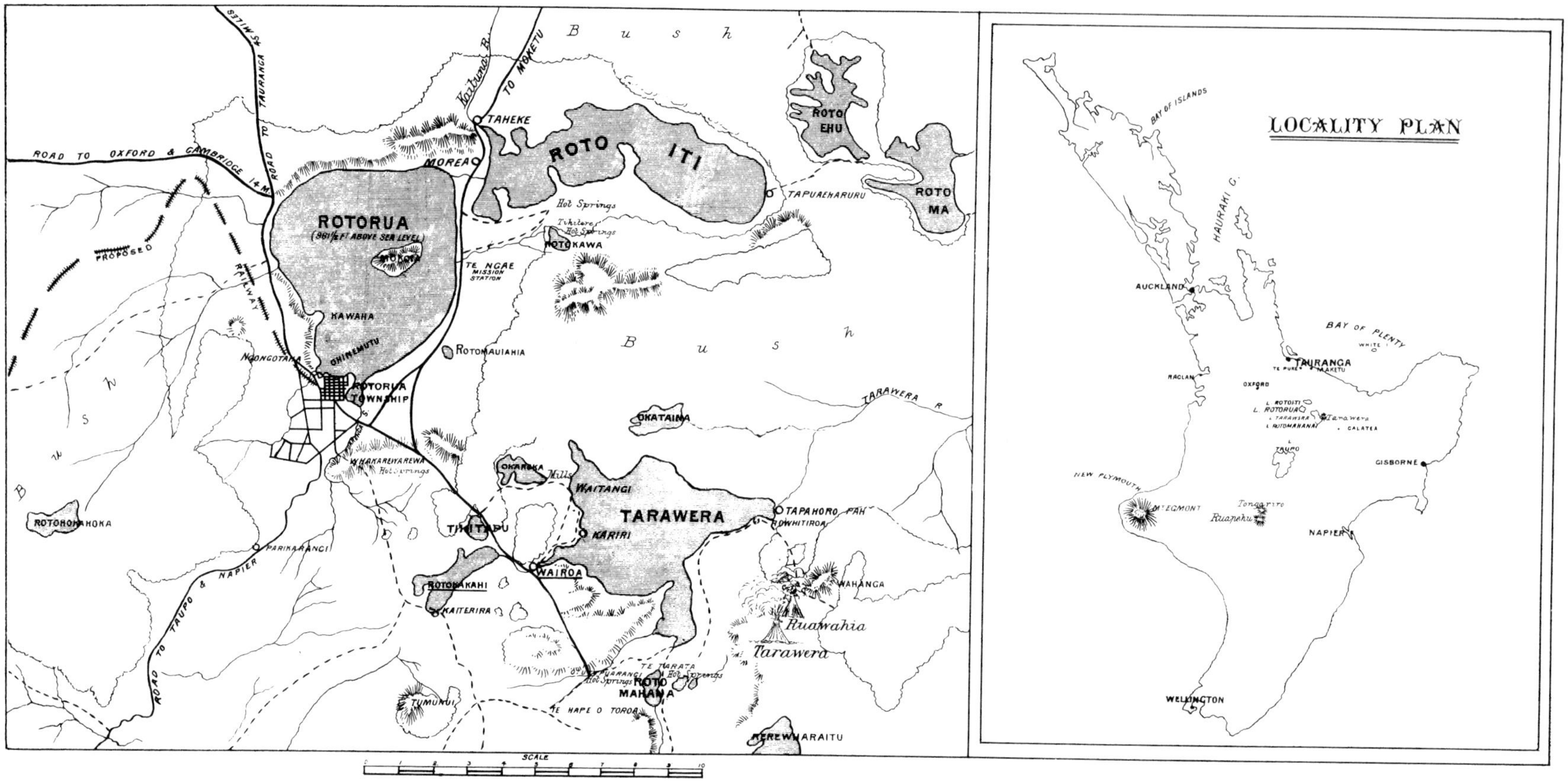

Map of North Island and Thermal District, 1886

had charged artists and photographers £5 for the privilege of working there, and as a consequence 'no important paintings had been attempted by any artist'. Custom also ruled that no one could visit the lake without a Māori guide, so Blomfield, 'determined', as he put it, 'to spend some weeks there, and do the thing properly', had found it 'necessary to make arrangements with the natives beforehand'. This was done through his friend at Te Wairoa, the schoolteacher Mr Haszard, who 'was in treaty with the different chiefs interested for some weeks, and at last a big meeting was called to decide the question. Finally after much talk, an agreement was come to. Upon the payment down of a lump sum, I was to be allowed to come and camp on the lake, to bring my own boat, to stay as long as I pleased, and not be interfered with by anybody.'

On his way to the Terraces, however, Blomfield was met by local chief Tamihana Te Keu (known also as 'Thompson') who, claiming the payment to the Te Wairoa chiefs had nothing to do with him, demanded from the artist an extra £5 10s a day to look after him. Despite threats of a soaking in the lake, Blomfield refused. He was greatly relieved by the arrival on horseback of Clara Haszard, his friend's eldest daughter, who in fluent Māori warned Tamihana Te Keu of bringing in the principal chief Te Rangipuawhe – a warning which soon brought an end to the demands.[6]

Uncertain as to what they themselves should expect,

Valentine and Chapman left Auckland on their two-day journey to the Thermal Region, travelling by rail to Cambridge, then by coach to Ōhinemutu.[7] The overland route was also preferred by invalids, a growing number of whom were heading to Ōhinemutu for the reputed healing virtues of the region's sulphur springs. Unfortunately their benefits did not extend to consumptives, but for Valentine, as for most who came, the region's chief attractions were its scenery. For this he was well prepared, with camera and tripod, a small number of wooden plate-holders and a fairly heavy, carefully packed case of pre-prepared 12" x 10" 'dry-plate' glass negatives.[8] While these glass plates were cumbersome, he was at least spared the need to travel with a portable darkroom, the recent innovation of 'dry-plate' photography allowing him to process exposed negatives more comfortably later.

A hundred miles from Auckland the rail journey ended at the fast-growing settlement of Cambridge, which was observed by British author James Froude as 'a village developing into a town on the edge of the Māori location to which it had once belonged'. Forfeited from its Māori owners in the sham justice following the 1860s wars, Cambridge was now the 'point of departure to the hot lakes, to and from which swarms of tourists were passing and repassing'. Following an overnight stay, they continued their journey through open, rolling, uncultivated country before they reached the quaintly named Oxford (Tirau), which Froude described as having 'Instead of domes and towers, and colleges and cloistered avenues ... a solitary wayside inn on the ridge of a high range of hills.'[9] A few miles further on was the entrance to a dense forest, and a road which had opened to wheeled traffic not many months before.

It would take all day for Valentine and Chapman to leave this forest and to reach the Hot Lakes District, where the road descended rapidly 'as if into a basin surrounded by hills and mountains, among which the sharp peaks of

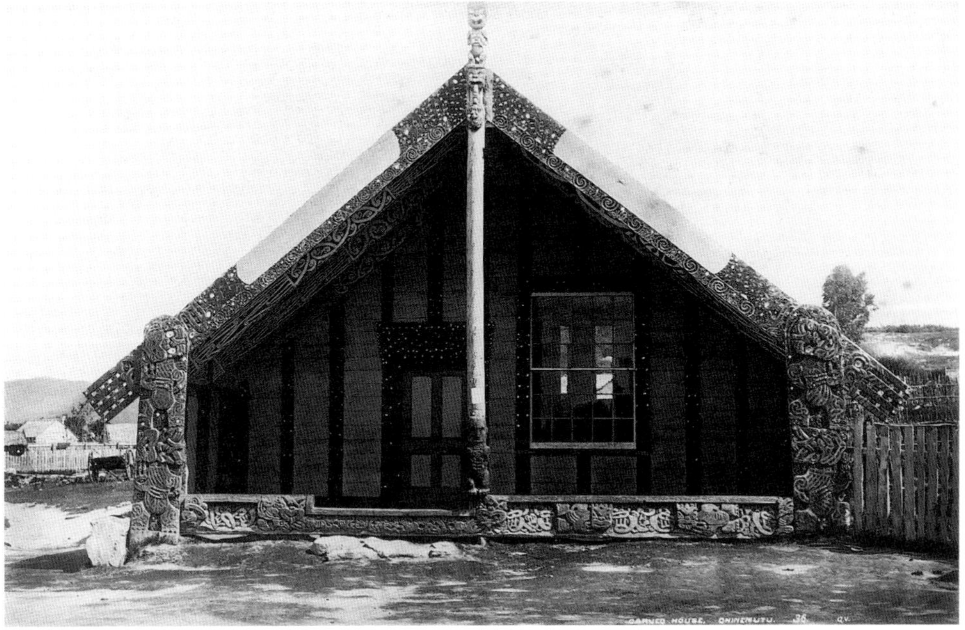

'Carved House, Ohinemutu', [Tamatekapua], 1885

famed Tarawera were conspicuous by their rugged grandeur. Right in front, the shining surface of Lake Rotorua caught the last rays of the setting sun, while on its shore the white houses of Ōhinemutu rose, one above the other, from rolling clouds of steam, when suddenly even the water flowing by the side of the road bubbled up and smoked, and, as we pulled up at Lake House, and the mists of evening mingled with the vapours around, we seemed to have arrived at a region of eternal fire.'[10] From the four hotels in the town, G.T. Chapman had favoured Robert Graham's Lake House for its 'commodious and comfortable' style and commanding view from 'one of the prettiest sites in Ohinemutu'.[11] Here were to be found well-heeled travellers from all parts of the globe – London, Capetown, Glasgow, Paris, Bombay and New York. Wishing to head straight for the Terraces after a night in the thermal village, Valentine and Chapman were hindered by poor weather, and decided to delay.[12]

In the meanwhile, Ōhinemutu held a fascination of its

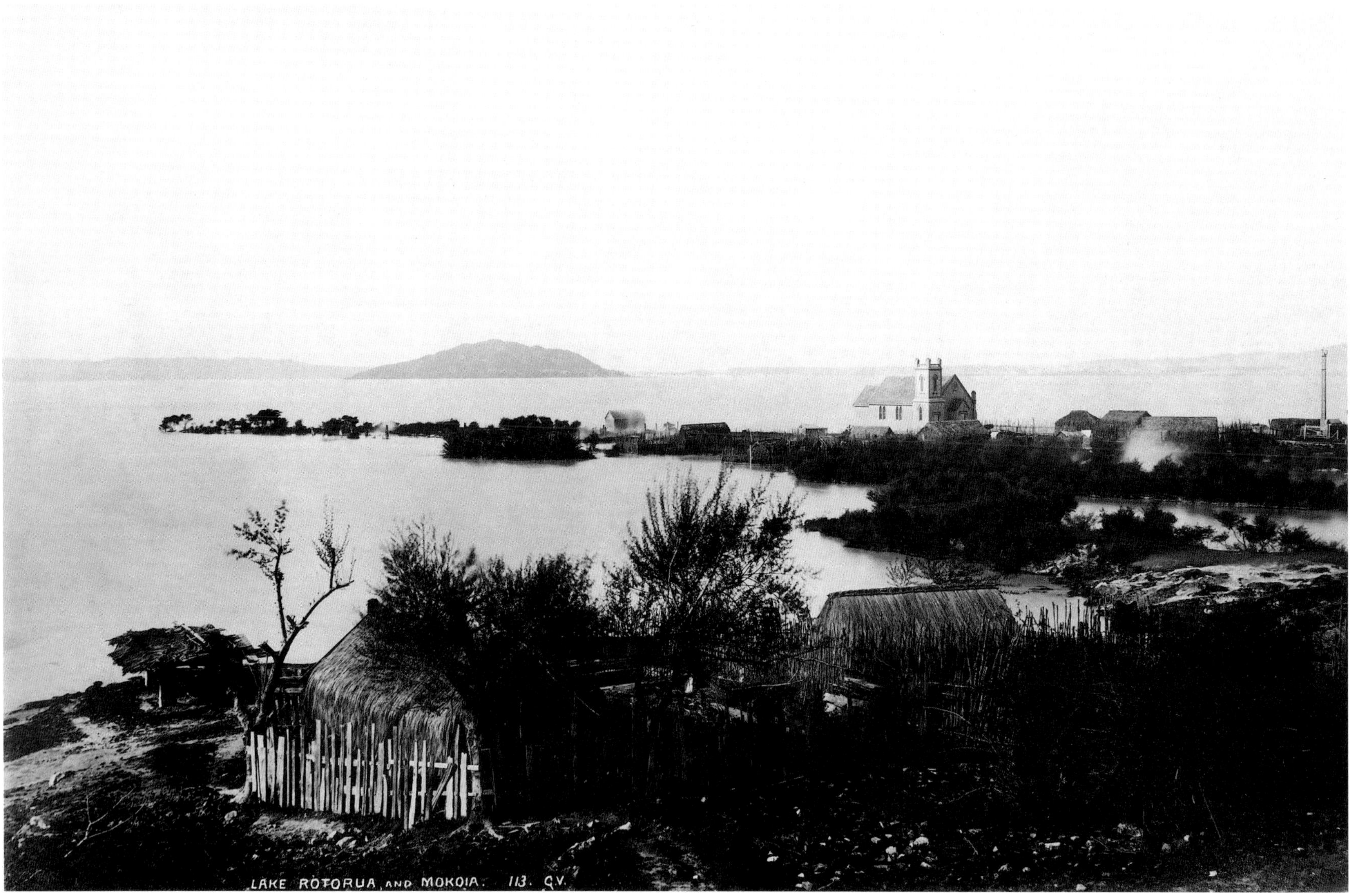

'Lake Rotorua and Mokoia', 1886

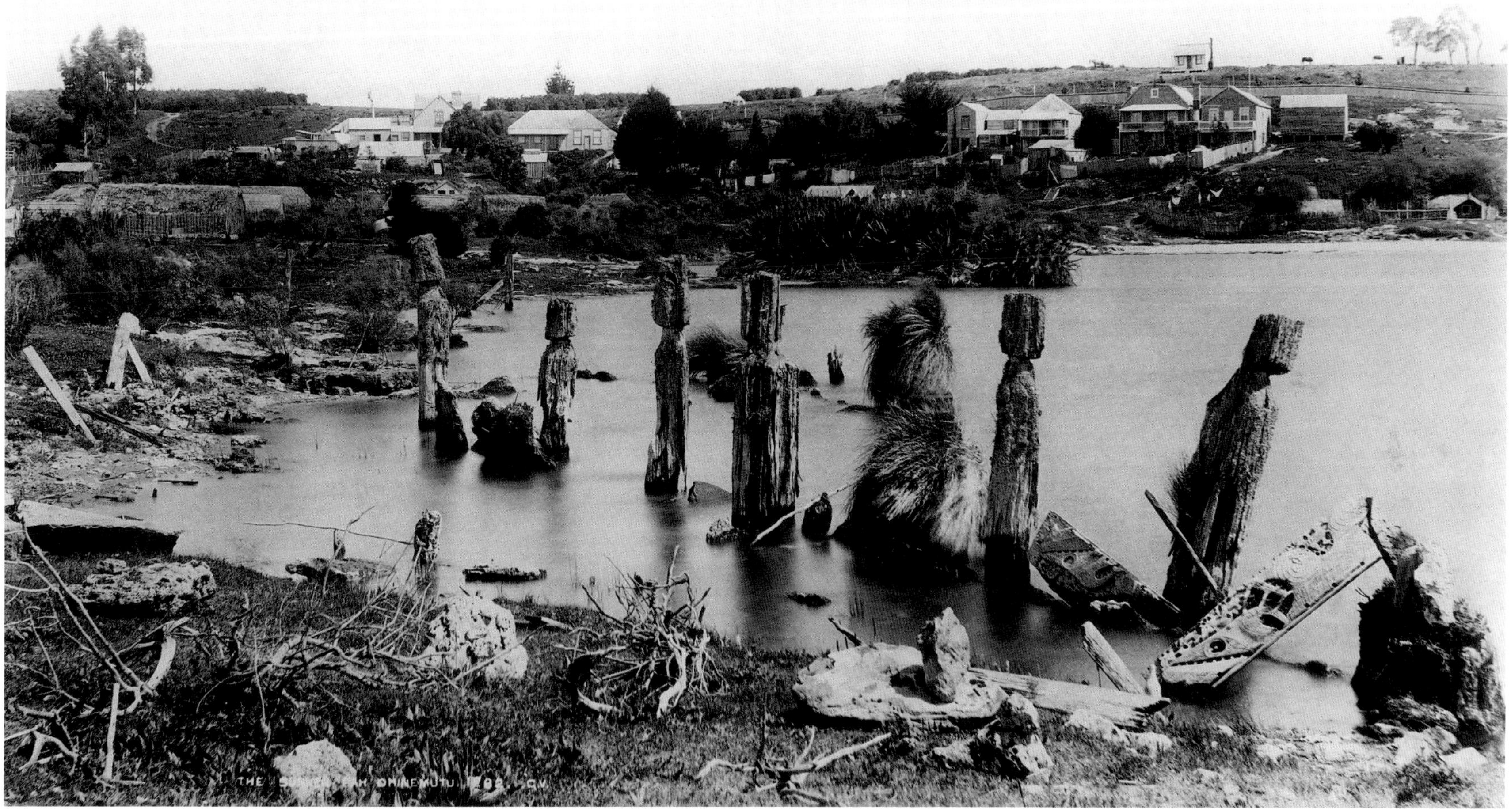

'The Sunken Pah, Ohinemutu', 1889

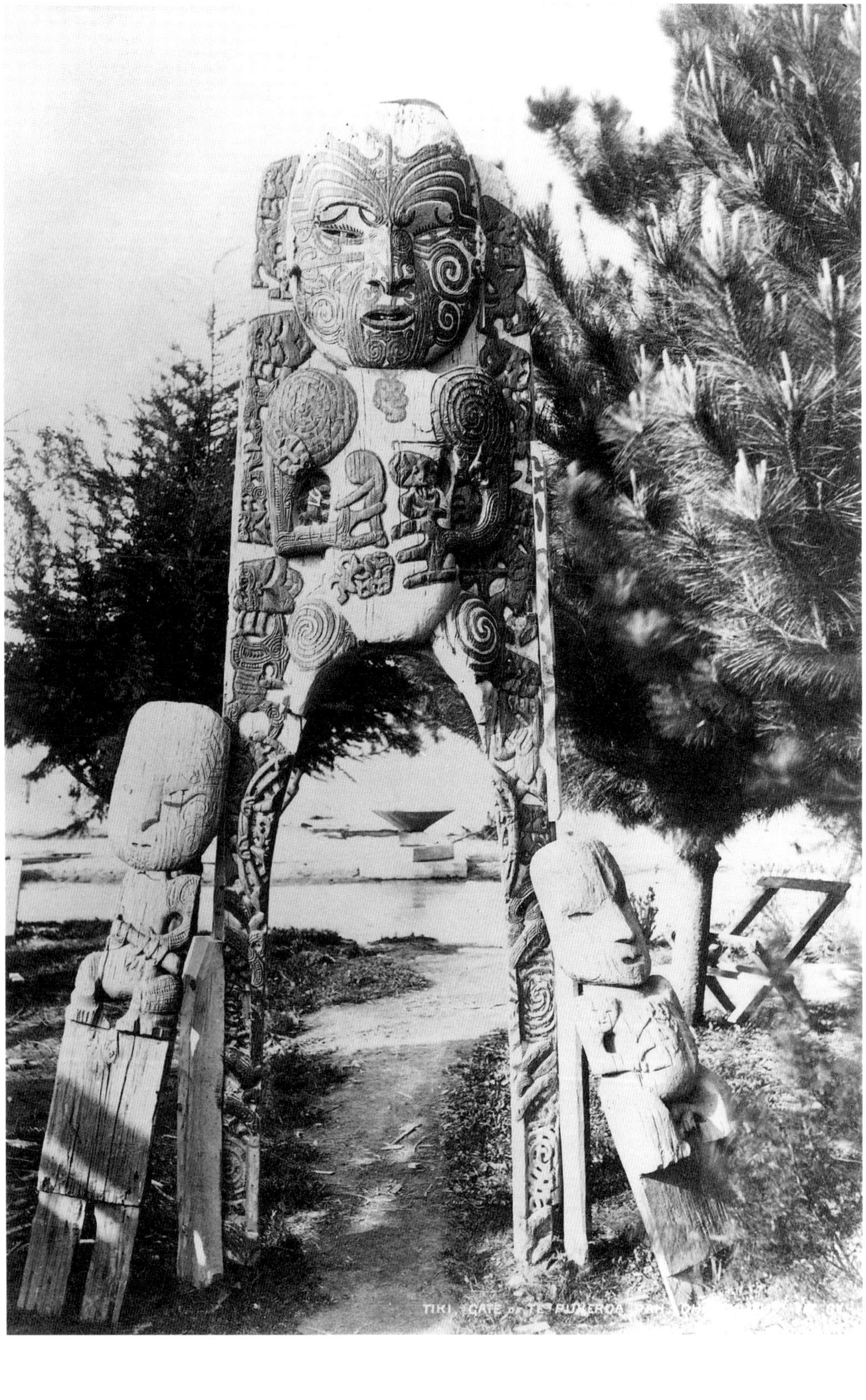

'Tiki, Gate of Te Pukeroa Pah, Ohinemutu', 1886

own. Most of its interest lay below the European part of the town in a Māori settlement stretched across a promontory of the lake, described by a government surveyor as 'a native village built on a thin crust of rock and soil roofing over one vast boiler'.[13] For at least 500 years, descendants of Te Arawa canoe voyagers had made good use of this thermal resource in a variety of ways, including cooking, bathing and heating their houses. In recent years the Arawa people had also opened this resource to the Colonial Government, resulting in the newly planned township of Rotorua a short distance to the south. So far this consisted of just a handful of buildings, including a government bath-house and hospital: its aim was to become 'a city of health' rivalling the great spas of Europe.[14]

Valentine's glass plates were reserved primarily for the Terraces on this journey, but later visits would enable him to capture Ōhinemutu's distinctive features, including Te Whare Karakia o te Whakapono Tapu, the newly finished wooden church near the end of the promontory and, further along, the remains of the ancient Muruika pā.[15] At the end of the promontory, partly submerged in the lake, stood six carved posts, testimony to a night some 120 years earlier when sudden, unexpected geothermal activity had caused the extensive pā to subside into the lake, taking with it about 30 inhabitants.[16] Other relics – 'Portions of curious carvings, old canoes, and grotesque figures in wood ... scattered about in every direction ...' – were to be seen nearby, and through their tapu status were left untouched.[17]

The impressive carved kūwaha or waharoa (gateway) Tiki, an ancestral guardian figure, would also later capture Valentine's attention. Standing guard at the entrance to the village cemetery, Tiki had once looked across the lake from a position above Ōhinemutu at the stockaded Pukeroa pā, before it was dismantled around 1867 to make way for a fort for the militia.[18] During this visit, Valentine photographed Tamatekapua, the ornately carved and painted wharerunanga or meeting house, named for the great captain of the Arawa canoe. Opening in the heart of Ōhinemutu in 1873, Tamatekapua presently served Ngāti Whakaue in the multiple purposes of church meeting place, schoolroom, concert hall for tourists and land court. In this latter function, the arrival of the Native Minister was being anticipated in order to pursue solutions to problems being experienced by the new Rotorua township's Māori landowners, including unpaid rents, defaulted lease agreements and many of the lessees determining to manoeuvre for freehold possession.[19]

As the weather cleared, Valentine and Chapman left for Te Wairoa, the village 11 miles to the southeast, from which the journey to the Terraces would be made. Crossing a sparse, fern-clad plain, distant glimpses of steam and the occasional spouting column of water could be seen at Whakarewarewa, a village where tourists with sufficient time could enjoy some of the world's most spectacular geysers. These and the more dreadful wonders of nearby Tikitere would be saved for later photographic journeys. Further on, Valentine stopped to photograph the Tikitapu Bush, which was unusual for having hardly been touched by logging or fire, with the cutting through it 'merely a track through a dense wood, broad enough for carriages to cross each other'.[20] Three-quarters of an hour on and the bush pulled back to reveal Lake Tikitapu, or the Blue Lake, which Valentine chose to photograph, then, further on, Rotokākahi, the Green Lake, which little more than a year before had risen in temperature 'to nearly boiling point, which was considered to be a remarkable phenomenon, as the lake was always cold before. There was also a very strong outflow down the Wairoa Valley into the Tarawera Lake, lasting for a day.'[21] Since that time the lake had apparently returned to its normal state.

Valentine and Chapman needed to spend the night at Te Wairoa before heading for the Terraces. Established as

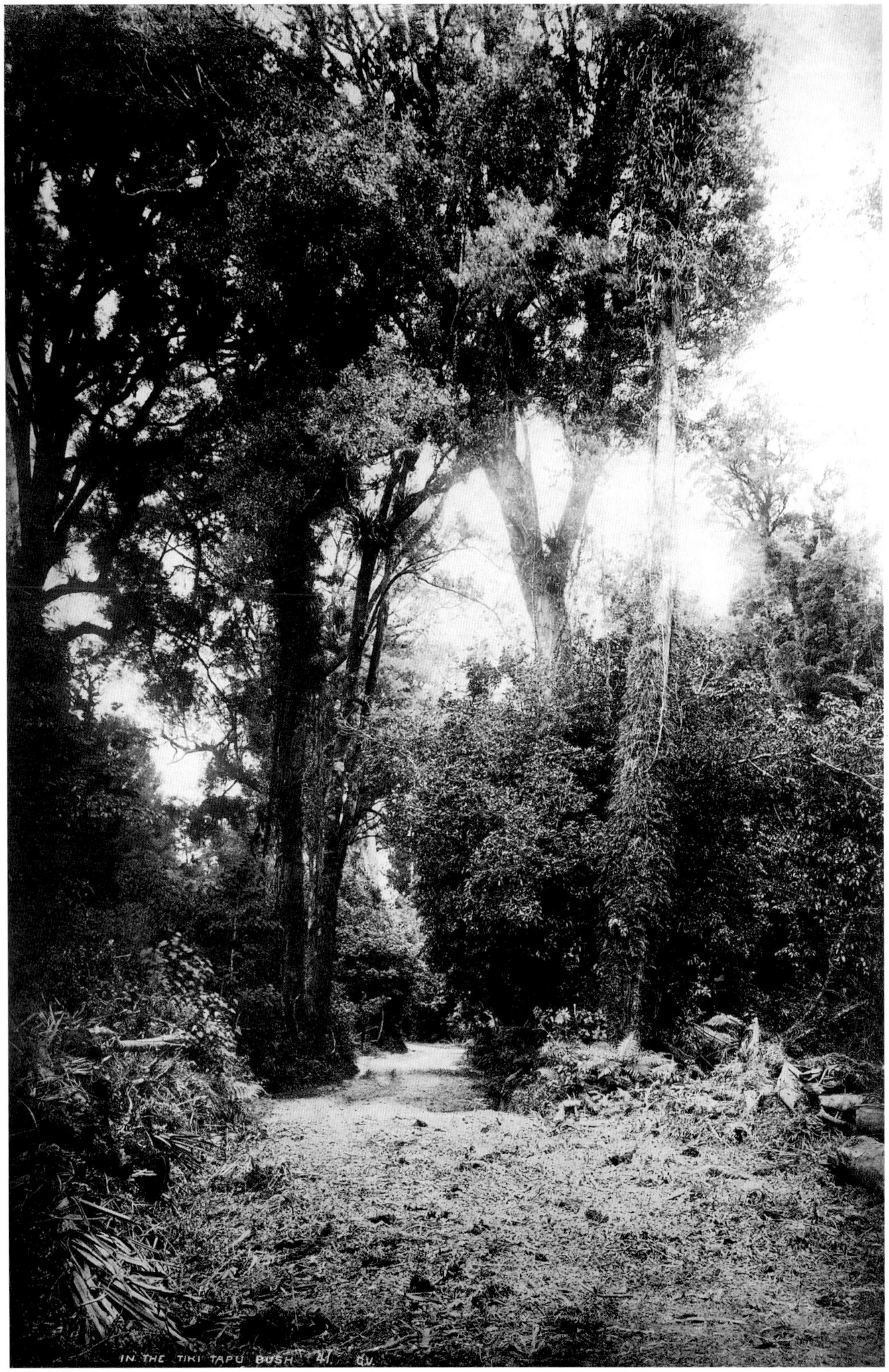

'In the Tiki Tapu Bush', 1885

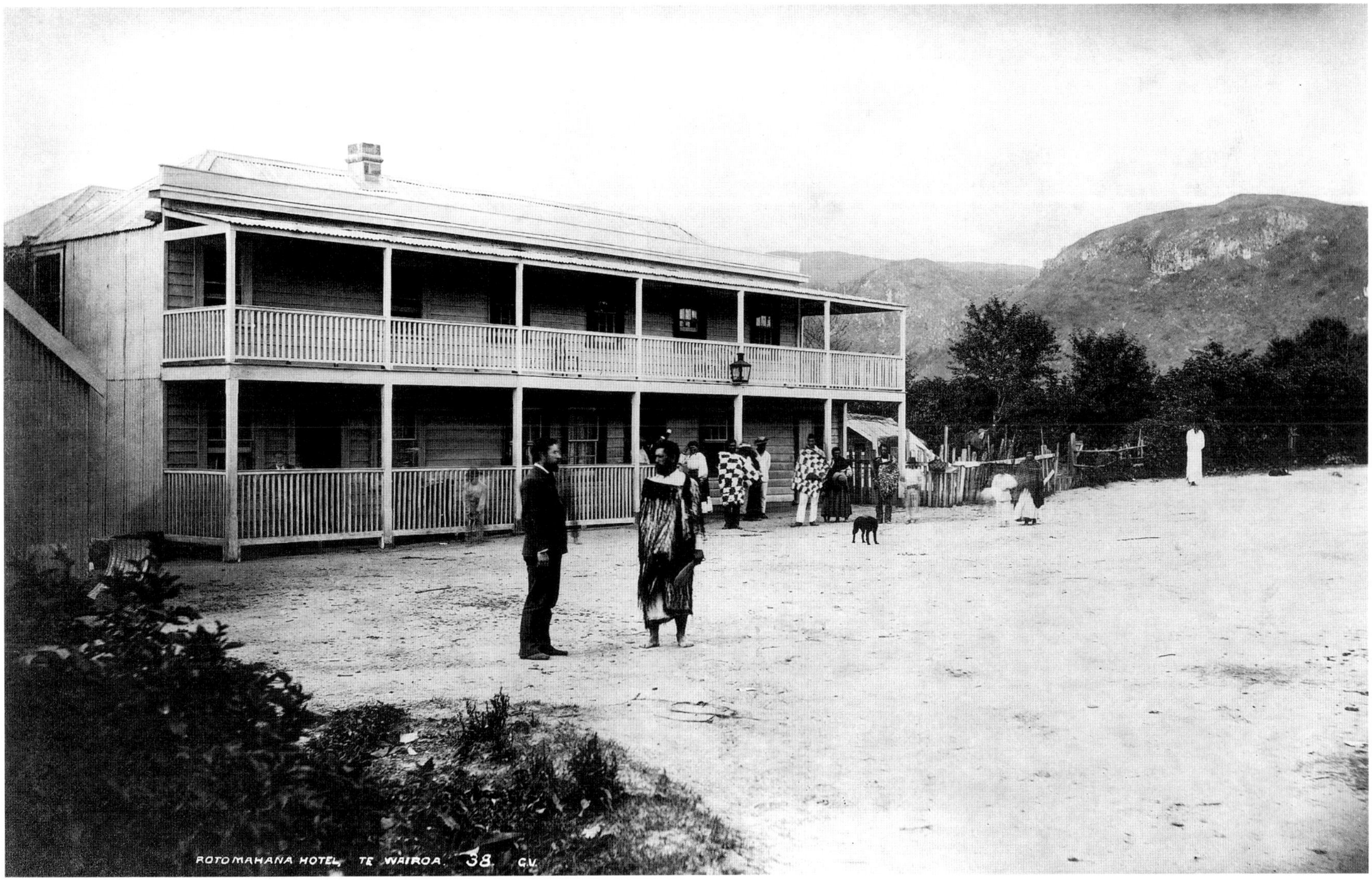

'Rotomahana Hotel, Te Wairoa', 1885
Hotel owner Joseph McRae is joined by chief Aporo Te Wharekaniwha. Guide Sophia is seen to the right of the chief.

a mission station on the shores of Lake Tarawera in 1850 by the American Seymour Spencer, Te Wairoa had its own distinctive flavour, with each whare in its own neatly fenced half-acre lot, and trees such as peach and cherry in abundance. At the start of the village on the left was an old flour mill, abandoned since the chaos of the 1860s wars. Peace had long since returned to the region, but everything now was altered, the flourishing trade in tourism overshadowing the industry of earlier years. Well-publicised visits from such people as Alfred, Duke of Edinburgh, and popular novelist Anthony Trollope had done much to boost the district's fame, with more than 2,000 people estimated to be passing through the village each year. [22]

Two hotels in Te Wairoa offered accommodation to tourists: Robert Graham's Terrace Hotel and, further on, Joseph McRae's licensed Rotomahana Hotel. McRae's was the more spacious and popular of the two, with its 15 bedrooms, three parlours, large dining room and 'splendidly-toned piano'. The Scottish McRae was an entertaining and popular host, with whom Valentine evidently struck up a rapport. A contemporary reporter found the establishment's landlord 'very attentive to the wants of his guests', but was rather less pleased with 'the noise consequent on the crowds of Maoris that swarm about its doors and windows'.[23] Others seemed to enjoy this presence. Surrounding the hotels was a mixture of traditional whare and wooden European-style dwellings, including that on the hill opposite owned by principal chief Wi Keepa Te Rangipuawhe.

Permission was required from local chiefs for Valentine and Chapman to stay at the Terraces – this had to wait until evening. In the meantime, they could see the Wairoa Falls, half a mile below the hotel, or the ivy-covered church complete with stained glass and bell tower, and an excellent view of the lake below. Another attraction was the carved meeting house Hinemihi, in which its Ngāti Hinemihi owners had placed coins in the eyes of carved ancestral figures. While much wealth had poured into the village, observers in general had seen little benefit for the wharepuni's owners, the house having gained a reputation for drunken displays and paid performances of what seemed a degenerate form of haka, the entertainers 'excited by rum and pakeha approval'.[24]

Valentine was to photograph both well-known guides to the Terraces: Sophia Hinerangi, described by a *Herald* reporter as 'a great favourite with the Europeans' for her 'pleasant chat and cheery ways', and Kate Middlemass, famous for having received a Royal Humane Society medal for her rescuing a drowning tourist.[25] Both had Scottish fathers, Sophia's parents an Alexander Gray from Aberdeen and Hinerangi Kotiro of Taranaki, and Kate's 'a Scotchman who was wrecked on the shore more than 70 years ago' by the name of Middlemass, and Rangitukia of Whakatāne. Both also wore the traditional moko: Sophia with lightly tattooed lips, and Kate the more elaborate chin adornment. A young tourist guided by the latter recorded: 'Kate's real name is Maggie Middlemas [sic] and right proud she is to think herself Scotch. She only gets "Kate" after an aunt who died. She is a widow – very shrewd, intelligent, kind and obliging – very considerate of those she sees little able for the fatigues of climbing & c.'[26] Wearing a highly treasured kahu huruhuru (feather cloak), Kate Middlemass became the subject of one of just four documented portraits made by Valentine in New Zealand.

Valentine and Chapman still needed permission from the owners of the Terraces to be able to camp there, and that night 'had a lot of trouble ... with the natives of Wairoa before they got their consent to come'.[27] The artist Blomfield's case and even his troubles may have helped, with the chiefs' diplomatic decision being for the newcomers to be chaperoned during their stay by Blomfield's 'Thompson', chief Tamihana Te Keu.[28]

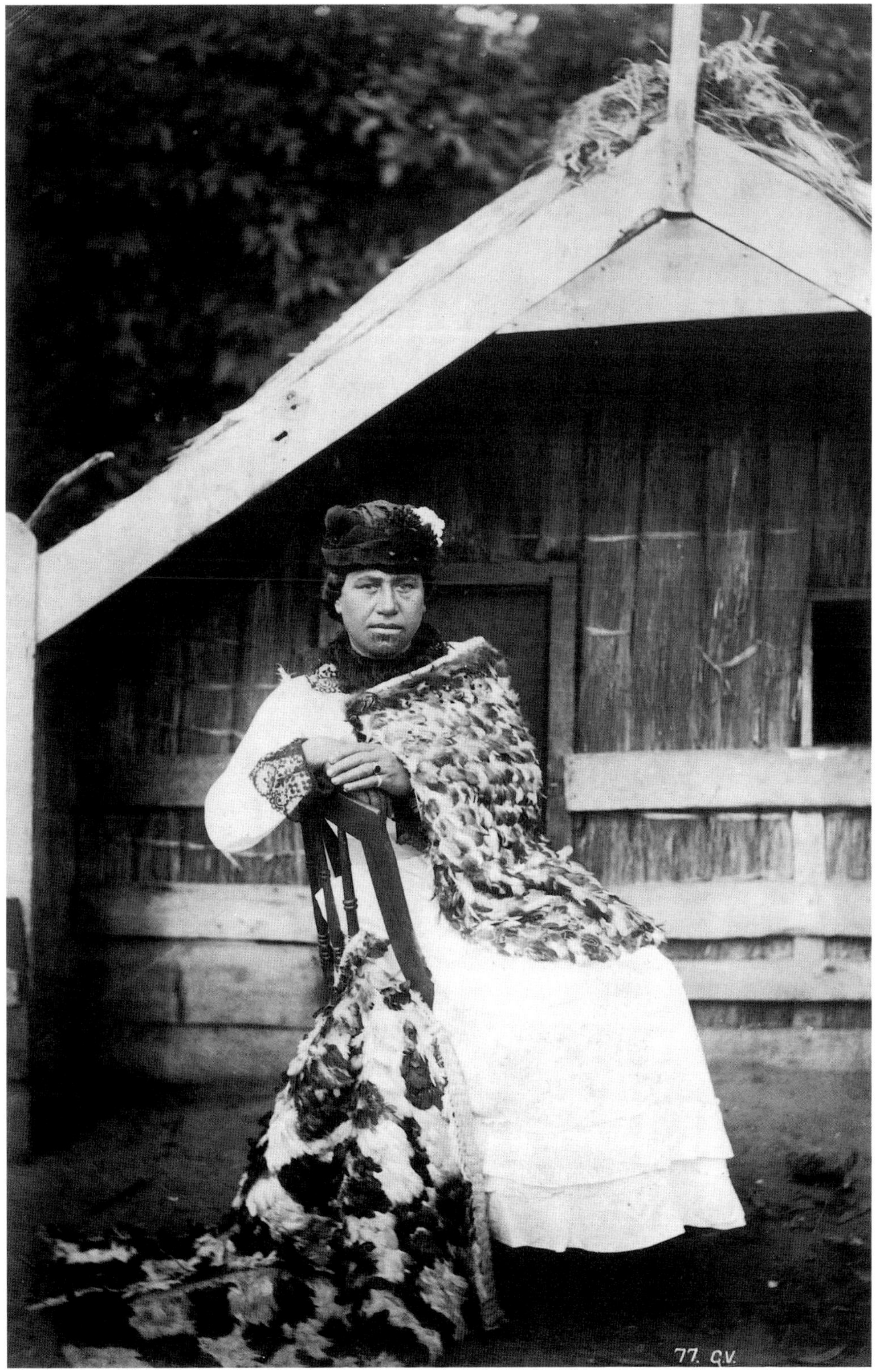

'Guide Kate', Kate Middlemass, Te Wairoa, 1885

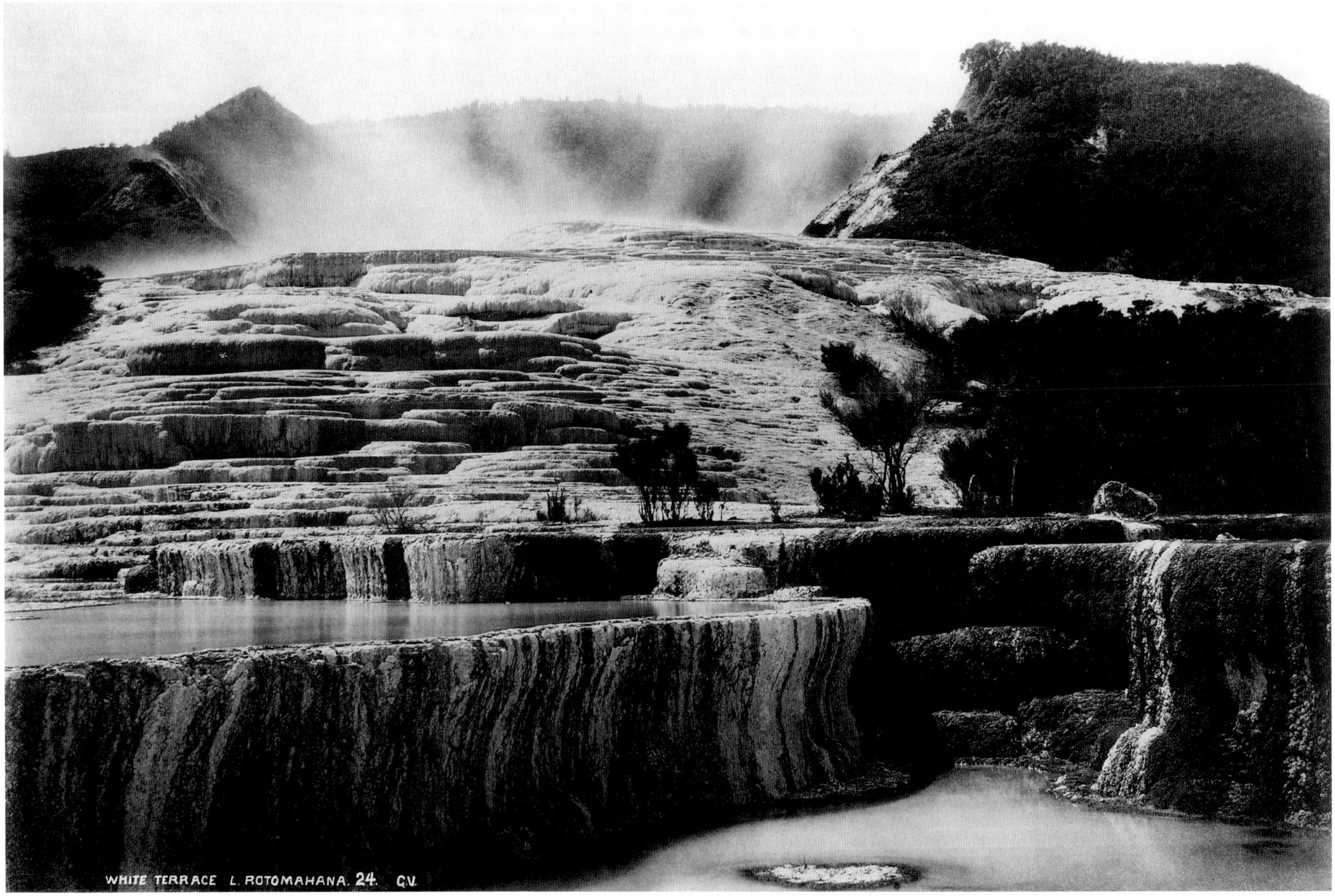

'White Terrace, L. Rotomahana', 1885

CHAPTER 5

THE PINK AND WHITE TERRACES

Tuesday 13 January 1885 began as a fine day for travelling to the Terraces.[1] After an early breakfast, Valentine, Chapman and a small party of tourists departed, heading down a steep winding path to the boat sheds to meet their waiting 'native contingent' – Guide Sophia, a steersman and six rowers for the whale-boat journey across Lake Tarawera.[2] An 11-mile haul then began, the boat staying close to the southern shore, while Sophia would delicately extract from her passengers (on behalf of Tūhourangi) payment for the day ahead. Minimum charge was £2 per boat, with an additional 5s per head. The guide's fee was 10s per group, and permission to view the Terraces and other wonders of the lake 2s 6d per tourist. A further 10s per group was charged after seeing the White Terrace, for the canoe ride across to the Pink.[3]

While such a steady flow of charges could leave some patrons gasping, most were from privileged backgrounds and this was an experience they could easily afford. The boat journey itself was something to savour, with the rhythmic singing of the crew, the dazzling red rata blossom on the headlands as they passed and, on the southeastern shore, looming larger as they progressed, Tarawera mountain. The mountain's three flat-topped domes – Wāhanga, Ruawāhia and Tarawera – would have been pointed out, as well as the fact that 15 generations of Arawa chiefs had been laid there to rest, their bodies carried and placed in the mountain's caves and recesses. The mountain was tapu, and climbing of it was forbidden. Such knowledge intensified for some the feeling that the setting was 'not very romantic ... the general aspect of the landscape on Tarawera is dull and sombre, an effect heightened by the dark frowning mountain'.[4]

After just over an hour the boat would round a point at the southern arm of the lake. Then, stopping by the small Ngāti Rangitihi settlement of Mourā, passengers would disembark to stretch their legs and buy peaches, apples or kōura (freshwater crayfish). Beyond Mourā, the whale boat would pass a steep shore fringed with red-flowering pōhutukawa, then head towards a large moss-clad stone standing out of the water. Led by a member of the crew, a customary offering of a few coins would be left to safeguard the waters for an uneventful return journey – a propitiation to 'taipo', to send favourable winds.[5] The rowing ended three miles from Mourā at Te Ariki, a settlement of Ngāti Taoi Tūhourangi, situated by the Kaiwaka ('canoe-devourer') stream which

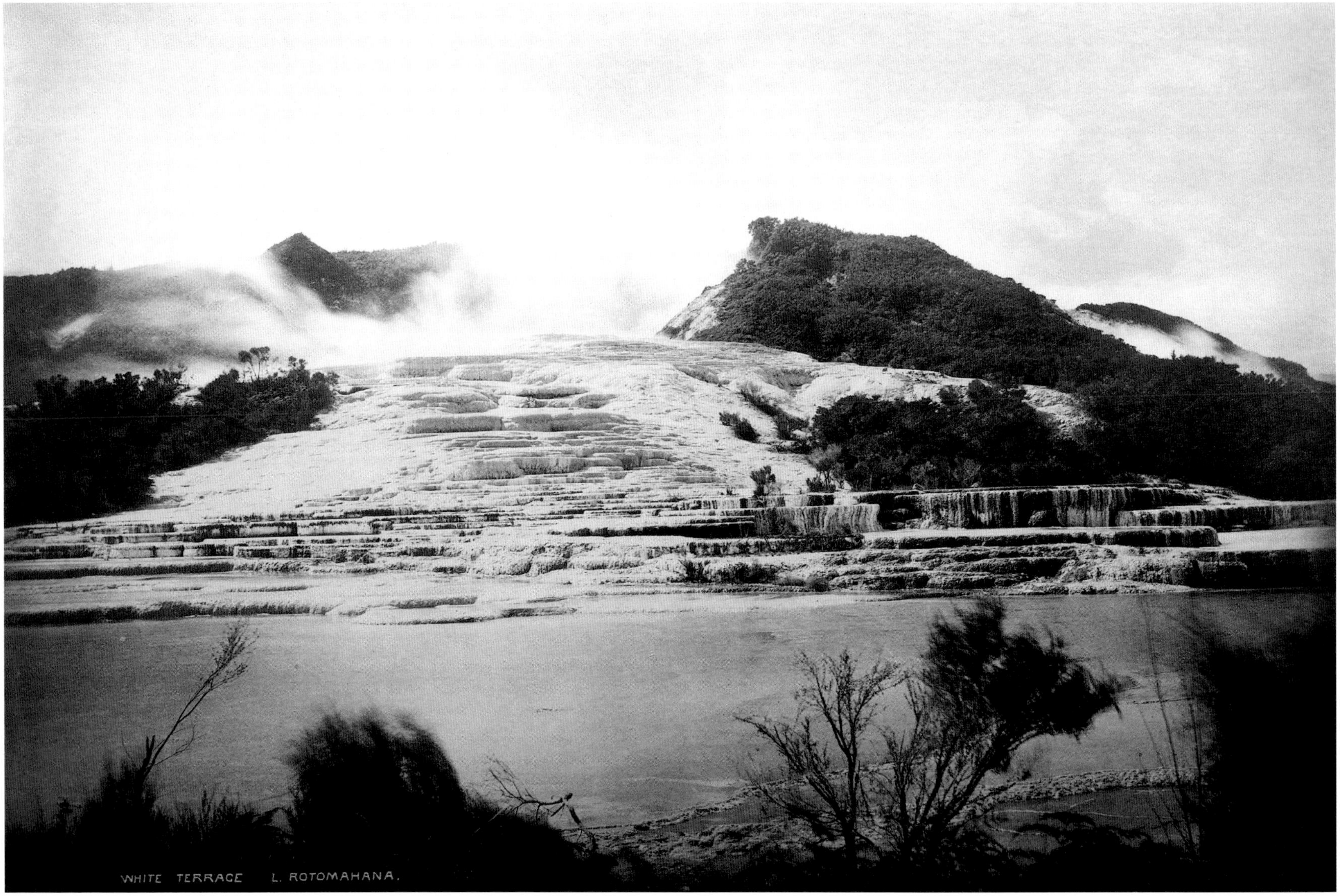

'White Terrace, L. Rotomahana', 1885

connected Lake Tarawera to 'the Warm Lake', Rotomahana. From here, most visitors would walk the half-mile between the lakes – a winding, hilly track through barren scrub. Valentine, with his provisions and equipment, was probably poled up the swift-flowing stream in a dugout canoe. On reaching Rotomahana – which at less than a mile long and less than a quarter of a mile wide was one of the smallest lakes in the district – he would have disembarked, then climbed a small bank. Suddenly stretched out now before him would be one of the wonders he had come to see: Te Tarata ('the Tattooed Rock'), the celebrated White Terrace.[6]

The White Terrace had been described by one visitor as 'grand enough to serve as steps to Heaven'.[7] Seven and a half acres of glassy, snow-white silica rose in stepped basins from a wide, curving sweep at its lowest point to a swirling mass of steam at its summit 150 feet above the lake. From the geyser basin at the top, terraced basins, 'thousands, of all sizes, from the segment of a cheese-plate to that of a twenty-ton galleon', filled with water of a semi-opaque turquoise: 'the purest blue of the sky melted down into its cups, and illuminated in some supernaturally beautiful fashion from beneath'.[8] In the lower basins the water was tepid, while at the top it was almost boiling, the silica-laden solution trickling over every part of the formation. Several basins were also suitable for bathing, although usually visitors were recommended to wait until they reached the smoother-surfaced baths of the Pink Terrace.

On the day of Valentine's arrival, possibly before he had reached Rotomahana, it is recorded that 'about ten o'clock it came on raining', making his introduction to the lake a less enjoyable affair.[9] Valentine, Chapman and Tamihana Te Keu established their canvas camp by Te Tarata's base and waited for the weather to clear. Sophia's party, meanwhile, continued on their way with topcoats and umbrellas at the ready. After the White Terrace, the guide would show them a number of nearby geysers and hot pools before stopping at the sinter platform Te Takapo for a modest feast of fresh kōura and potatoes, boiled in a nearby spring. Next they would be taken to the quarter-mile-long Waikānapanapa ravine, with its numerous boiling pools and mud volcanoes, and then to the cave Ngāwanga, before a shaky ferry ride by canoe – carved from a single log – across the lake to the Pink Terrace.

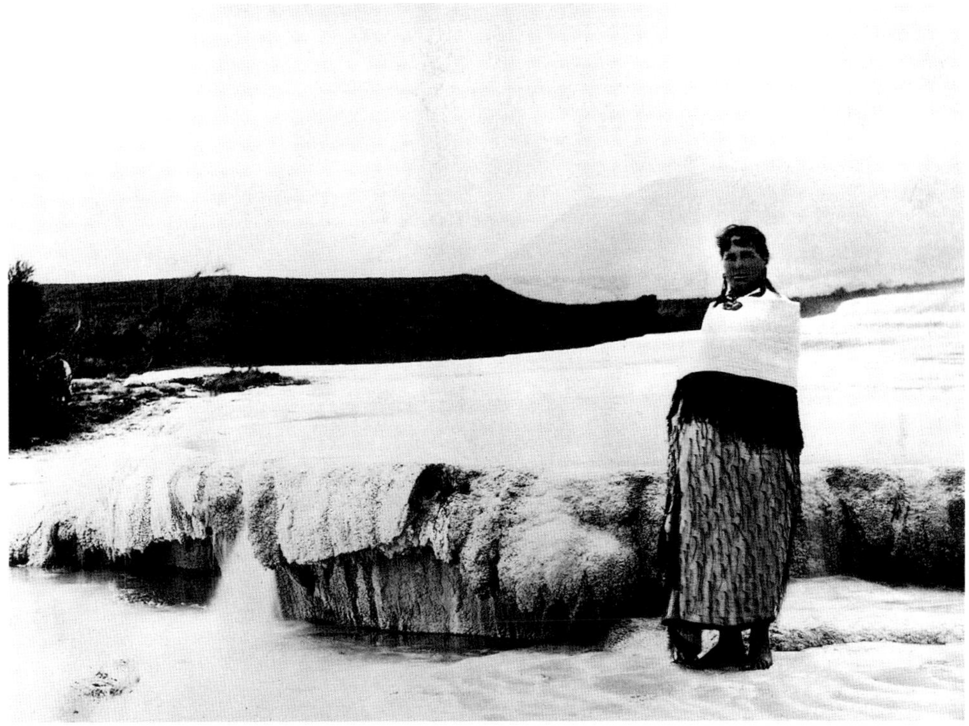

'Guide Sophia', 1885. Sophia Hinerangi by Te Tarata's hot baths, not far from the geyser cauldron

At 80 feet high and covering an area of five and a half acres, the Pink Terrace, or Ōtūkapuarangi ('Fountain of the Clouded Sky'), was smaller than the White, though with its more spectacular colouring, visitors were left undecided as to which of the two was the greater. Widening as it ascended to a cloudy summit obscured by steam, it was more regularly formed than the White, with its marble-like steps level and buttressed rather than cupped. At the bottom, the colour

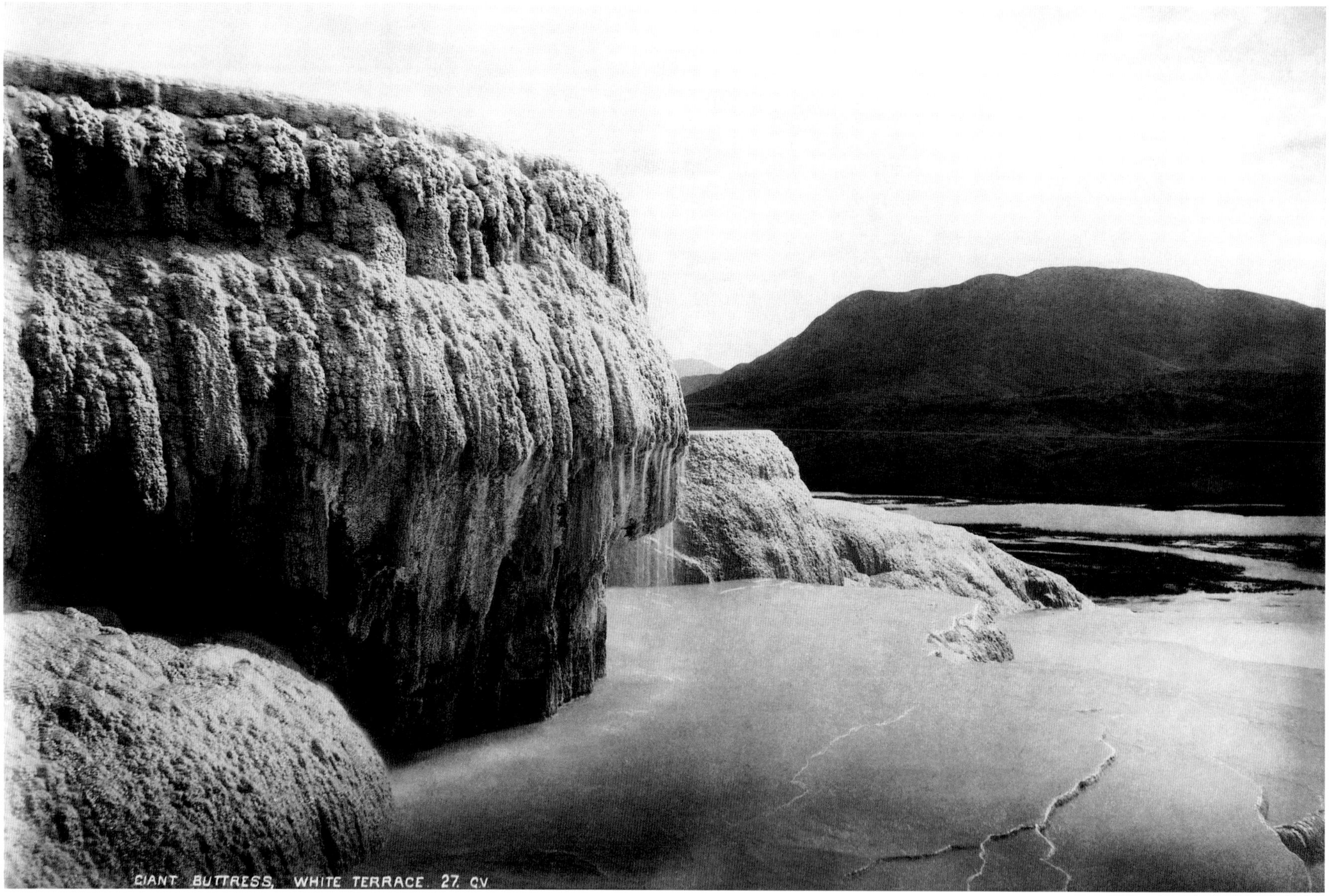

'Giant Buttress, White Terrace', 1885

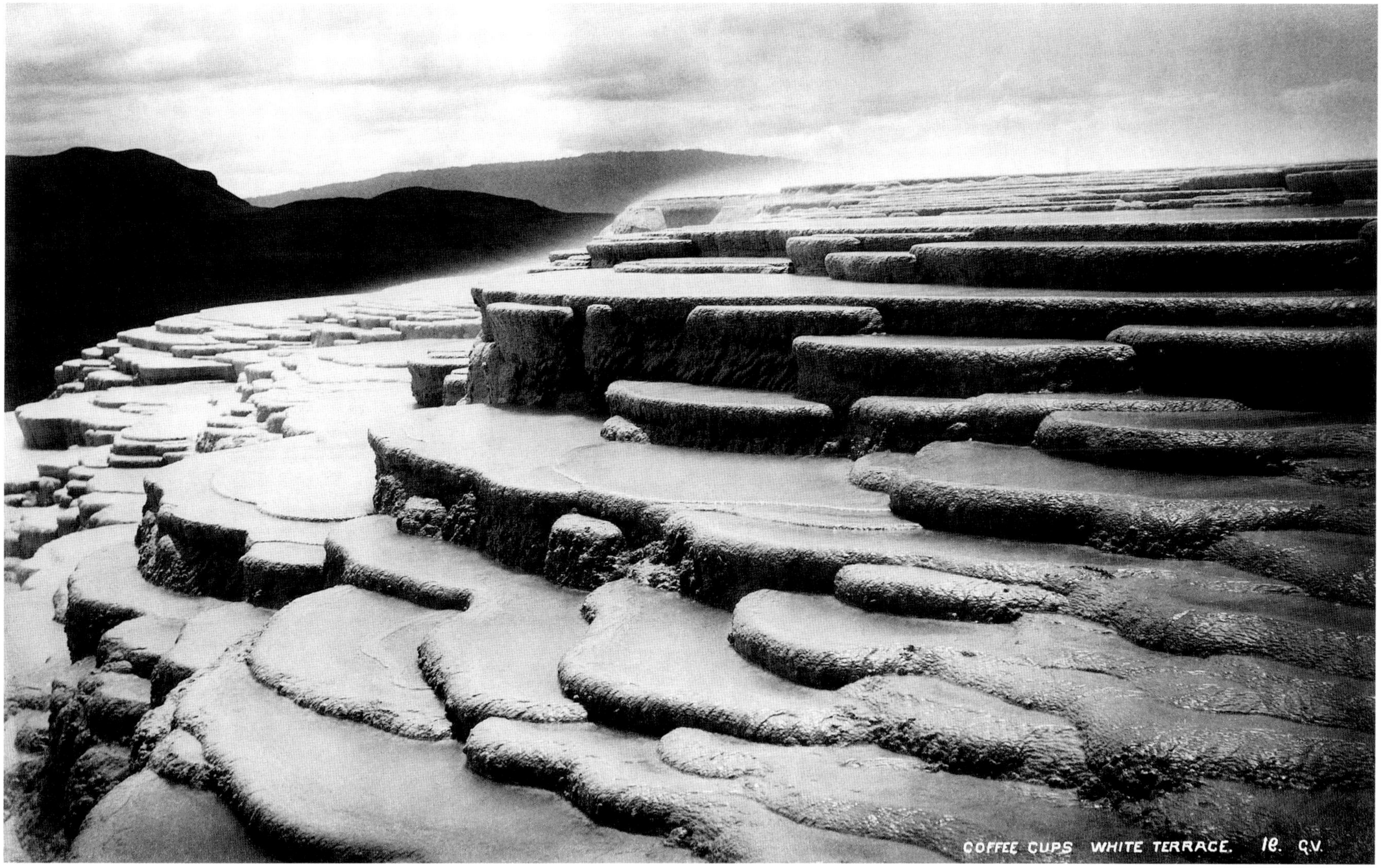

'Coffee Cups, White Terrace', 1885

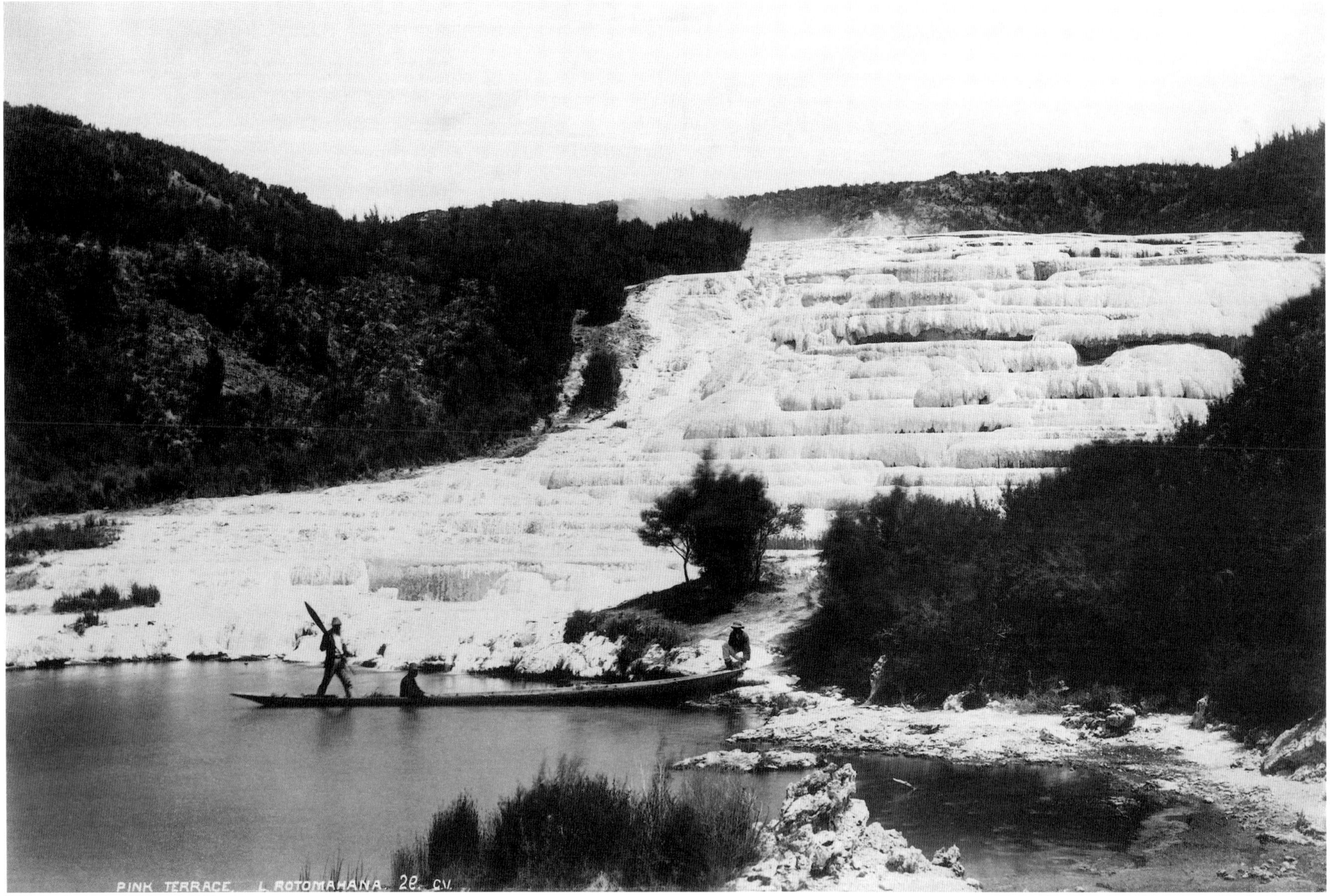

'Pink Terrace, L. Rotomahana', 1885

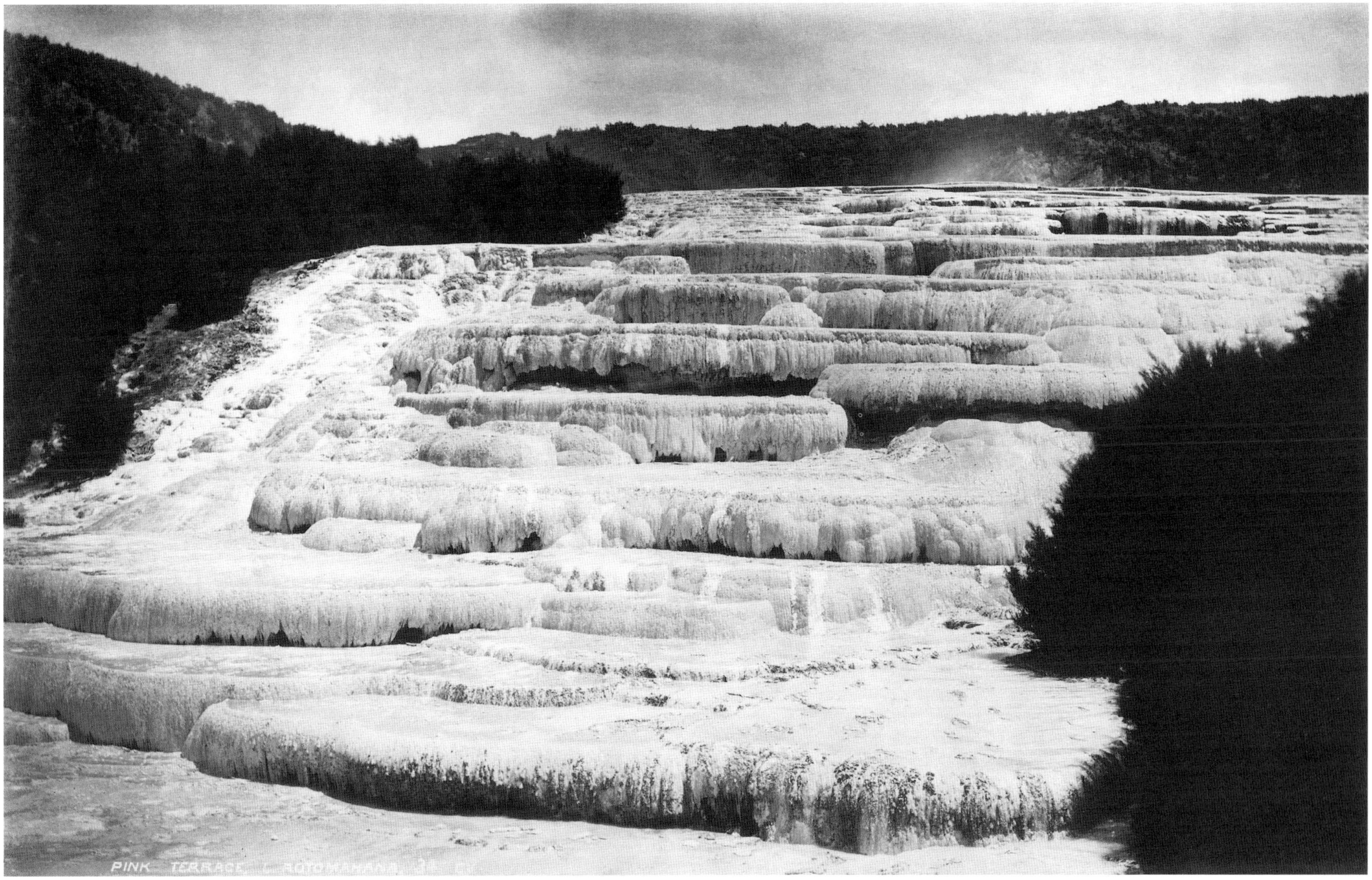

'Pink Terrace, L. Rotomahana', 1885

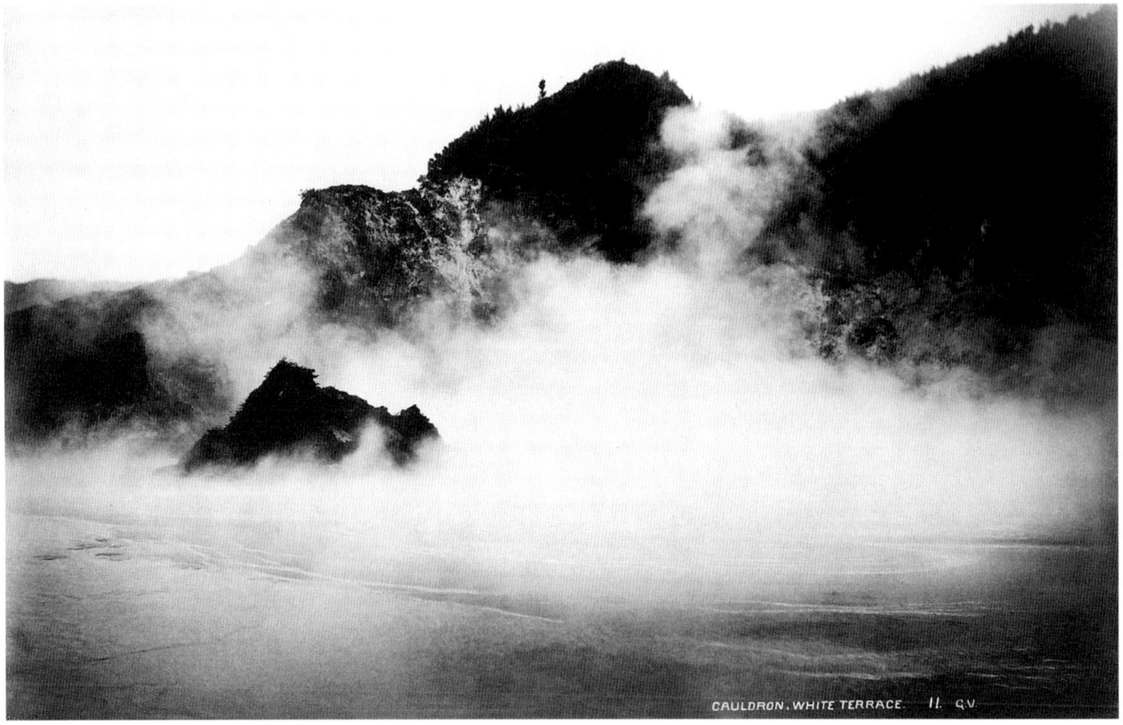

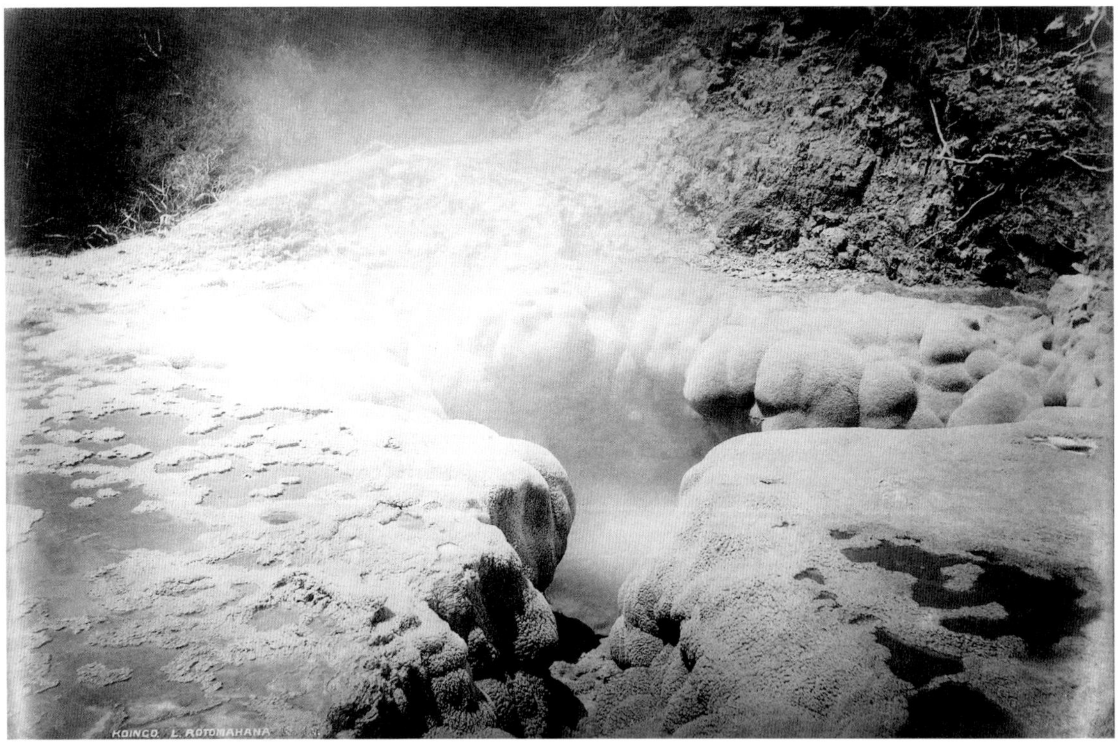

Top: 'Cauldron, White Terrace'
1885
Bottom: 'Koingo, L. Rotomahana',
1885

"...the sighing Koingo intermittent fountain, from which discharges of water take place three or four times a day." – G.T. Chapman

was a glassy white; a little higher it was tinged with pink; and higher still it was a salmon hue deepening to a rosy tint. Ascending the Pink Terrace via a natural staircase on the left, a tourist party could in places observe signatures and other graffiti – indelible from its glassy covering – and be discouraged from any similar urge of their own to desecrate.[10] Near the top beside a wide, open platform were Ōtūkapuarangi's several bathing pools, with basins between three and four feet deep and a choice of temperature from lukewarm to as hot as could be endured. At the top was the boiling cauldron – a large circular basin of clear sapphire blue. Next came the much-anticipated bath, with ladies first to enjoy the luxury of open-air bathing in a warm pool overlooking the lake.

Meanwhile, Guide Sophia met Charles Blomfield and was able to tell him of the newcomers at the White Terrace – 'photographers' who had come to stay ten days. Blomfield was halfway through his planned six weeks at the lake and had nearly finished his work on the Pink Terrace. Early that morning, in preparation for his move to the White Terrace, he had spent time clearing a space in the fern and bracken near its base, and of the visitors wrote to his wife: 'they appear to have jumped our claim, and I believe pitched their tent in the very place I cleared for ours'. That evening ('the rain held off for a little about half past six'), Blomfield and his daughter rowed the half-mile across the lake to meet 'the new arrivals, and found that they had not got our place, but just close to it, in among some teatree. One of them is Mr. Chapman of Auckland, bookseller, and another, [whom he calls] Ballantyne, a photographer. Thompson the Dreadful [Tamihana Te Keu] is with them taking care of them, and so he will be happy. He looked half frightened when he saw me.' The newcomers 'said they had heard all about me in Auckland and the trouble I had had with the Maoris', and recounted their own troubles from the previous evening. Blomfield recorded their disappointment over the 'very unpromising' weather; Valentine, he said, informed him that 'another wet day would be enough for him, and he would clear out'. Heading back in their boat to the Pink Terrace, Charles Blomfield and his daughter were caught in a heavy shower, and 'got very wet rowing'.[11]

Wednesday 14 January evidently cleared for the photographer, yielding to his plans to work in one of the most exceptional landscape settings in the world. Blomfield and his daughter joined the newcomers on this day, the artist ready to complete a series of 12 canvases of Rotomahana's wonders. Clearly Valentine found himself captivated, exposing each day up to five or six plates in his temporary new environs. A solid placement for the sturdy view-camera's feet and tripod was essential before Valentine could disappear beneath the black velvet photographer's cloth. There he could carefully consider each composition upside-down on the camera's ground-glass back, before fixing it onto sensitised glass by the deft removal – for the appropriate number of seconds – of the black metal slide.

Over the next few days, George Valentine was able to create what is considered to be the most complete and artistically interesting collection of photographic images from Rotomahana. Every day as he worked, new wonders were explored and recorded: a plateau of mini-volcanoes in Waikānapanapa ravine; the nearby intermittent sighing geyser Kōingo, 30 yards above the lake; and its noisy alternating partner, Te Whatapohu, or 'Pain in the Stomach', named for its rumbling, indigestive groan. Across the lake, not far from the base of the Pink Terrace, he photographed the sulphur-encrusted fumarole Whakataratara.

During their stay at Rotomahana, the group were able to watch the tourists come and go, 'every weekday, from ten to thirty of them, mostly moneyed people, from all parts of the world'.[12] Visitors arrived at the White Terrace at around 11 a.m., stayed for nearly an hour, then left to view the sights nearby and have a picnic luncheon by the edge of the lake. While most people's encounters with Rotomahana were therefore brief, any such visit would leave an abundance of memories and observations. In the week of Valentine's visit these would include the antics of Mary Blomfield who amused herself by 'bathing in the hot basins, making mud pies, plastering up the baby mud volcanoes with clay to hear them go off with a pop, hunting for petrified ferns and birds' feathers in the hot water. She got so used to the strange, weird sights that she skipped about fearlessly among the geysers, greatly to the horror of the visitors, who hardly dared venture out of the guide's footsteps.'[13]

Valentine achieved some of his most memorable results from the White Terrace. Notable among them is a frontal view, 'White Terrace, L. Rotomahana. 24', in which its extraordinary monumental form and radiating crown of vapour are transformed into a powerful, abstracted composition. From near the top of the White Terrace, 'Giant Buttress, White Terrace. 27' is likewise remarkable, a considered study of monolithic strength and fine honeycomb detail, with the buttress trimmed by a delicate, trickling veil. Further across and looking down, in 'Coffee Cups, White Terrace. 19' – one of his most unforgettable works – Valentine arrested the shell-like silica basins, adjoined and overlapping in banked-up repetition, as the steam on the summit drifts away from the lake.

Valentine and Chapman remained at Rotomahana for less than a week, but in that time Valentine made more than 40 plates of Rotomahana and its wonders. Having originally allowed for ten days at the Terraces, there was also time to visit Wairākei, where Valentine and Chapman stayed a night before returning to their respective homes in Nelson and Auckland.[14] Back in Nelson, Valentine processed his glass-plate negatives in a rented or borrowed darkroom – very possibly Tyree's studio – and developed his mostly 7½" x 11½" albumen contact prints under sunlight. Not long afterwards, on 23 March 1885, George and Mina's second son, Arnot Stirling Valentine, was born.[15]

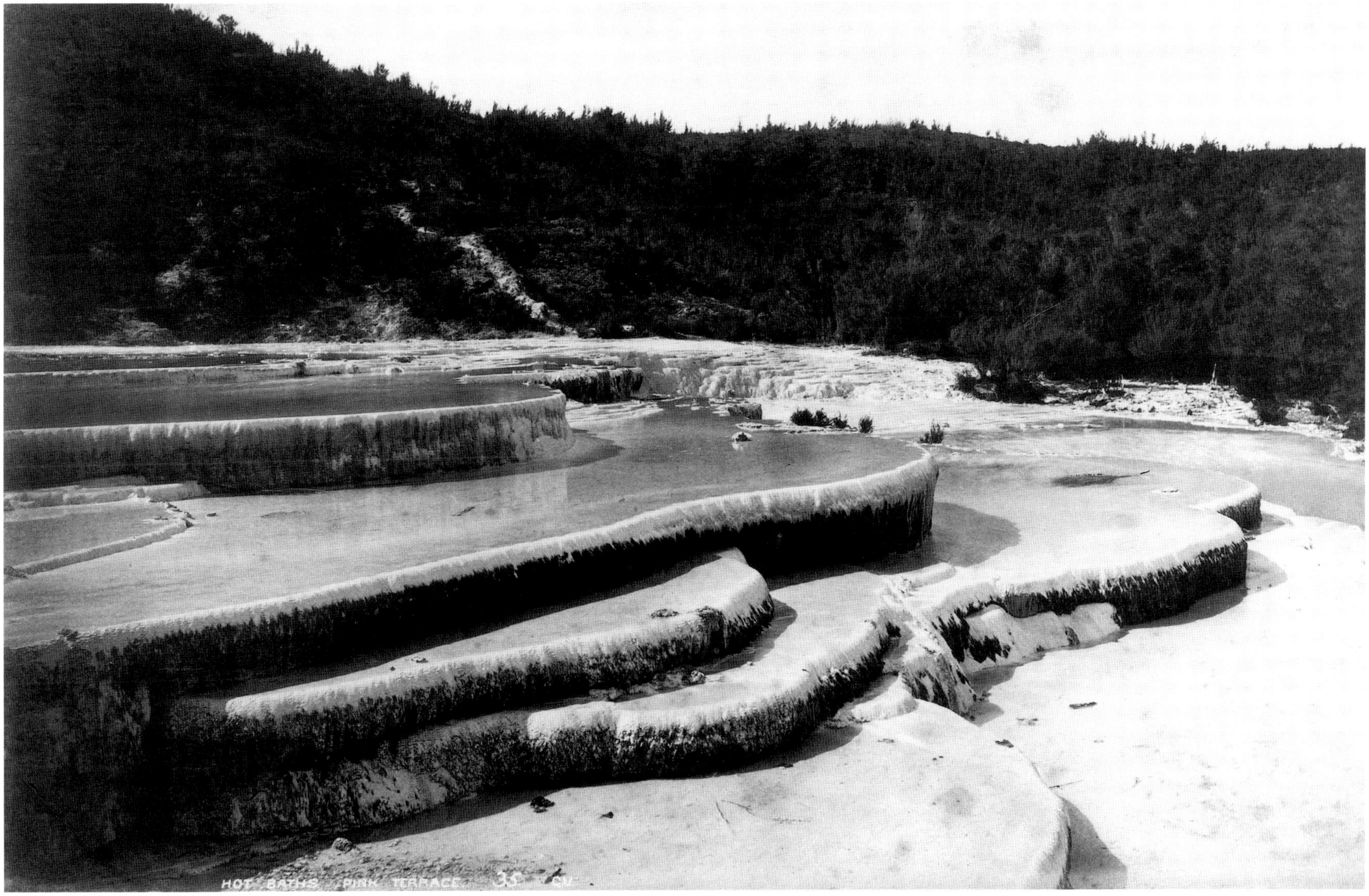

'Hot Baths, Pink Terrace', 1885

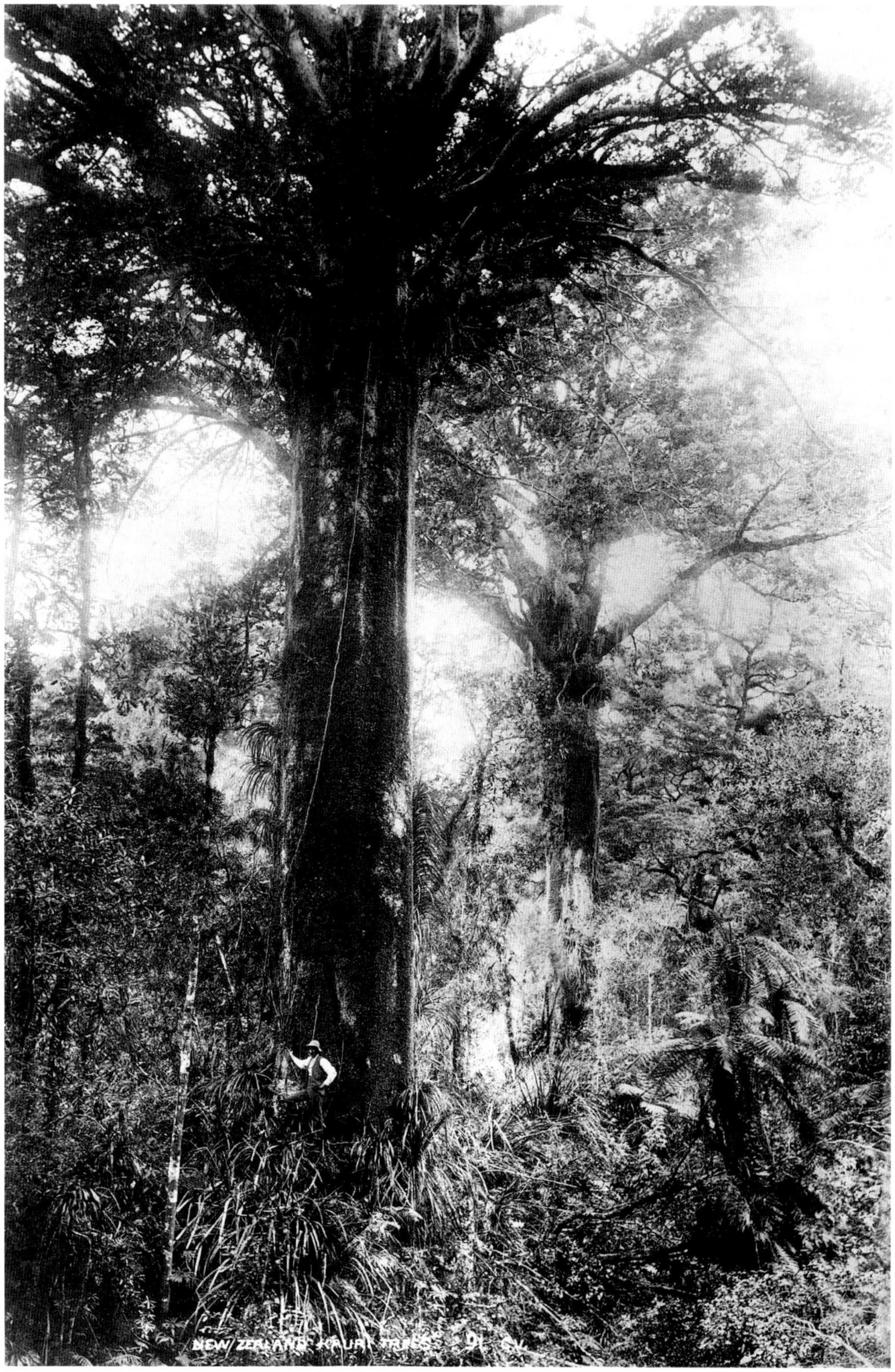

'New Zealand Kauri Trees', 1885

CHAPTER 6

ACCLAIM

A booming naval artillery salute was the signal that the Governor-General, Major-General Sir William Francis Drummond Jervois, was leaving Wellington's Government House, 2.25 p.m., 1st of August 1885, for the much-awaited New Zealand Industrial Exhibition opening. The clock chimed the half-hour and the Garrison Band burst into 'God Save the Queen' as the Governor-General alighted from his carriage. As he entered the building to join a capacity crowd of 2,000, the orchestra and 200-strong choir gave a rousing national anthem, followed by pieces by Wagner and Handel. In unfurling his inaugural speech, Premier Sir Julius Vogel was eager to establish that while this was not the first such exhibition to be held in the colony, it was 'the first held entirely under the charge and control of the colonial government, and confined to local productions'. No few words were added by His Excellency the Governor-General, until at last all that remained was for the Exhibition to be opened, with a triumphant, echoing 'Hallelujah Chorus'.[1] Three cheers from the crowd, three more for Sir William (and another for Sir Julius), and the assemblage was dispersed to admire and inspect the finest collection of pickles and preserves, corn-crushers and horizontal steam winches, saddles and bootstraps, tarred rope and drain pipes, macrame mantle drapes and brass binnacles, inlaid tabletops and ornamental castings, heel and toe plates, knitted stockings and tam-o'-shanters, account books and rubber stamps, barbed wire and scrub-cutting machines, blackboards and marine charts, wigs and washstands, corned beef and cod liver oil, artificial limbs, etc., etc., that the colony had ever seen.[2]

When the inaugural crowd had dispersed, a further 5,000 opening-day visitors flooded the display halls to view this splendid array of industry, in the midst of which was also an Art Department, with photography by the country's leading exponents. Three entries for the Exhibition's Photography Section had been despatched from Nelson, and the *Nelson Evening Mail* had been confident these 'should make a good show. One of them contains some beautiful views of the Hot Lakes and neighbourhood taken by Mr. Valentine; and the other two are Mr. Tyree's, one of them consisting of portraits and the other of views of Nelson scenery'.[3] The panel of judges was to agree: in the Landscape section, George Valentine's entry gained second prize, beaten only by the remarkably prolific Alfred Burton, whose entry included recent extensive coverage of the little-known Māori 'King Country', as well as results from his 1884 tour of the South Pacific.[4]

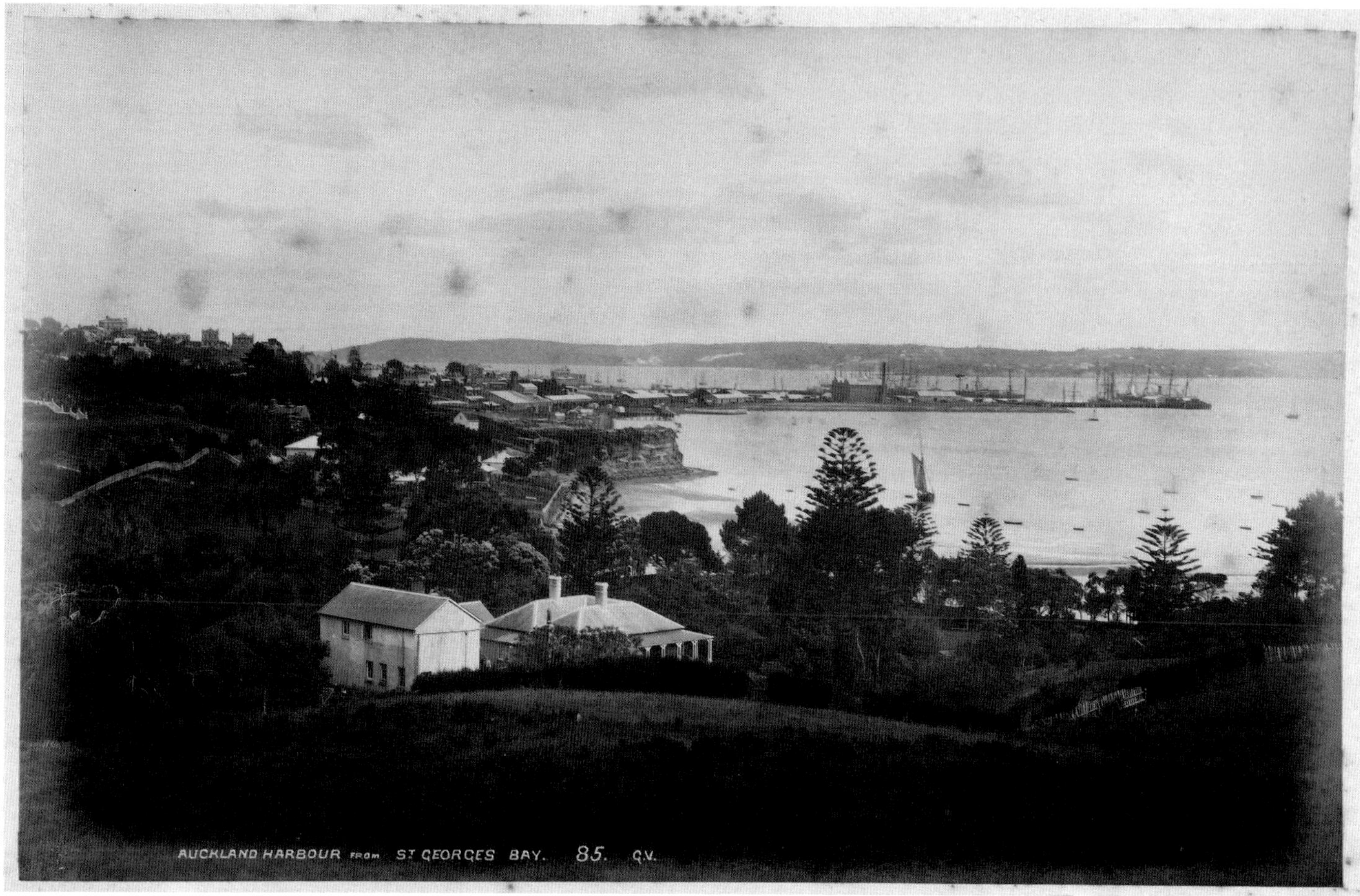

'Auckland Harbour from St. Georges Bay', c.1885
The view from George and Mina Valentine's home in Cleveland Road, Parnell.

By the time Valentine learned of his award, it was October and he and his family had recently moved to Auckland.[5] The Valentines had been in the new setting for less than a fortnight when Auckland claimed the prize-winning photographer as its own, the *New Zealand Herald* noting George Valentine's award as 'the only prize in this class which came to Auckland'. It was also announced that 'Mr. Valentine (of Valentine and Sons, Dundee)' was about to take a series of views in Auckland, and that

> He has already taken a large series of views of Lake Rotomahana and surrounding districts. The photographic views are clear and sharp, and among those specially noticeable in these respects may be mentioned the view of Tarawera Lake – the White and Pink Terraces, the 'Coffee Cups,' the 'Umbrella Buttress,' the cold water basins, and the cauldrons and geysers. They are an excellent illustration of the natural wonders of the Lake Country.

Mr Chapman, bookseller, of Queen Street, would be sole agent for the photographs.[6]

Despite the encouragement of this sudden acclaim,

George Valentine's arrival in Auckland in late September had been traumatic, a rough passage from Nelson having put him, for the first time since he had been in New Zealand, not only in need of a doctor but also fearing for his life. Certainly any enjoyment of George and Mina's new home 'Balgay' (after the park and district in Dundee) had been all but removed. Letters by the pair written in November 1885, to Helen Dobson, the favourite aunt, reveal something of these circumstances:

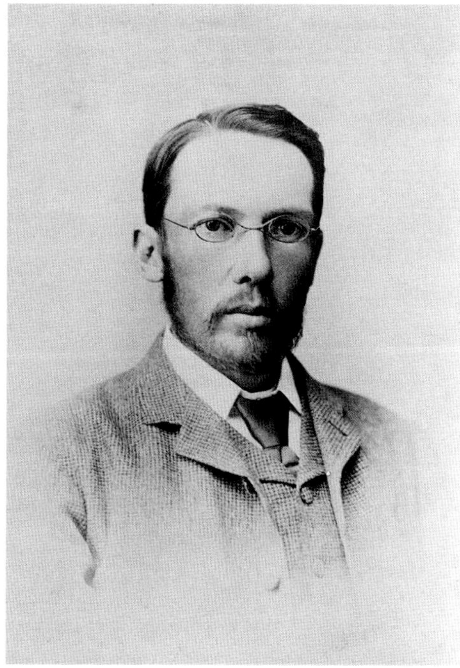

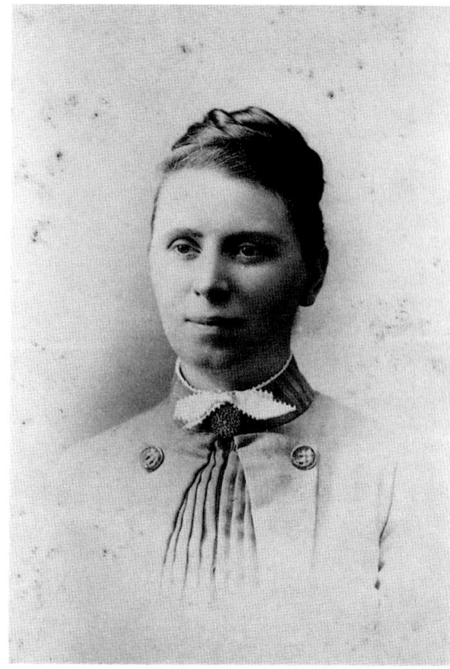

George and Mina Valentine, by J.R. Hanna, c.1885

> Cleveland Rd., Parnell, Auckland 4/11 1885
>
> Dear Aunt, ... Well we have got to Auckland at last and are finally settled down in what is I hope to be our home for good. Let's hope in more ways than one. "They" say that good beginnings are bad endings and vice versa, so we have had our fill of bad beginnings and we hope for the fulfilment of the other part.
>
> To begin with we had a very bad passage up from Nelson and with attending to the others who were very sick I turned up as well. There were a good many passengers and so the Stewardess could not give Mina so much attention as she would have required. The Baby alone was happy all the time. We arrived in Auckland or rather Onehunga, 8 miles from Auckland, on Sunday forenoon. Mr. Chapman met us with a very comfortable roomy cab and we drove to the Star Hotel Auckland where we stayed for two nights when we got into our own house.
>
> Unfortunately I managed to get a severe cold and was laid on my back, and had for the first time since leaving home to call in a Doctor and he is still attending me, with I am glad to say good results as I have now got over the worst and altho' very weak I think am improving rapidly. This is the worst knock I have had and gave us all a start.
>
> I have got all the workmen out of the House, and workshops are about ready for work – I only wish I was the same as it keeps my mind from my troubles which are not so few as I would like.
>
> I am sorry to say that owing to the great expense I have been at and will be for some time and nothing coming in that I will not be able this year to send you my little present of money – if all is well I hope by another year to be in a better position...
>
> When Easton has time a letter from him would be acceptable, and now with best wishes of the Season to you all,
>
> I am your affectionate Nephew, George

> Cleveland Road, Parnell Auckland, 6th Nov 1885.
>
> Dear Aunt Ellen, Your last letter was very welcome. It reached us just before we left Nelson. Geo. has told you of the miserable passage we had – we shall not soon forget its horrors. Geo. has told you of his illness, he has been very

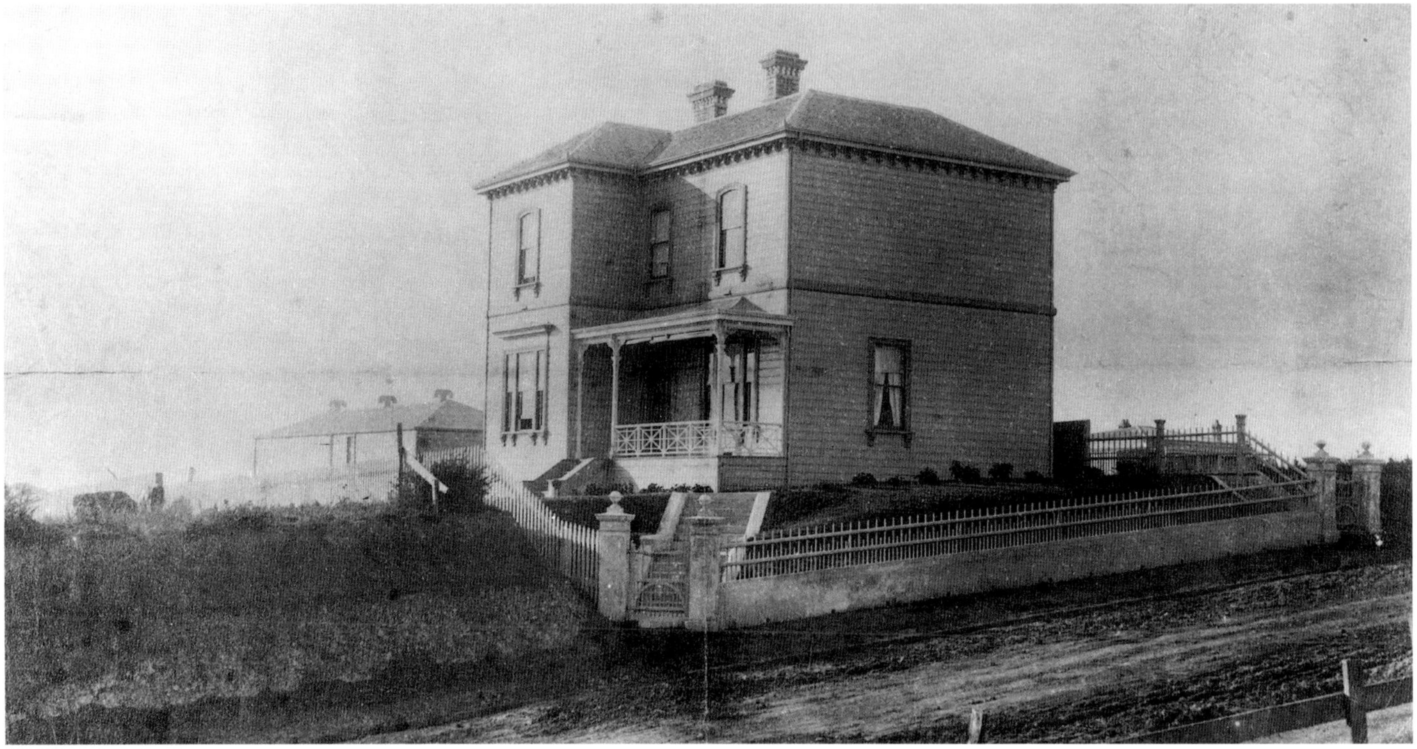

'Balgay', Cleveland Road, Parnell, c.1885–86

ill indeed, so ill he thought he was to die. We were both very alarmed. Geo. never was so ill, and I felt oh so lonely here in this strange place, was so thankful for the return of day. It has taken away the pleasure of our new house but if Geo. keeps improving he will pick up again but all the strength gained has been lost in this last illness. We think we are sorely tried, and have felt quite disheartened this time.

Geo. has thought on everything for our comfort and convenience and if he were well we would be happy in our pretty new house. It is a serious matter travelling here – it is so very expensive, but Geo. says this is the last move he will make. We hope we may be permitted to live in this nice new home for many a long year together. We have been very unfortunate as regards weather, rain and wind since ever we came: only a few perfect days and they were a treat. It is milder here than in Nelson. Geo. was not sorry to leave Nelson. I must say I was, changing about is not very pleasant, but it will be better for us to be here ...

These distances are terrible. We feel that I assure you. Mary and James go to school here – they like it so much and are getting on very nicely. Mary is learning to sew – she is to do all sorts of things with her way of it. Baby is well just now... Aunt Smith kindly knitted two pairs of sleeves for baby and sent them by post, so I must write her by this mail and thank her for them. I trust Aunt Isa is keeping pretty well. You will have dreary weather likely. I must now stop and with the best of wishes for Xmas and New Year,

I am, Yours sincerely, Mina Valentine.[7]

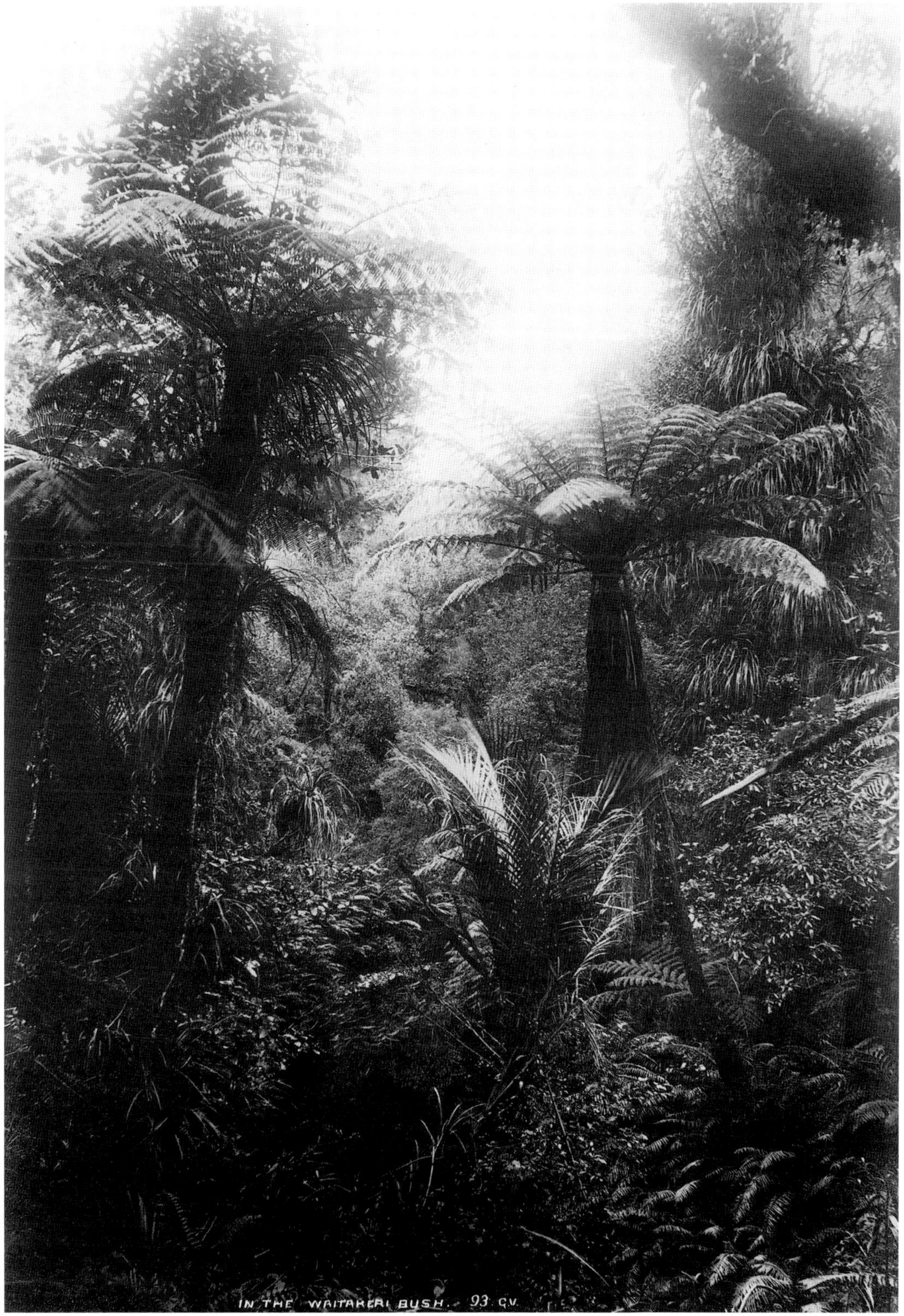

'In the Waitakere Bush', 1885

Auckland with its subtropical climate was to suit the Valentines and George's health requirements well. Their large new home in Parnell Borough's Cleveland Road commanded a view across the harbour, and George was under doctor's instructions to go horse riding every day.[8] Behind the house were a stable and well-equipped workshops which enabled him to experiment with technical innovations for his craft. A darkroom was almost certainly included, though large print runs are likely to have been handled elsewhere, considering the unhealthy and tiring nature of photographic printing.

Apart from these pursuits, George seems to have taken life at a quiet and steady pace, enjoying reading (poetry and Dickens were among his favourites) and involving himself thoroughly in the life of the Parnell Congregational Church. The Valentines' arrival in Auckland had timed well with the church's first service, and George became 'one of its most earnest supporters', taking 'a leading part in the work since its commencement'.[9] Like the rest of his family, George had long been involved in the Congregational movement which, along with its commitment to temperance and other social reforms, encouraged an unaffected belief in Christ and 'Christian decision' in the undecided.[10]

The move to Auckland was also to hold commercial advantages for Valentine. Prospects for sales of work were greatly improved in a town that had four times the population of Nelson, and that was situated on all the major international steamer routes – it was therefore the place from which most visits to the Hot Lakes would start and end. Benefit would also come from an increased access to the Thermal Region.

As his strength and health improved, Valentine embarked upon his series of Auckland views, starting with the harbour, then returning to the qualities of the New Zealand bush that so fascinated him in the nearby Waitakere ranges. '18 miles from Auckland – a most delightful picnic reserve', was the inscription he gave a superb image of the Waitakere Falls in one album. The Waitakere ranges also held many fine specimens of the mighty kauri – the last vestige of vast ancient forests – as well as much other unspoilt subtropical bush. The series recommenced at the harbour, at Queen Street Wharf, continuing with the city and harbour from Mount Eden, to Auckland from the North Shore, and a view of the heart of the city from the bottom of Queen Street. All of this was to establish him as an Auckland photographer.[11] Finished results were sold through G.T. Chapman's, either as single prints or made up into albums, usually with the plain, gold-embossed title *Photographs of New Zealand, by G.D. Valentine*. Around this time, Valentine also sent a collection of photographs to London for inclusion in the New Zealand section of the 'Colonial & Indian' Exhibition to open at South Kensington in May 1886.[12]

The author James Froude, on his world tour of British colonies in 1885, had dismissed Auckland's streets as 'not interesting'. At the same time, he noted in the shops that 'Photography was in fashion', with 'marvellous landscapes, lakes, mountains, waterfalls, or, coming to human subjects, Maori chiefs and Maori villages'.[13] Such imagery gave the author a good idea of what he should expect on his travels: later, at Te Wairoa, he met Guides Kate and Sophia, whose portraits he had 'studied in the Auckland photograph shops'.[14] After Froude's visit to Rotomahana, two of George Valentine's photographs were chosen to illustrate the Terraces, in the form of engravings, for his best-selling *Oceana, or England and Her Colonies*, 75,000 of which were sold within six months of first publication. Such publicity only increased the growing world-wide interest in the Terraces. According to some, the numbers of those visiting were now doubling every few months.[15]

Paying especial attention to such numbers was the Colonial Government which, along with numerous investors and

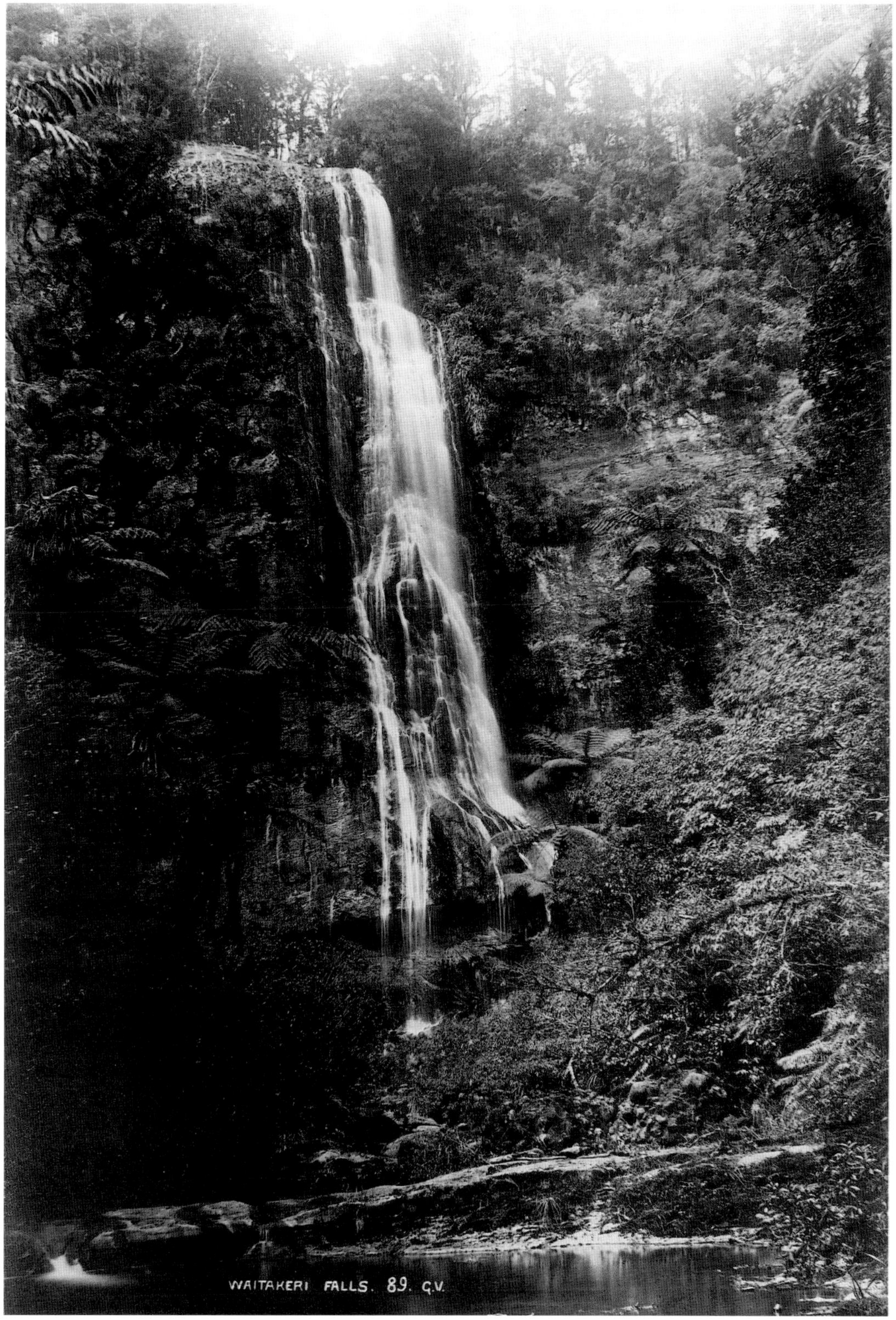

'Waitakere Falls', 1885

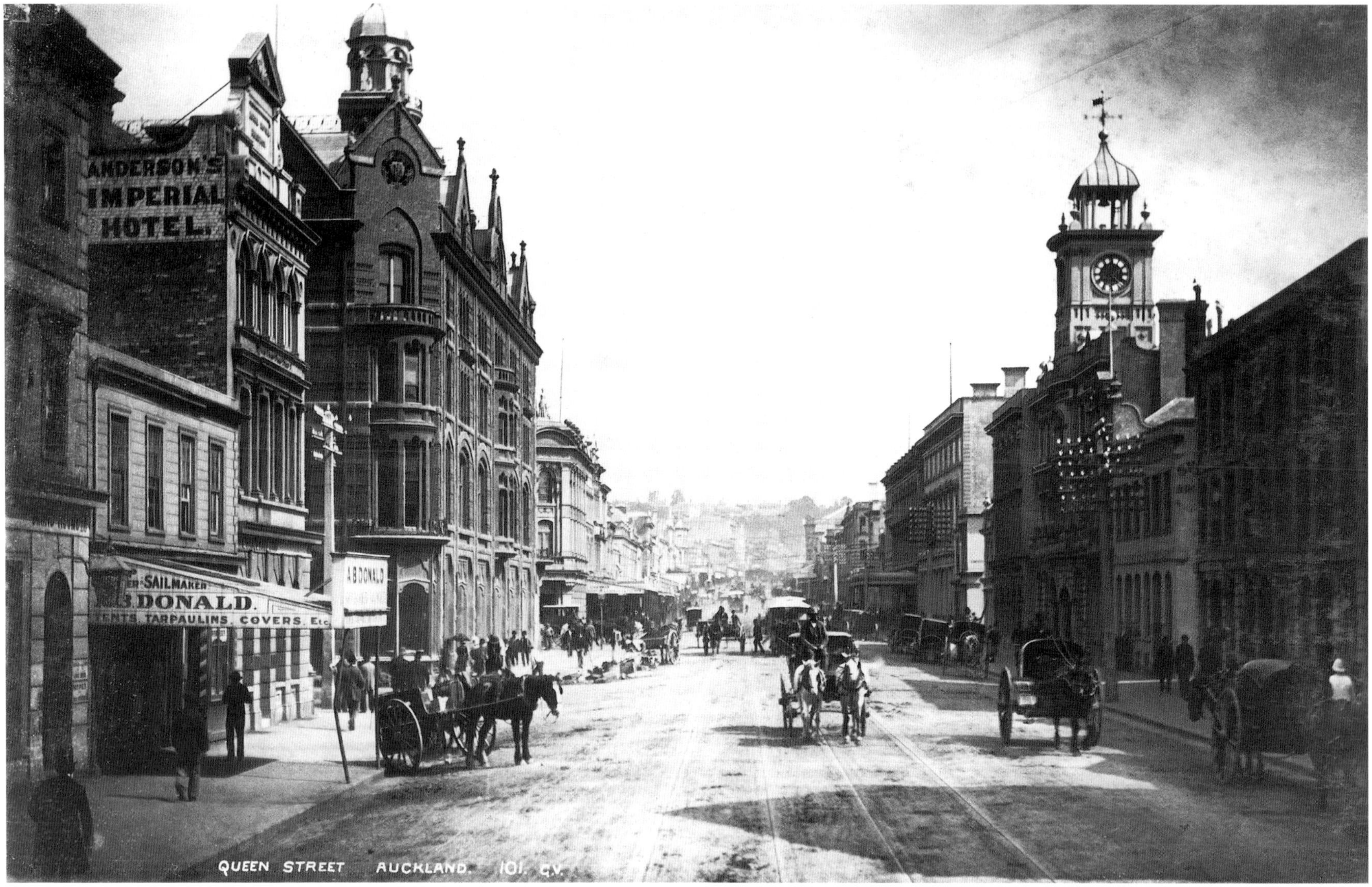

'Queen Street, Auckland', c.1885

speculators, had long held it 'a matter of general interest and of desirability ... [to] possess land in the neighbourhood of Rotomahana.[16] In 1874, the Premier William Fox had been one of the most forthright in wanting the Terraces under government control 'as soon as the Native title may be extinguished'.[17] In pressing its case for public ownership, the Government had of course always managed to claim the public good.[18] So far the Tūhourangi council of chiefs had been able to maintain an effective resistance to such efforts – with a little unbidden help from a rival tribe's claim to the land's actual title.

The start of 1886, however, had seen something new in the region, with Government Surveyor John Blythe at work on plans for a new road between Te Wairoa and Napier, and 'a coach road to the Terraces as soon as the Native Lands Court is held and the title to the land determined. In all probability this road will not be completed for a couple of years yet, but when finished, and a tourists' hotel established at the Pink Terrace, it will then be possible to make the visit to the Terraces leisurely and comfortably'.[19] The initiative for a hotel at the Pink Terrace had come from the principal Tūhourangi chief, Wi Keepa Te Rangipuawhe, in partnership with Terrace Hotel proprietor Charles Humphreys. Both had good reason for wishing it to go ahead and were confident that the licence to build would be granted. Accordingly, ground beside the Pink Terrace had been prepared for the erection of a large licensed hotel.[20] At the Terrace Hotel, Humphreys and intending business partner Alfred Minett had stored £600 worth of furniture and goods.[21] All now that held up the licence from being granted were opposing claims over the land from the neighbouring Ngāti Rangitihi, with hearings being worked through the system.

Back in Auckland, on the early morning of Thursday 10 June 1886, many of the city's residents were awoken from their sleep by sounds of distant explosions and thundering booms. Most who heard the noises were unsettled by the disturbance and looked forward to learning from the next morning's press exactly what had caused them. As the explosions continued, reporters finishing off the morning edition of the *New Zealand Herald* had their own ideas as to their source, and enough time to put out a hasty report:

> SUPPOSED SHIPPING DISASTER IN MANUKAU. ALARM GUNS HEARD IN AUCKLAND THIS MORNING. About half-past two o'clock this morning the firing of alarm guns was heard in Auckland by the watchman on the Queen-street Wharf, the police on duty, and the crews of vessels in harbour. The first impression was that it was a vessel in danger off Takapuna, but as the firing went on at intervals it was believed to be at the Manukau, especially as telephone messages came in from Remuera stating that residents had heard the sound of guns being fired in that quarter... The officer at Onehunga stated that he had seen a flash in the direction of the Manukau, and that it was believed a vessel was on shore at the Manukau Heads. From the continuousness of the firing, the loudness of the reports, and the fact that there were occasional salvoes of guns, it is the impression, that they must have proceeded from a man-of-war, and the supposition is that it might be the Russian cruiser Vestnik, which was believed to be coming up the West Coast. Up to time of going to press (four o'clock) the firing was proceeding, though seemingly slackening ... The flash of the guns firing was plainly visible from the cupola of the HERALD office.[22]

CHAPTER 7

ERUPTION

'This is the most awful moment of my life,' wrote 20-year-old Edwin Bainbridge in his diary from the smoking room of McRae's Rotomahana Hotel. 'I cannot tell when I may be called upon to meet my God. I am thankful that I find His strength sufficient for me. We are under heavy falls of volcano...'[1] From the rear of the building there came a heavy crash. The young English tourist closed his writing-case and turned his thoughts to those around him ...

June was off-peak season for visitors to the Terraces, and Bainbridge was the only tourist staying at Te Wairoa. Three days earlier he had enjoyed all the wonders of Rotomahana, including a bathe in the Pink Terrace. Since then he had chosen to linger, shooting pheasant with his host and acquainting himself with the inhabitants of the village. At around 1.15 a.m. on the intensely cold and clear starlit morning of Thursday 10 June 1886, Bainbridge was shaken from his sleep in an upstairs room in the Rotomahana Hotel by the movements of a heavy earthquake. From concern for his guest, hotel proprietor Joseph McRae went to his room and called through the door that it was '...just one of their earthquakes'.[2]

The shaking continued, however, and with it a rumbling noise like a heavy storm of wind.[3] As the young tourist got up to dress, the rumbling grew to 'a tremendous roar, rapidly increasing in volume like the sound of a tornado approaching'.[4] Outside, Joseph McRae discovered that the source of the disturbance was five miles away in the direction of Tarawera, which, when seen at first was 'just like a small' cloud on the mountain, with flashes of lightning of great brilliancy'.[5] Those sleeping at the hotel were roused from their beds and, together with McRae and Bainbridge, went up to the old Mission Station on the hill to better investigate the occurrence. McRae's brother-in-law William Bird noted everyone's feelings at this time as being 'more of awe than fear. No one thought of escaping from the place. The majesty of the spectacle held us spellbound.'[6]

At the Terrace Hotel, proprietor Charles Humphreys also roused his lodgers Charles Stubbs and intending business partner Alfred Minett. Minett heard

> a loud voice call up the staircase: 'Stubbs, Stubbs, come and see Tarawera blow up,' it was Humphreys calling, and I was dressed and out in the street in about half a minute,

> and soon Stubbs and Humphreys joined me. We looked in the direction of Tarawera, and there we saw a cloud gradually rising, black as ink, behind the hill that shelters Wairoa; it was flashing with lightning in every direction, while occasionally fireballs, like rockets, dashed from it; the number of these and their vivacity increased to a fearful extent while we were gazing. The cloud kept slowly and steadily rising, and gradually bent over in our direction. Stubbs and I proceeded to where we thought we should get a good view over the lake ...[7]

Seventeen miles to the northwest of Tarawera, another observer, 'About 1.45 ... was startled by a steady roar, like that produced by a blast furnace, or a great waterfall ... upon looking out I saw that all the eastern side of the heavens was aglow, and there seemed to be a great column of fire rising to a height of about fifteen or twenty degrees, while above it was a dense column of black smoke.'[8] Two miles closer to the blast, Rotorua postmaster Roger Dansey observed in the same direction to his 'intense amazement ... an immense column of fire ... rushing up heavenwards with a frightful roar ... an immense solid column of fire rushing up perpendicularly. Its sides were not jagged, but even, as the edges of a board. It appeared to be from 300 to 400 yards in width ... and of even width from its base right up to the very top, where it was cut off square with its sides. Huge streaks of yellow, red, black and grey ran straight up the column.'[9]

In his foray with Stubbs, Minett found 'the darkness was intense, the cold piercing, and it appeared dangerous to go forward, as we were getting more and more under the cloud and its dropping fires'. Back at the hotel to collect his coat, he found on arriving that he could not keep a candle alight: the wind was forcing the doors open and the building shaking violently. Turning again to the road in search of McRae and his party, 'the lightning seemed to strike the road in so many places before me that I turned back again and up the Mu road'. Joining up with McRae, Minett headed for a vantage point by Te Mu, the church on the hill, and observed 'the Tarawera mountain belching out flames thousands of feet into the air, and illumining the whole heavens; clouds of steam and smoke rose above this, and a molten shining mass rolled down the sides'.[10] To McRae it was a sight 'that no man who saw it can ever forget. Apparently the mount had three craters, and flames of fire were shooting up fully a thousand feet high. There seemed to be a continuous shower of balls of fire for miles around.'[11]

With Tarawera's summit 'a mound of fire', the lake was 'a copper mirror, reflecting the mount from base to summit in a lurid glare. Dominating all, hung the great cloud-curtain, gloomy and dark above, saffron and orange on its undersurface. From the cloud great balls of flaming rock dropped from time to time, descending with a splash into the waters of the lake.'[12] Still, Mrs Humphreys observed, the small party 'did not feel frightened then. There were twelve of us, and we remained about ten minutes watching the magnificent view, for it was magnificent.'[13]

The group on the hill were not the only ones in Te Wairoa to be awed by the spectacle: school teacher Charles Haszard found it 'the most wonderful sight I have ever seen';[14] to his daughter Ina, 'fiery electric balls darted in every direction and looked like brilliant fireworks as they burst'.[15] From their large whare behind the Terrace Hotel, Guide Sophia and her husband Tiawihio also witnessed the event, watching in amazement as 'the sky seemed to be on fire, beautiful balls of light blue, green and red ... shot into the air at each explosion's roar'.[16]

Gradually the mushroom cloud above the watchers lengthened, its edges illumined by a quivering electrical display: 'The black cloud was driven slowly in on the light, dropping over it like a veil, and by degrees blotting it out.

For a time the lightning flashed through the murky mass, and then there came on the most utter and appalling darkness.'[17] Now there also came a strong and sudden wind blowing down the valley to the lake, then what at first was seemed to be rain but was soon discovered to be mud. McRae's group decided to head back.[18]

With Tarawera glowing red behind the stretching curtain, Joseph McRae led his party to the Rotomahana Hotel, the group of 12 Europeans and several Māori reaching the hotel just before 3 a.m. They were scarcely inside before the wind increased and it began to rain heavily.[19] Earthquake shocks also recommenced, and then 'Shortly after, what seemed to be heavy hailstones came pouring on the roof, and this continued about a quarter of an hour. This was succeeded by a fall of heavy stones, and fire balls, and mud and lava, falling after the manner of rain.'[20] 'The windows were smashed in, and we found that what we had taken for rain was scoria and stone. The wind, blowing violently, was veering and shifting in every direction, stones and scoria were dashing on the house with deafening noise, and the roaring of the crater was tremendous.'[21]

'Meanwhile the eruption had increased at Tarawera. The smoke again rolling away disclosed the whole length of the mountain still in action, throwing up even larger quantities of red-hot stones and scoria and immense volumes of black smoke.' Around 3.30 a.m. Lake Rotomahana itself erupted in a huge explosion, joining a line of craters nearly ten miles long; 'a dense heavy grey cloud of smoke, or more probably steam and dust, shot up from a point some six or seven miles to westward of Tarawera and came rolling down with the wind. Spreading eastward and northward, it soon enveloped the whole landscape.'[22]

'The downpour of mud and stone continued for about half an hour, and Mr. McRae and Mr. Humphreys went upstairs to ascertain whether the roof was alright. They found that the windows were all smashed, and that the roof was partly smashed in through the weight of mud.'[23] McRae and Humphreys were kept busy ensuring that the house did not catch alight: twice they had to extinguish flames caused by 'the upsetting of two kerosene oil lamps, one in the smoking-room and the other in the tap-room'.[24] McRae also put out 'at least ten balls of fire, which came crashing through his roof ... igniting everything they came in contact with'.[25] Soon the weight upon the roof began to tell upon it. At around 4 a.m. 'the first portion that gave way was a detached kitchen and pantry, and then we all collected in the smoking-room'.[26] Still 'there was no panic, no noticeable excitement. All of us were resigned to whatever the future held. Bainbridge finished his writing, closed his diary and proposed prayer. We were very ordinary people in an extraordinary situation, but we all joined in that prayer for safety.'[27]

McRae found a Bible for Bainbridge, who then read to the gathering

> several passages ... and preached 'a most beautiful sermon'... He told them that he believed God had given them this respite before the end came, that they might prepare themselves to go into His presence: and exhorted them all if they had not given their hearts to God, to do so now; and if any of them should escape, to let it be the turning-point in their lives. He pointed out that at the last moment Christ heard the prayer of the thief upon the Cross, and said to him, 'This day shalt thou be with Me in Paradise'; and that if they would only now just accept Jesus, He would be with them at the end.[28]

In Minett's words,

> Some moments elapsed; and we were all silent. I went up to him, and thanked him for having thought for us all in

> these dread moments; for during the whole time we were expecting death at any moment – either by being buried alive by the sand, mud, and stones that were overwhelming the house; or by suffocation with the sulphurous gases which pervaded the atmosphere; or by being crushed under the falling timbers; or swallowed up by the opening ground as it trembled beneath our feet. There was also the additional danger of being burned to death by the fireballs which were dashing over and through the building. Mr. Bainbridge, though calm, seemed to feel that he would not survive the night ...[29]

At around 4.30 a.m. McRae and Humphreys, still going about with their fire buckets, had just returned from upstairs when, from just above the stairs, close to where everyone was gathered, 'The roof of the hotel gave way ... with a loud crash, and the whole of the upper storey collapsed, the debris falling into the rooms below. We left the smoking-room and went into the drawing-room, which as it was the newest part of the house, we thought would stand the longest, but it was with the greatest difficulty that we got there, owing to falling stones and mud which impeded us. When we went outside, everybody, without exception, was cool and self possessed.'[30] Filing beneath the balcony and along the verandah, the party found they 'could not keep lights burning, the wind was so great, and stones and mud were still showering down in great quantities'.[31]

They had been no longer than ten minutes in the drawing room when part of the balcony fell in, just in front of where they sat sheltered. 'The only light now came from the intermittent flashes of vivid lightning and a pale momentary gleam as matches were struck to examine the heavily loaded ceiling beams of our shelter. And again we waited – just a few people cut off from the rest of the world ... waiting and longing most of all for daylight.'[32] 'Looking out, we perceived a fire on the opposite side of the road, which reminded us of the danger we were in from this same cause, and in about five minutes we saw a still larger fire to our right, which we at once made out to be Mr. Haszard's house all in a blaze ... we dared not stir out to attempt assistance; between earthquake and fire we stood expecting death ourselves.'[33]

Up on the hill, with the schoolhouse burning and the rest of her family trapped, Clara Haszard escaped the house with her father's guests, the surveyors Blythe and Lundius: 'When the flames got too strong we ran outside with no settled idea where to go. We stumbled amongst the trees in the garden until the flames lighted us to make for the paddock.'[34] Briefly were they warmed by an outburst with 'a fearful sulphurous smell ... scorching hot but [it] did not last long', before they managed to find shelter in a nearby hen-house.[35]

At the hotel, 'The back part of the house, in which was the dining-room gave way next, and suddenly we heard a fearful crash and roar as if thousands of tons of stuff were falling';[36] the roof and upstairs portion of the house had completely caved in. With this, McRae decided to evacuate the doomed hotel:

> I then thought it was not safe to stay inside longer. We thought it better to brave the showers that were falling than to be crushed to death in the house. We got whatever shawls and mats were in the room and wrapped them round our heads to protect them from falling stones. We arranged that we should make for either Sophia's house or the whare-puni ... Mr. and Mrs. Humphries went out first, [Bainbridge followed, then McRae] and the two servant maids and the rest of the party... it was so dark that you could not see your hand three inches from your face – it was raining mud and stones, without any intermission. I got over the balcony which had fallen down in front of

> the house, and assisted the girls over... We then started for Sophia's whare ...[37]

Dimly a light shone from the whare on a rise some 400 yards away, and through mud and hurtling debris, McRae managed to reach the refuge: 'when I got there I found William Bird and John Bird, myself and the two girls – five of us arrived at the one time'.[38] William Bird joined his wife Kiekie and their child with relief, but Bainbridge, George Baker the cook, and Mr and Mrs Humphreys had still not arrived. Under Sophia and Tiawihio's steeply pitched roof more than 60 people were now gathered; as whare after whare had collapsed or been buried, villagers had struggled through mud and ash to the security of this haven. Others attempted to reach the carved house Hinemihi, while settlements closer to the volcano such as Te Ariki and Moura were offered no such relief as tons of ash, red-hot rocks and mud poured forth to bury their inhabitants.

Tiawihio and several of the young men strengthened the supports of the house, while McRae went out to find the rest of his party: 'I got a rug and wrapped it round my head and went to look for the others and kept shouting all the time.'[39] 'The shower of debris was great. I was knocked down, but getting up again, called as loud as possible ... I was rewarded by coming in contact with George Baker, my cook, who was standing against a tree, and got him to the whare.'[40] Through the blackness McRae found his way 'back to the hotel to find the others. I found that Messrs Stubbs and Minett, having groped about for some time in the rain, had returned to the drawing room.'[41] Helping them through the storm to Sophia's place, he then went out again to seek those still missing; a nearby whare burst into flame, helping him to see.[42] Towards Hinemihi, McRae found Mr and Mrs Humphreys heading for the carved house. 'I went back to the whare, looking for Mr. Bainbridge, but could get no answer, and I have not seen him since.'[43]

CHAPTER 8

AFTERMATH

As daylight broke in Auckland, newspaper offices were already crowded with those wanting to know more about the early-morning explosions. The news of a shipping disaster involving the *Vestnik*, a Russian man-of-war to which New Zealand had recently been unexpected host, had left the public hungry for details.[1] In to the midst of this concern, however, there came news of 'a catastrophe, far surpassing in horror even the most terrible of shipwrecks'.[2] Mount Tarawera, never known before to be active, was in violent eruption, the whole area was in darkness and people were fleeing the district. Hundreds of new boiling springs had broken out, some in the streets of Rotorua, and great loss of life was feared among those at Te Wairoa and around Lake Tarawera.[3]

The Rotorua telegraphic office message was a bombshell, and word of it spread even before it could be published. The result was an immediate rush of even larger crowds at the two Auckland newspaper offices, which by 9 a.m. had issued 'extras' containing Rotorua postmaster Roger Dansey's full message. At the *Herald*, 'the office and the street in its vicinity were crowded with people anxiously awaiting the receipt of the successive telegrams which arrived from the seat of the disaster ... Tens of thousands of copies of extras, issued on receipt of each fresh telegram from Rotorua, was eagerly contested for by an excited crowd of numbers of individuals.'[4]

> ROTORUA, 9.30 a.m. The township of Rotorua and the surrounding country are enveloped in dense smoke. Maoris and Europeans are rushing about in a state of great excitement. Property of all kinds will be completely destroyed. People are fleeing in crowds from the district, but they do not know whither to turn, as the whole country from Lake Taupo to Tauranga is covered with a thick smoke, which makes it as dark as midnight.[5]
>
> THE OFFICIAL REPORT FROM WELLINGTON. LARGE LOSS OF NATIVES ... The Native Minister has received a telegram to the effect that the house of Mr. Haszard, schoolmaster, Wairoa ... was struck by lightning, and the whole family killed except the two eldest daughters ... Mr. McRae's hotel was completely wrecked. One tourist is missing. Several natives have lost their lives, but the exact number is not known ...[6]
>
> ROTORUA, 11 a.m. Terrible night. At Wairoa there is

ten feet of mud and stones ... The schoolhouse at Wairoa was fired by the lightning, and then smothered in mud and stones. The two hotels there are all in ruins ... Mrs Haszard has just been rescued, but is injured. Four of her children were found dead alongside of her. Mr. Haszard is missing. It is reported that all Rotomahana has disappeared.[7]

ROTORUA, 1.58 p.m. ... From Wairoa I learn disastrous news. Nearly every house in the village is levelled to the ground, and the country spread for miles with fully two feet of mud, boulders, and sand. The lovely Tikitapu bush is like a desert waste ... Mr. McRae's people all escaped, but the schoolmaster and family are reported as killed, with the exception of two children. Ten or twelve Maoris are reported killed, and many dying ... A report just arrived states that Mrs. Haszard was rescued from the debris, but the child at her breast is dead. All the natives living at Te Ariki have perished.[8]

ROTORUA, 4.35 p.m. ... The Terraces are all gone. The Te Ariki natives are reported to be all lost ...[9]

LATEST FROM ROTORUA. ROTORUA, Thursday ...The two eldest Misses Haszard were brought in, and it was then thought they were the sole survivors of the late respected native school teacher's family. Mrs. Humphries and the servants from Mr. McRae's hotel were all brought in ... The party were very glad to learn that Mrs. Haszard had been dug out alive, and comparatively uninjured ... Two of the children were found dead beside her ... Several natives are known to be killed, but the number is not definitely known. It is supposed to be about a dozen ... there is very little hope that any of the natives in the Moura and Te Ariki settlement, near Tarawera mountain, could possibly have escaped ... A tourist who was stopping at McRae's, name at present unknown, is missing, and is supposed to have been knocked down and covered up by the falling mud. Mr. Blythe and others describe the scene as most appalling.[10]

SPECIAL REPORT FROM OHINEMUTU, TAURANGA, 9 p.m. ... There has been no communication with Te Wairoa, but many have gone out to there from here ... Two buggies have just returned from Wairoa with some of the inhabitants, who report the place as being destroyed ... Mr. McRae and his servants have escaped, but one tourist, named Bainbridge, is reported missing. Mr. McRae's conduct during the time is spoken of in the highest praise ... Those who have come in from Wairoa are females, and they present a sad appearance, looking pale and ghastly. Their dresses are smeared with lava. No doubt the terraces will be destroyed. How the whole thing will finish, and when, is quite perplexing.[11]

Details of the eruption continued to pour in and the public was struck by the disaster's awful magnitude. One editorial stated '... with certainty ... that never before has the attention of the whole of New Zealand been so concentrated on a single subject as it was throughout the whole of the day'.[12] From his home in Parnell, George Valentine's reaction to the event can only be imagined. His own story was now also part of a much greater one, and the results of his journey 18 months before completely altered in their significance. If the subject matter of the bulk of his work in New Zealand was destroyed, the most terrible realisation would be in the fates of those whom he had met on the visit, including Tūhourangi chief Tamihana Te Keu, who must surely have perished with his family at the settlement of Totarariki.

Soon first-hand accounts by survivors were being published throughout the country. Guide Sophia as she was interviewed 'wept copiously' for Te Wairoa and the loss of lives, her house being one of the few still standing in the village. Joseph McRae's first interview was surprising, given that the previous day's news had reported his being 'blown

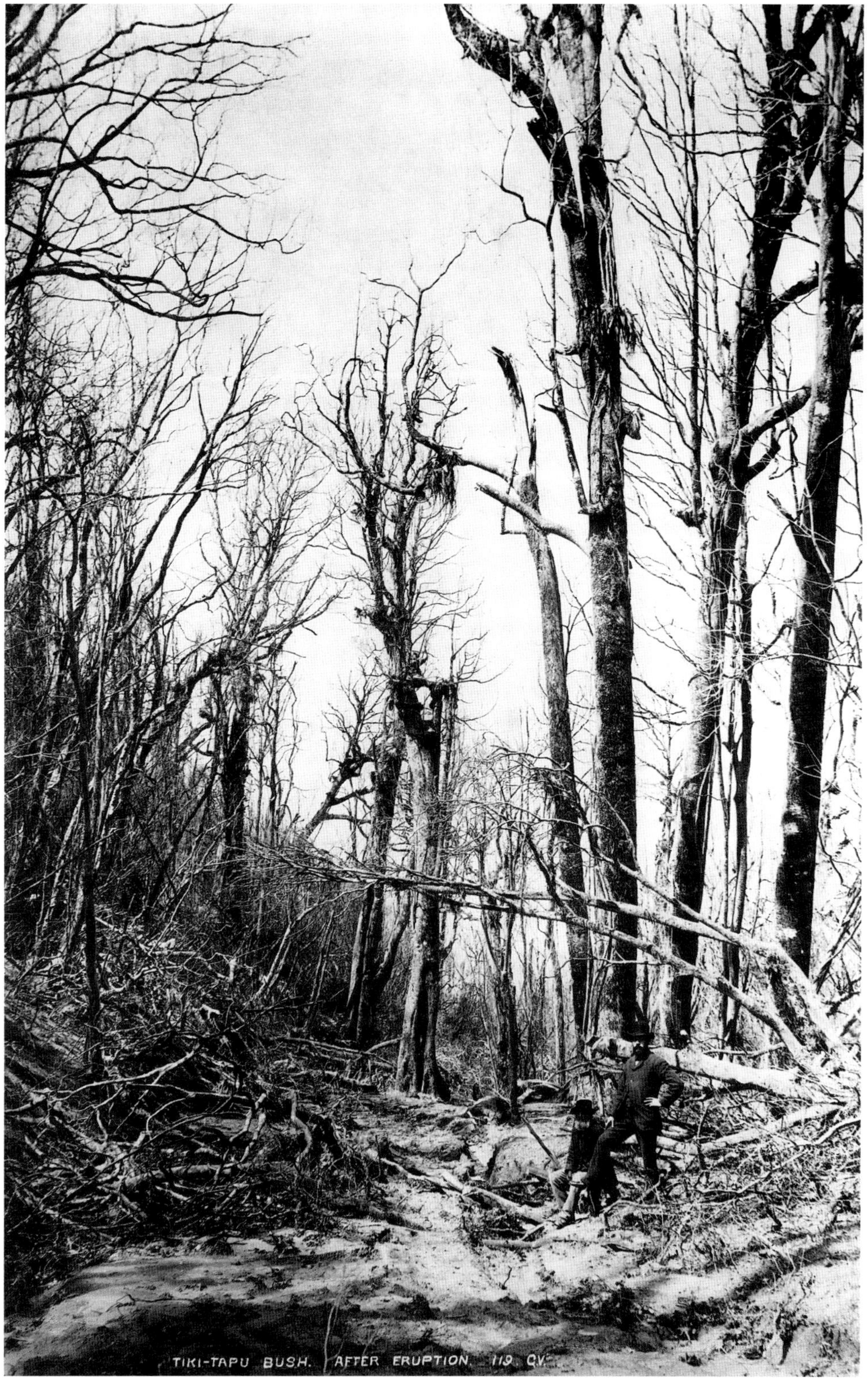

'Tiki-Tapu Bush, after Eruption', 1886

up'. The search for Bainbridge was still unsuccessful, but McRae confirmed the safety of Clara and Ina Haszard and his astonishment at finding their mother Amelia alive and 'not greatly injured'.[13] Tragically, the rest of the family had died in the house. Three days later in Rotorua, a burial service was held for Charles Haszard, the four young children and Edwin Bainbridge, whose body was at last found beneath a balcony of the Rotomahana Hotel: he had evidently been crushed in the act of escape.

Many other tragic stories were to surface. Seven Europeans and an estimated 110–120 Māori had lost their lives.[14] A group of Tūhourangi camping on one of the islands at Rotomahana had been overwhelmed as the lake had turned into a crater. Those in Te Ariki and Mourā villages were buried under 75 feet of mud and debris. At Ōhinemutu, a huge tangi was held, with the displaced of Te Wairoa taking up temporary residence at Tamatekapua. Survivors were given generous supplies of potatoes, flour and pigs by local Māori, while Pākehā ('not our fellow-settlers only, but also the thousands in Europe and in America who have found delight in the attractions of Rotorua, or health in its springs')[15] were urged to follow their open-handedness.

Surprising in the face of such human tragedy was the intensity with which the loss of the Pink and White Terraces was immediately felt. The day after the eruption, a newspaper editor summed up the feelings of many:

> In the face of such a painful loss of human life it seems almost out of place to lament the destruction of the lovely scenery which was the cynosure of thousands of tourists from every part of the world. But there are few who will not sincerely regret the loss of the beautiful Terraces. They are gone, and their site is the scene of a raging volcano ... nothing will ever take the place of the lovely handiwork of Nature, the matchless veil of lacework that she had been weaving for a thousand years, and thrown over the Pink and White Terraces, now to be seen no more for ever. It is unbecoming, perhaps, to grieve for inanimate nature, when so many of our fellow-creatures have been lost, but the feeling for our Terraces was something akin to love; and while their disappearance will be regarded as a misfortune to New Zealand, their loss will come home to every citizen of Auckland like a personal sorrow.[16]

From Rotorua, however, there came a report from surveyor John Blythe that perhaps the eulogy had come too soon. With gladness he stated the news received 'from a native who passed them on his way here, that the White and Pink Terraces are uninjured. Their loss would have been a world-wide calamity.' It seemed incredible, especially since 'The native, who came from Rotomahana last night [11 June] and reported the safety of the Terraces, says that Rotomahana is a seething boiling pool, and he believes the native settlements on Tarawera are completely buried.'[17] Nevertheless the report was immediately despatched by telegram to Parliament, where it was hailed in the House with loud applause.[18]

Three expedition parties left Rotorua on the Saturday to gain a confirmation of the facts, despite Rotomahana now being 'a seething roaring mass of water, the clouds of steam from which are several thousand feet high'.[19] The first party to leave, which was also searching for survivors, came close enough to see 'immense volumes of steam and smoke rolling up from the spot on which the lake once stood'.[20] The second party got no closer than six or seven miles from Rotomahana before being halted by 'a tract of volcanic dust as fine as flour, into which their horses sank up to their bellies'.[21]

Comprising a dozen or so individuals, the third party was equipped for a longer journey and headed by Rotorua railway surveyor James Stewart. Also in the group was eruption survivor Harry Lundius, and the two Auckland news-

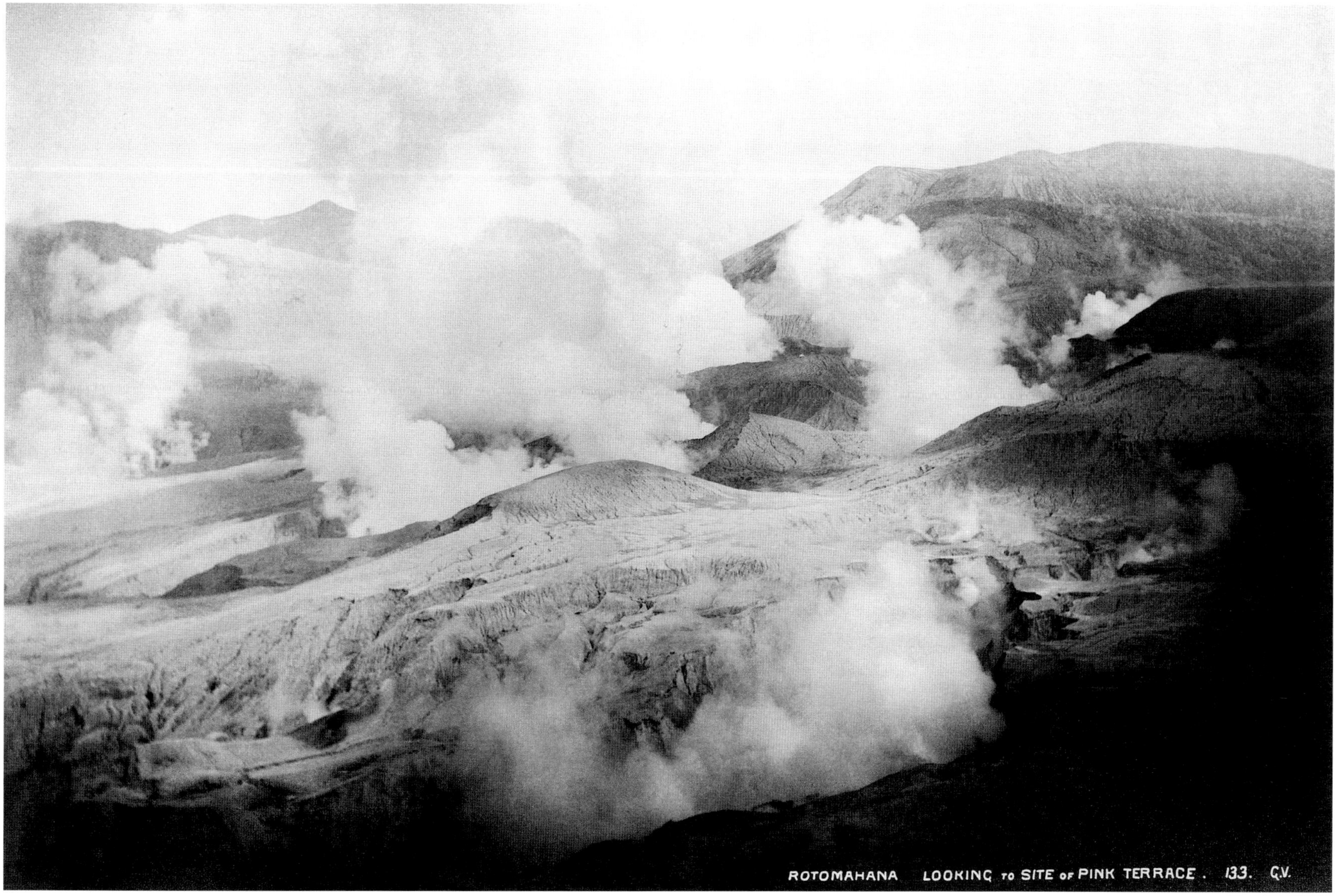

'Rotomahana, looking to site of Pink Terrace', 1886
"This View is taken White Terrace site showing Hape-o-toroa Mt. on right" – George Valentine.

paper editors, William Berry from the *New Zealand Herald* and Thomson Leys from the *Auckland Evening Star*. Reaching Te Wairoa by coach with some difficulty, the group returned to Lake Tikitapu, then left the vehicle to commence a toilsome march across the mud-covered hills. With every footstep they sank to their ankles, but they were determined to find out the fate of the Terraces, 'even at the cost of some fatigue or even danger'. The walk continued over hills and valleys, 'over fields of dust as fine as flour, over expanse of rough stones, over hillsides which had been washed with showers of hot water from the volcano', until at last a vantage point was gained

> from which we looked down upon an awful scene. All the ground about the Pink Terrace had fallen in. We looked down upon some thirteen or fourteen craters, all belching forth stone and ashes. We could not count the separate craters exactly owing to the smoke and steam, but it seemed to me that the whole area which had been occupied by the White and Pink Terraces and the Lake Rotomahana was now occupied with vast craters all roaring and belching forth stones and cinders... We could not see the site of the White Terrace, the steam and smoke quite concealed it. We were all of opinion that nothing of the kind could remain intact. We fear that Te Tarata and its loveliness has passed away.[22]

Thomson Leys' report was equally despairing. He found the whole configuration of the place

> so completely altered, that those who were most familiar with its features hesitated in locating the site of the Pink Terrace. The spot finally settled upon was one of especial activity, dense masses of steam and smoke completely obscuring the view in that direction ... That the Terraces were utterly destroyed was manifest enough to everyone, and we gazed in silence and in sorrow upon this spectacle of fierce and destructive turmoil ... The whole mountainside was strewn with fragments of terrace-formation, but as the surroundings of the old lake at many points were marked by areas of silicious deposit there was no clear evidence that these fragments came from either of the great Terraces, and there was still the narrow chance that the Terraces were not blown out but were covered up beneath the deep deposits of ejected matter.[23]

Hope surfaced again in William Berry's report from the following day: 'We saw the place where Otukapuarangi (the Pink Terrace) stands. The Terrace, I believe, to be safe. Steam was issuing from it, but I do not think that any crater has burst there. I do not think the Terraces are broken. The steam was coming from the original springs. One of the craters was sending out fiery flames. We could see the fire through the smoke ... I saw the Pink Terrace for a short time. I believe this structure is all right, but it was covered with ashes.'[24]

Uncertainties continued. On the Monday morning William Berry was able to report that 'Wahanga, one of the ranges of Tarawera, looked to be quieter, but Tarawera proper was still busy. The great volcanic activity, however, appeared to be at the Terraces, which were in more violent eruption than yesterday. Immense clouds of steam went up all day, and in the forenoon two high black columns shot up in the air in the shape of a waterspout, and must have been several thousand feet high.' Berry also recorded his rather poignant encounter with a Māori who expressed 'with some bitterness, "You pakehas have been striving and fighting to get hold of the Terraces. I make you a present of them."'[25]

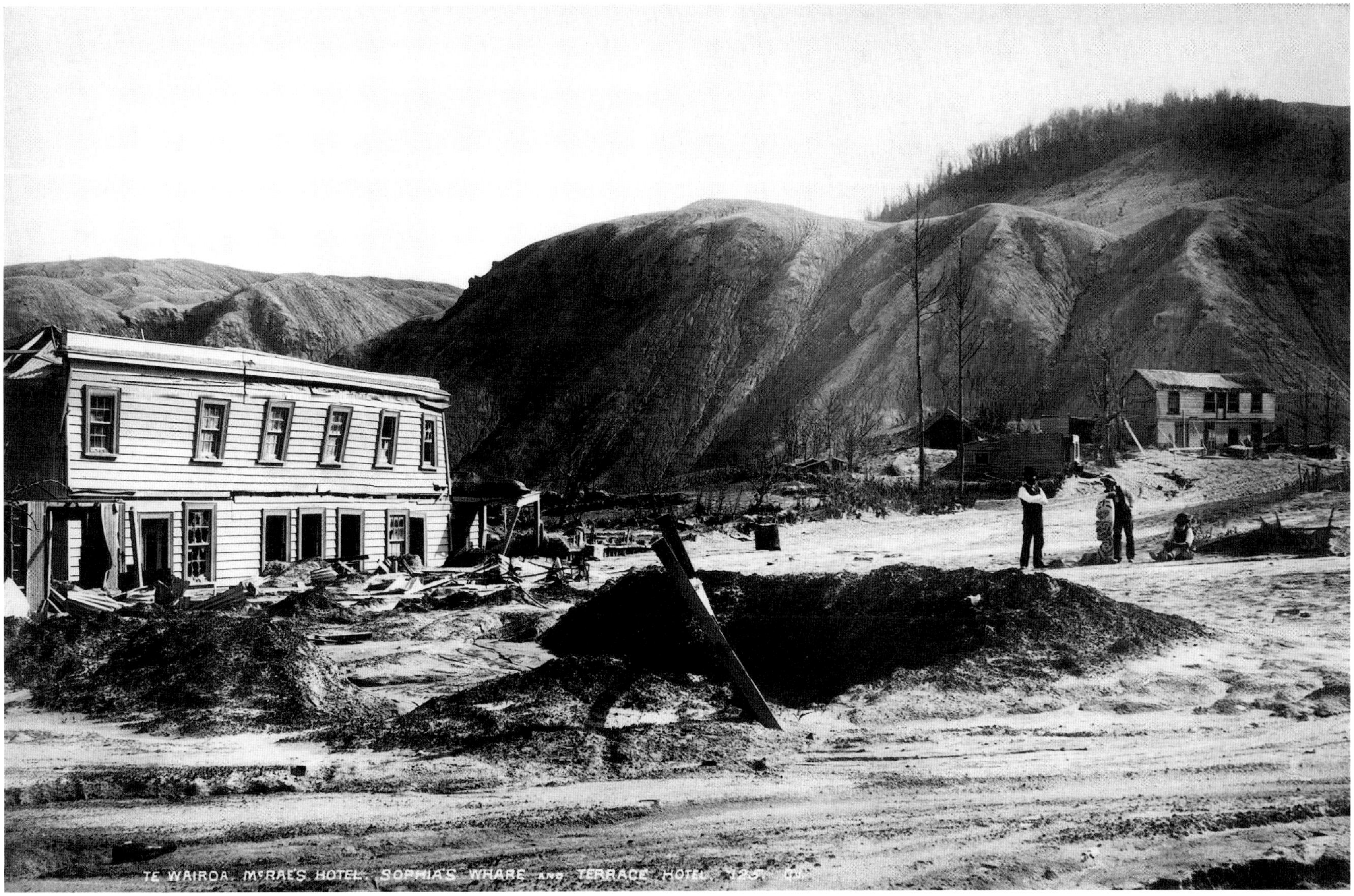

'Te Wairoa, McRae's Hotel, Sophia's Whare and Terrace Hotel', 1886

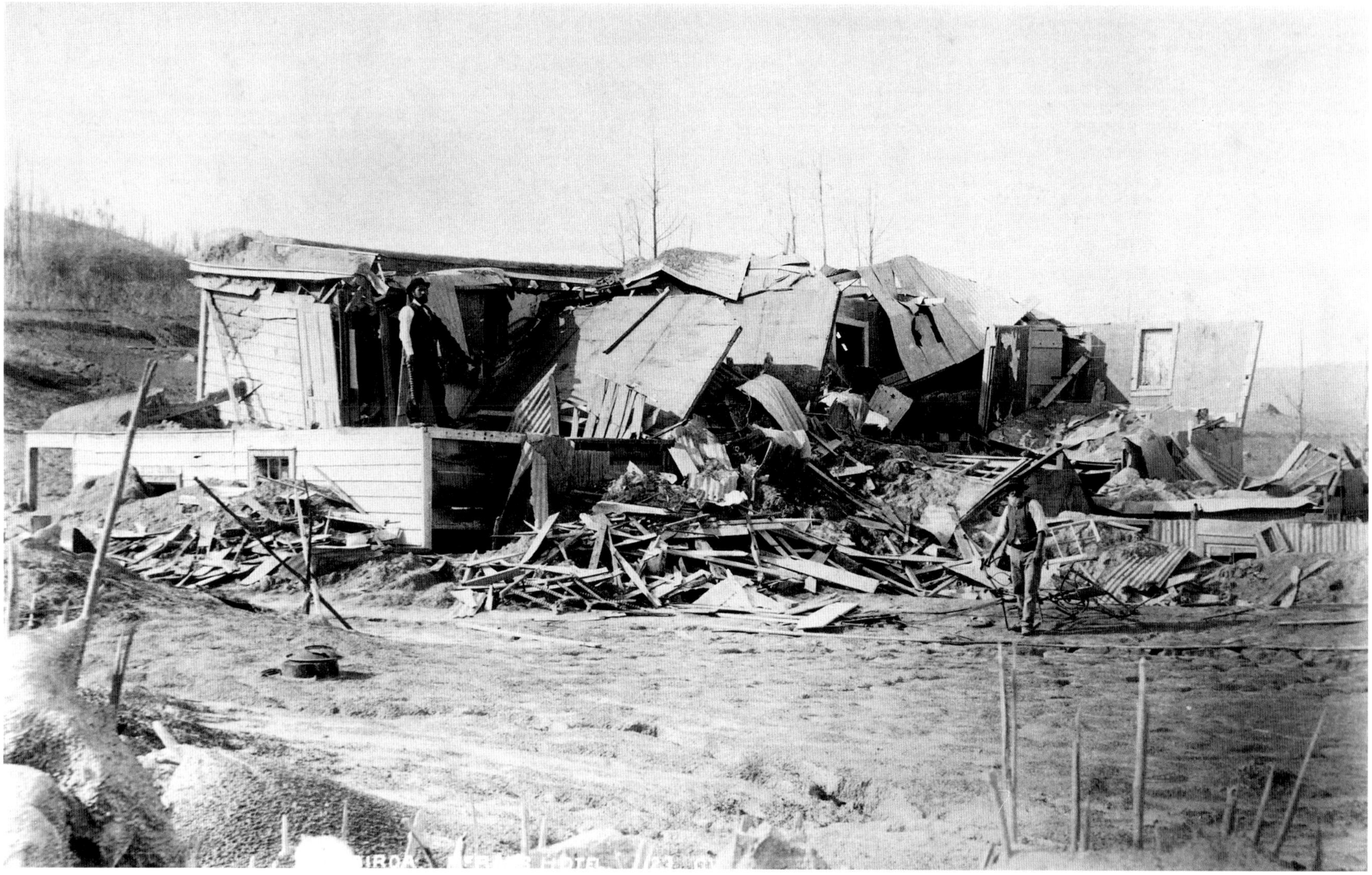

'Te Wairoa, McRae's Hotel', 1886

Photographers had been at Te Wairoa from just three days after the eruption, and photographs of the devastation were ready for the Auckland public four days after that.[26] However, George Valentine, with winter conditions and his health to consider, was confined to his home in Parnell, and would have to wait before making his own investigations.[27] The sudden and desperate demand for photographs of the Terraces, though, may have kept him occupied. One day after the eruption, at the other end of the country in Dunedin, photographer Alfred Burton had found his window display of photographs from a recent visit to Rotomahana crowded with spectators, and was later 'utterly unable' to keep up with public demand.[28] Soon Burton would make illustrated lectures throughout the country, before heading to Britain to do the same – contributing to a satirist's view that: 'Two things now engage the public attention in the matter of the Tarawera eruption: One is to explain it and the other to turn an honest penny by it. At present only the photographers have discovered how to do the latter, and probably it will turn out in the end that the eruption occurred chiefly in the interest of photographers.'[29]

In explaining the eruption, there seemed no shortage of mysteries – both physical and supernatural – upon which to ponder. One of the strangest was a 'phantom canoe' which had been seen on Lake Tarawera by a party on the way to the Terraces ten days before the eruption.[30] The sighting had been taken as an omen of disaster to come, and this was confirmed by the ancient tohunga Tuhoto, who had then predicted the region's very destruction. Now the centenarian tohunga was believed by many Māori to have caused the eruption – a belief only reinforced when four days after the event he was found alive in his buried whare, muttering, and apparently not very anxious to come out. His being unearthed was looked upon with dread and amazement by the Tūhourangi, who now wanted nothing more to do with him.[31]

Over the next few months there came a trickle of photographers to the district, but as the warmer weather of spring approached the photographers and artists of Auckland were said to be making a bee-line for the region.[32] George Valentine, again accompanied by his publisher Charles Chapman, was slightly ahead of the pack, leaving Auckland in early October. At Ōhinemutu they joined Joseph McRae, who was now living there and, though widely commended for his bravery during the eruption, facing bankruptcy. Valentine, Chapman and McRae took the recommended Te Wairoa route, stopping at the Tikitapu Bush to record the forest standing skeletal and bare. Approaching Te Wairoa, Valentine photographed the disused mill, half-buried in a sea of mud. Further along was the still-habitable Terrace Hotel where they would shelter for the night. Valentine's view of the back of the Rotomahana Hotel captured McRae, his one-time host, standing amidst the crushed and splintered ruins. In another photograph he arrested the general scene, with Sophia's whare and both hotels surrounded by devastation, and trees and landmarks stripped of familiarity.

Evidently there were still hopes for a flow of tourist traffic to the region. After a night in the ruined village, Valentine and Chapman, joined by local half-Māori guide Alfred Warbrick, were hauled over Lake Tarawera to Te Ariki in Warbrick's new boat, which had been 'built to carry a party of eight tourists in addition to the crew'. From the site of the buried settlement, Valentine captured one of his most potent images, as the boatman in the foreground held his pose in front of distant hills stripped of life, a gaping wound in Tarawera's side.

From the Te Ariki site the party was able to walk the

bed of the old Kaiwaka Creek with ease, 'the channel being better walking than the mud, even when hard. There are still a few places where the mud is heavy, and which are pointed out by the guides.' Between Rotomakariri and the site of the White Terrace they observed a number of small lakelets 'of various colours – light and dark blue, light green, mauve, black, and pure white'. At Rotomahana, Valentine was able to get 'one photographic view, which, when compared with the outlines of the hills as taken previously to the eruption, proved tolerably conclusively that a lake now exists on the site of the White Terrace'. From above the site of the White Terrace, he took a view looking to the site of the Pink Terrace: vast tracts of smouldering earth levelled, split apart and heaved aside. With the geysers in the lake basin reasonably quiescent, the party was able to walk almost to the site of the Pink Terrace, which general opinion held to be still existing.

The party witnessed four jets of smoke thrown up from the Tarawera craters during the journey. Returning to Rotorua via the back-road Pareheru route, Valentine and Chapman were later able to recommend the Te Wairoa route as 'the easiest of the two, and giving the tourists the best view of the rift at Tarawera, and of the scene of volcanic eruption in the bed of Rotomahana Lake'. Back in Auckland on 11 October, with 'a good series of photographs of all the principal features of interest', details of the journey were published two days later. Potential visitors were informed that 'No provision has yet been made at Pareheru for the accommodation of tourists, and it is still necessary to ride back to Rotorua the same day, making a journey in all of 34 miles, which leaves little time in the one day to inspect the "lions" of the New Wonderland.'[33]

Just a few weeks later, at the end of November, Valentine left for his second post-eruption journey, this time to photograph along the line of craters.[34] This trip would be a longer one, and again demanding for a man in delicate health. It was also to prove timely: 'On the arrival of Mr. Valentine, the celebrated photographer, at Rotorua, arrangements were promptly made by Mr. Blythe, Government Engineer, to enable him to accompany his survey staff, which was just starting on an expedition to the volcanic centre at Rotomahana for the purpose of making observations and taking notes of any alteration or change that might have occurred since Mr. Percy Smith's last visit, and reporting such to the Government.' Here the group was also joined by a *Herald* reporter and the adventurous Mrs Blythe – John Blythe being one of the surveyors to have sheltered from the eruption under the Haszard's hen-house.

> Two packhorses and men thoroughly equipped proceeded, shortly followed by Mr. Valentine and Mr. and Mrs. Blythe on horseback. (I may here note that this was a very plucky venture for a lady to make, one which required a considerable amount of endurance, but Mrs. Blythe proved equal to the task and kept pace with the best of us). The overland route following Mr. McIntosh's line of road was taken, which we found to be in excellent repair. After crossing the Waipa stream and about three miles ahead, the road diverged into the new Government line to Galatea, recently surveyed by Mr. Blythe, and at present under construction, following which, at easy grades, a fertile valley is reached, leading up to the native village of Pakaraka, prettily situated on a rising bushy hill. This place is now the adopted home of the Ngatitu, a tribe driven from their old settlement at Kaiteriria by the recent eruption. Traversing along a number of easy but uninteresting gulleys for over three miles and a half, Pareheru is reached, and it is from here that the first view of the vast and desolate panorama of volcanic destruction is obtained. Passing this to the left, the curious and wonderful mountain of Maungakakaramea crops

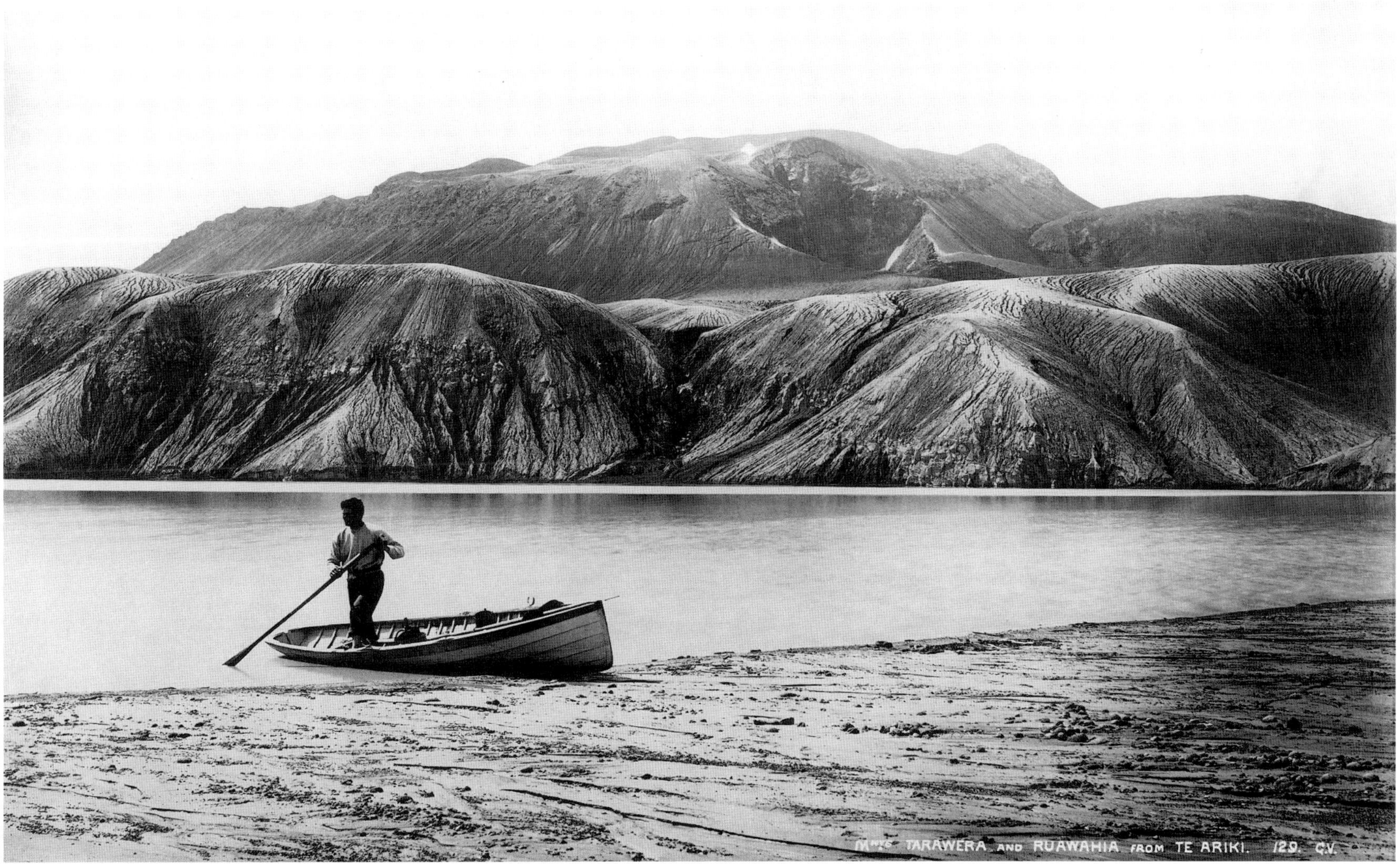

'Mnts. Tarawera and Ruawahia from Te Ariki', 1886

up, at the foot of which and at the head of the Waiotapu Valley, lies the survey camp, our destination for the night and headquarters for the future.

We have travelled all this distance (about twenty-five miles) just on the fringe of the volcanic deposit, the journey having been accomplished at a walking pace in five hours. The camp consisted of five tents, comfortably fitted up with beds. Just in front a purling little brook of the clearest water came rippling past, alongside of which ran another of a milky muddy colour ... This place, to my fancy, will, before long prove to be a most attractive spot, being a central and convenient station for making detours to the various surrounding wonders.

Next morning opened out hot and sultry. Most of this day was spent in leisurely exploring within a radius of five miles down the Waiotapu Valley. The view down this is very extensive, and numerous jets of steam are to be seen issuing from some of the most lovely tinted springs, and some of the most abominable mud fumaroles in existence; the natives say there are over 150 of them, and but few have been either visited or christened ... The first solfatara we came across – which, for lack of a name, we christened No. 1 – was a large circular basin, with irregular sides of bright-coloured clays, at the bottom of which, from a number of minor basins, spouts up steam and water in various shades and degrees in boiling. This is a pretty sight; but, in viewing and walking around it, great care is necessary in footing it, as the ground is exceedingly treacherous and hot underneath – a break through the crust, and the chances are a scalded foot. A little further on brings you to a most repulsive-looking abyss, which Mr. Valentine christened the 'Porridge Pots'. Basins, cones, and fumaroles of black, boiling mud spluttered here in all directions. Several others of a similar nature were passed ...

Turning in a homeward direction we suddenly emerged on a dark coloured pool, part of which was covered with a dirty, soapy-looking froth, quite still, but apparently boiling underneath, as the following painful incident will show:- One of our faithful followers, a young retriever mastiff named Pepper, in its eagerness to reach the water, and mistaking the surface for solid ground, bolted in, and with a yelp disappeared head downwards. A few struggles and all was over, leaving only a round hole as if broken through ice to mark the spot. The poor brute could not have suffered much pain, as its head never came up; death must have been instantaneous. Better this than if rescued in a parboiled state. We turned our backs upon the scene with feelings of horror and disgust, and for the rest of the day our ardent spirits were completely damped. We christened that pool 'Pepper,' after the dog ...

Languidly retracing our steps, a strong sensation of drowsiness overcame us, doubtless caused by the abominable surrounding gaseous vapours, which made us push on, and scrambling through tall tea tree, breaks, and tangled scrub, we arrived at our camp, thoroughly exhausted ... and so passed day No. 2. Next morning was bright and sunny. Skirting Lake Ngahuia to the right, and getting to the crest of the last fern-covered hills at the northern base of Maungakakaramea, we touched upon the mud deposit which extended as far as the eye could reach. This coating is firm and hard, the innumerable ridges being furrowed as if ploughed, but in the valleys the mud is soft and treacherous, at least in some places, which quickly brings one to knee-drill, and renders a certain amount of caution necessary, especially after rain. Rounding the eastern end of Lake Okaro, once a pretty sheet of water, fringed with trees and rich vegetation, but now a veritable quagmire, we steered in almost a bee-line to the southern crater.

At a point near here, which is virtually the extreme south end of the great rent, the finest and most compre-

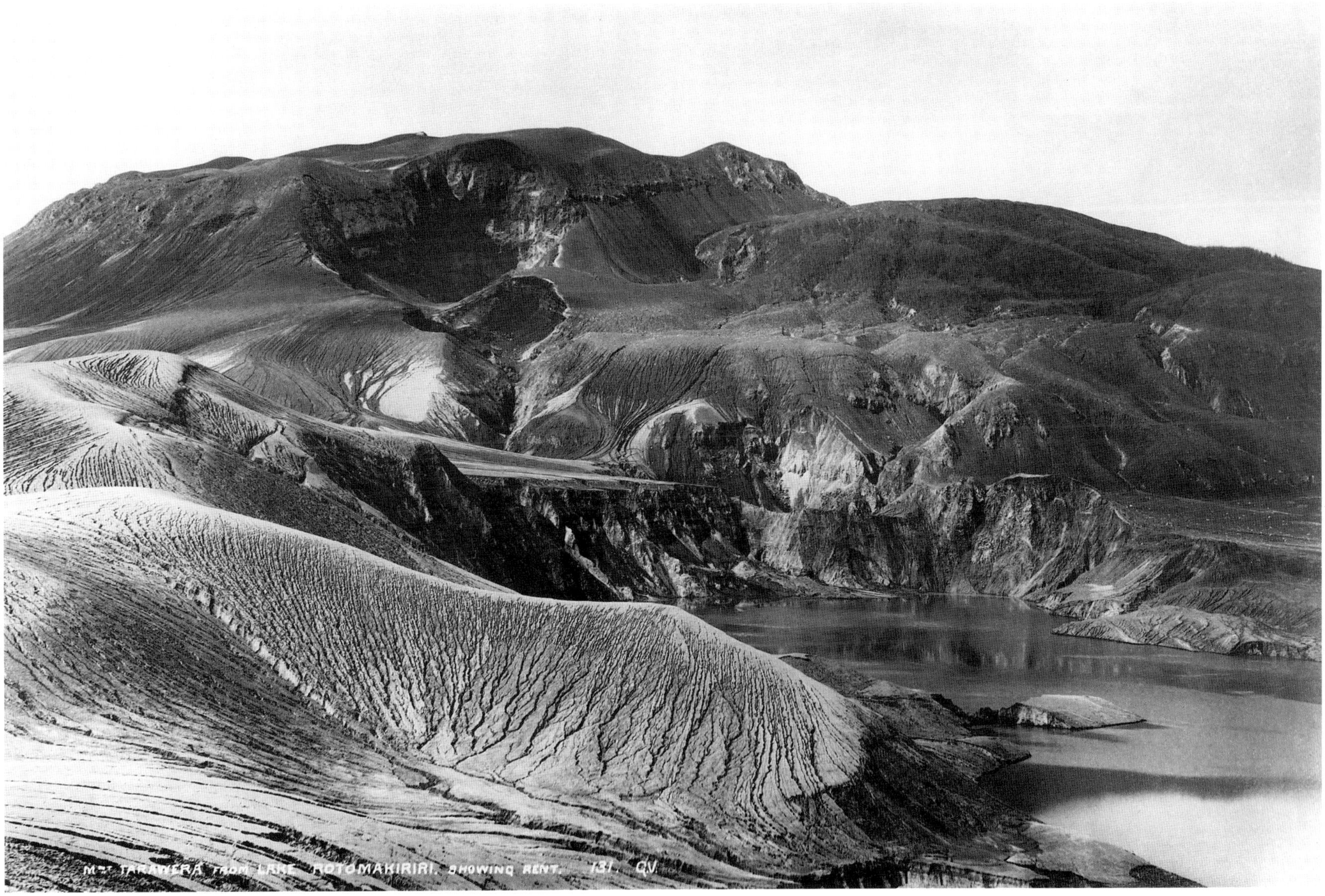

'Mt. Tarawera from Lake Rotomakariri, showing Rent', 1886

From a point west of Rotomakariri, looking northeast towards the great rent in Tarawera.

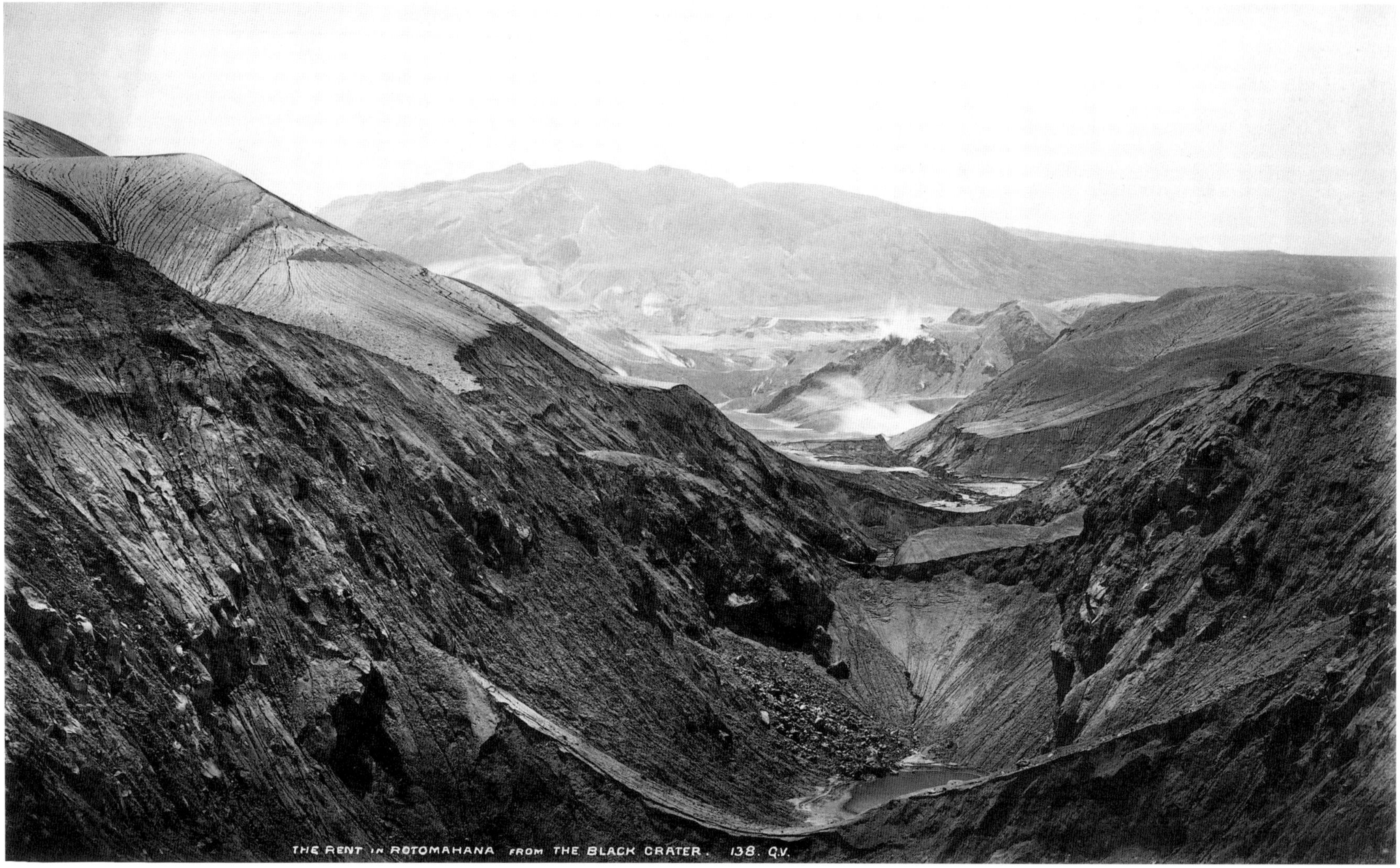

'The Rent in Rotomahana from the Black Crater', 1886
A column of steam approximately 15,000 ft high came from this crater during the eruption. This view looks towards Rotomahana, Rotomakariri and Tarawera.

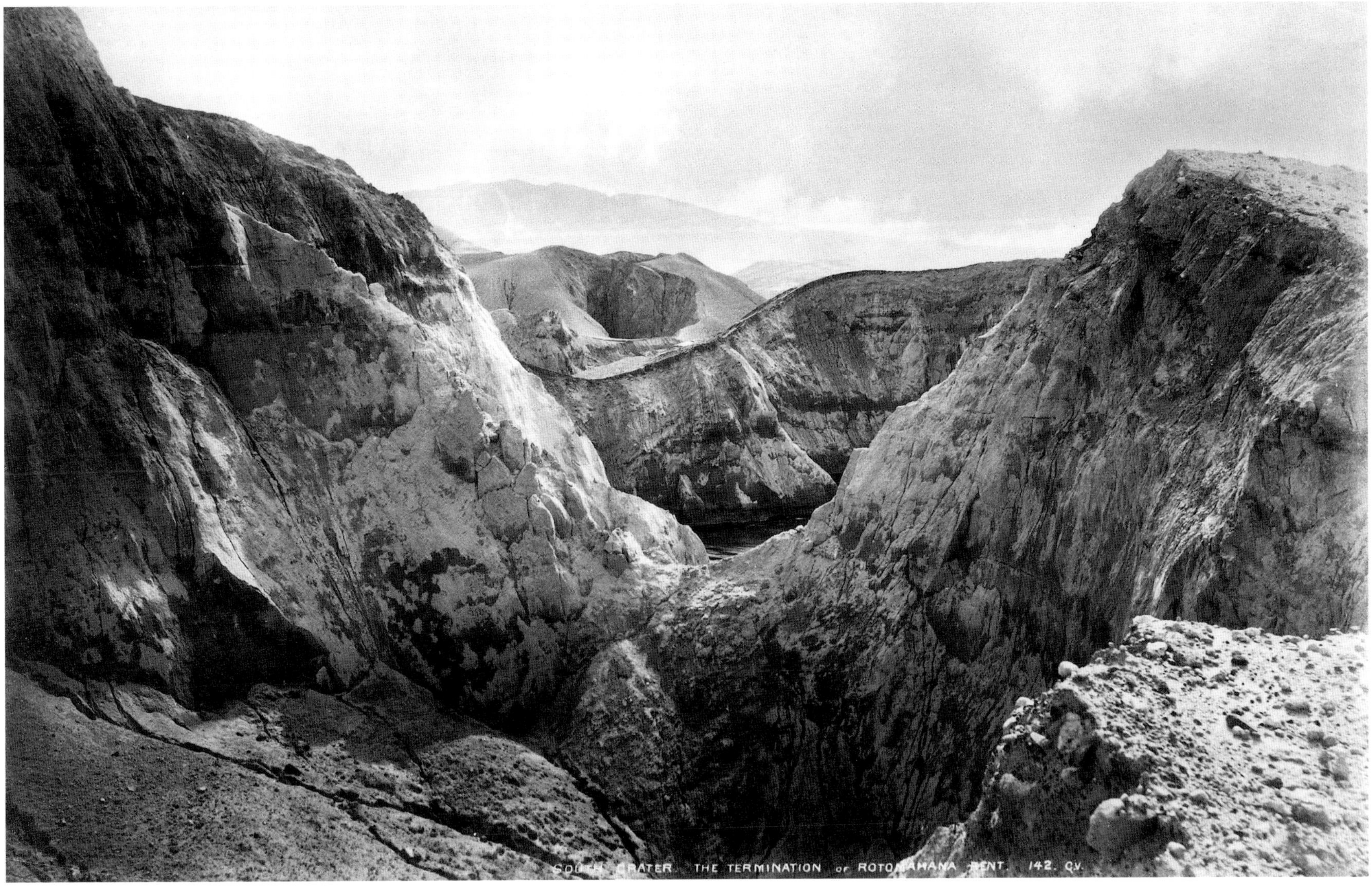

'South Crater, the Termination of Rotomahana Rent', 1886
Looking northeast towards Tarawera, taken from the edge of the southern-most crater.

hensive view of the whole eruption is to be obtained, as you look through the complete line of fissure, extending over Rotomahana and right up to the summit of Ruawahia. The activity in the southern craters, Black Crater, and Koho Lake, has almost subsided. There is water at the bottom of them all, but only in spots in a state of ebullition. Immense avalanches of mud appear to be constantly falling in, and the spot you stand on to-day is probably gone to-morrow ...

On Friday morning we were all astir, being roused from our well-earned sleep at four a.m. by the call of 'breakfast ready.' At half-past six a.m. we were all equipped and a start was made. The weather was all that could be desired, and we jogged briskly on, pursuing the same course we had taken on the previous day. Arriving at the extreme southern end of the rent at twenty-five minutes to eight a.m., a glorious sight presented itself. The sun had just risen over the hills, casting a grand light and shade along the whole line of rent towards Ruawahia, sufficient to make the heart of an artist rejoice. After a rough and tumble sort of a walk up hill and down dale, we came upon the Black Crater, on getting up to the lips of which, we passed over an extraordinary slope of jumbled up mud, just as if a rough sea had become suddenly petrified. Over this the walking was both disagreeable and fatiguing; however, we were amply rewarded on reaching the top, which we did at forty-five minutes past nine a.m. The view obtained from here was simply magnificent. The bottom of this crater is a most abominable-looking abyss, filled with coffee-coloured water, and boiling in places. It is a hazardous venture to peer over the edge, and I should not advise anyone to do so, as the sides are constantly falling in.

We then wandered in direction of the Rotomahana craters. Coming to the foot of Hape o Toroa, we clambered up the crater end of this hill, resting half way by digging our heels into the mud and turning round on our backs, not far short of a perpendicular position. But there was still a more sensational exploit in front of me, as I found we had to make an almost perpendicular descent on the northern side. I eventually succeeded in reaching the bottom in a high state of nervous perspiration. There we were on a comparatively level plateau, overlooking the spot on which the lovely Pink Terrace once stood. Most of the ngawhas and fumaroles were quiescent – many quite extinct. Natives had arrived by this time with horses to assist us in getting back. Mr. Blythe thought it advisable (in order to be at Te Ariki by sunrise) to camp for the night at Pareheru, which we did, Mrs. Blythe returning to our old quarters at Maungakakaramea.

Pareheru camp is situated on a fern-clad hill, close to the bush, and on the borders of the mud deposit. A splendid view of the whole arena lies at one's feet, and it appears to me that before long this will become an important station, if not the head centre for tourists visiting Wonderland. A spur or a gully runs down from here leading to almost any crater in the field, which can be followed on horseback, an immense advantage. We found a Maori here named Penetito, who is preparing to start an hostelry on this spot and provide horses as well.

Next morning, on looking around, every indication of a nor'-easter appeared, so our meditated visit to Te Ariki had to be abandoned, and we hastened as quickly as we could back to our old camp at Kakaramea. Next day, Sunday, was spent pleasantly in camp, and we rested from all our labour. Monday morning looked more promising, but a good deal of rain had fallen, so we thought it advisable to give the mud time to dry and harden, and leave Te Ariki alone for a day or two.

Wednesday morning was beautifully fine, and after

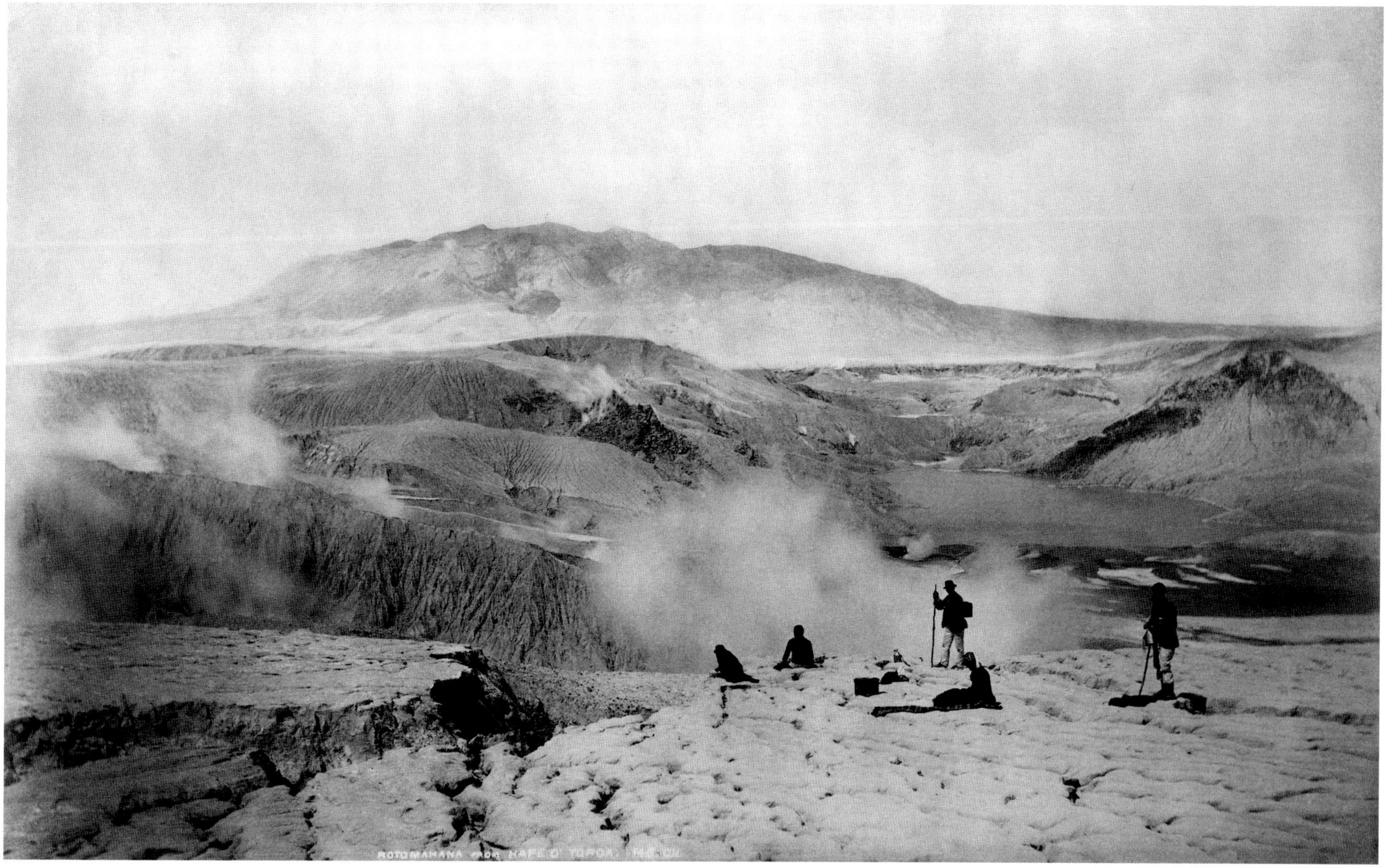

'Rotomahana from Hape O'Toroa', 1886

another four o'clock breakfast, we managed to get away from the camp a little before five a.m. This was to be our Te Ariki trip. Pursuing our old course, past the southern end of the rent, we kept well to the left, getting into a leading gorge running towards Pareheru. At the bottom of this an immense deep rut, averaging 3 feet across, with upright sides of solid mud 30 feet high, traversed the gorge. Following up this weird-looking defile we found it gently led us over the leading spur to Hape-o-Toroa.

Keeping the Black Terrace Crater to our right, and passing over some hot and dangerous ground, emitting the most abominable gaseous vapours, we reached Te Ariki at twenty minutes past nine a.m.. There was very little steam rising to obstruct the vision, and everything could be seen so clearly. A placid little bluish green lake lay at the bottom, a miniature mountain of black rugged rocks steaming all over lay at the extreme southward end, which we christened the 'Fumarole Peaks' (an awful feature in the abyss), and away round on the opposite side rose a high mound of burnt-looking clay, near the base of which jets of steam shot out horizontally, and all on a regular level, in appearance as if a salute was being fired from the lower ramparts of a bombarded castle. Another place showed an immense volume of steam ascending from a furiously boiling lakelet. This we determined was originally the site of the once glorious White Terrace; but oh, what a transformation! ... Next morning was a general pack-up, and we started homewards on our journey back to Rotorua the same way as we came, each one feeling delighted with the success attending and the pleasure afforded by a never-to-be-forgotten meander in Wonderland.[35]

Upon George Valentine's return to Auckland in early December, the success of his journey was announced and the more detailed account published four weeks later:

Perhaps the finest set of photographic views which has yet been obtained of the line of volcanic craters, and of the great eruption of Tarawera, has just been secured by Mr. Valentine, photographer, of this city, during his recent trip to the Lake Country, and from which he returned last week. As showing the care manifested to obtain the views under the best atmospheric conditions, only seven have been obtained in the whole fortnight ... Mr. Valentine states that the craters are changing greatly, both through volcanic action and landslips, and in the four days he wandered among them several material alterations occurred. He happened to be at the Rotomahana basin the other day, when the brown smoke arose from the top of Tarawera, which gave rise to the rumour of a fresh eruption, but he states there was nothing in it, the condition of the atmosphere simply presenting the ordinary steaming appearances in a new form.[36]

As well as making his results available to the public, Valentine's work was also to illustrate *The Eruption of Tarawera, New Zealand*, an official government report by Assistant Surveyor-General Percy Smith. Seven photographs (at the reduced size of 4½" x 7½") were chosen by Smith, who was 'greatly pleased with them'.[37] George Valentine was also kept occupied in the production of wet-plate collodion copies of his work, to be made into lantern slides for Colonial Museum Director Dr James Hector.[38] Another set of these would be despatched to Scotland to be shown at the next meeting of the Dundee and East of Scotland Photographic Association, and would be well received both for artistic merit and for the interest in the effects of the eruption.[39]

George Valentine's photography was to serve a more exacting purpose when taken in hand by the Hon. John Ballance, Minister of Native Affairs, Defence, and of Lands, on his investigative visit to Rotomahana on 24 January 1887.

Under the charge of Alfred Warbrick, Ballance was taken to Rotomahana, where Valentine's photographs of the White Terrace location – from before and after the eruption – were superimposed 'with a view of localizing the site of the Terrace as far as possible'. From the photographs, and from his knowledge of the region before the eruption, Ballance was able to form the opinion 'that the White Terrace is still in existence, though possibly buried 40 or 50 feet deep under mud'. Plans would be set in place 'to have cross bearings taken, and trial borings made, with a view of ascertaining the site', the Minister stating his view that 'there would be no difficulty, even if there were a deposit of 50 feet of mud, of getting it cleared away, as a foot or so below the exterior crust the volcanic deposit is perfectly soft. Warbrick, the guide, and Sophia, the late guide, are both of opinion the White Terrace still exists. Mr. Ballance is also under the impression that a portion of the Pink Terrace is standing – namely, some of the cups or basins.'

John Ballance also managed to travel down into the Rotomahana basin to see the new wonders close at hand. 'On returning, the wind changed, coming from Lake Tarawera, and in a few minutes a hundred geysers were in full play in the Rotomahana basin, throwing up jets over a hundred feet high, and forming one of the most wonderful scenes he had seen in his life.' Happily the Minister was able to prophesy 'that the stream of tourists will be as great as ever – even without the Terraces – especially if a good guide system be established, and a moderate tariff of charges fixed'.[40]

After Ballance's visit, Alfred Warbrick approached the Government with a request that the survival of the White Terrace be more fully investigated. From here, the decision was made that if Warbrick's assertions could be proved correct, work should begin immediately in unearthing the Terrace from the layer of mud. By 16 April, Assistant Surveyor-General Percy Smith was back at Rotomahana, ready to survey the lake bed. In fixing the position of the White Terrace through its projected original bearings, 'it was found that the bearings ran across the great deep chasm which now occupies the original position of Rotomahana Lake and the terraces, and as the bottom of this chasm is 500 feet lower than the former level of the surface it follows that the White Terrace is in mid air ...'[41] And so for the meantime, the matter was closed.

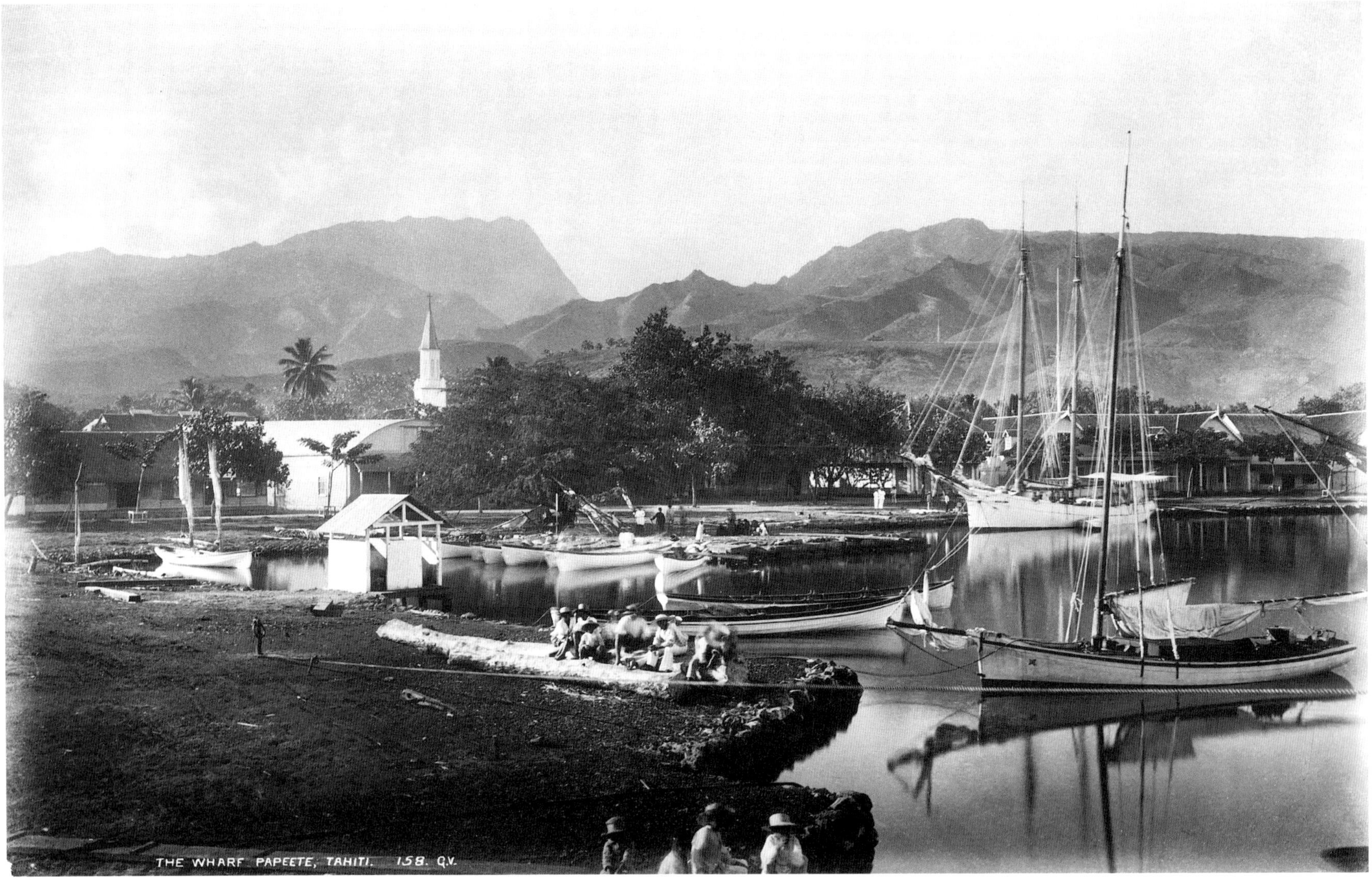

'The Wharf. Papeete, Tahiti', 1887

CHAPTER 9

THE SOUTH SEA ISLANDS

The novelty of the scenery, the primitive character of the aborigines, as seen in their dress, manners, and habits; the luxuriance of the foliage, the gorgeousness of the flowers, the luscious freshness of the fruits, the tranquil peacefulness with which the vessel lies listlessly at anchor upon the unruffled surface of the lagoon-like harbour ...

A South Seas voyage on Auckland's newest steamer was advertised as the perfect way to avoid New Zealand's winter months, and especially recommended for 'invalids and convalescents, or for persons overworked, or out of sorts and needing change'.[1] George Valentine found himself on the S.S. *Richmond*'s maiden voyage on 8 July 1887, ready for a 38-day trip through the islands of Tonga, Samoa, Tahiti and Rarotonga.[2] As one of 20 passengers on board, his distinguished presence was noted by the press:

> Among the passengers by the steamer Richmond yesterday, for the Islands, was Mr. Valentine, the well-known photographer, who goes the round trip on a photographic tour, on somewhat similar lines to that initiated by Burton Brothers, of Dunedin, photographers – 'The Coral Islands Through the Camera' – during the annual Islands' excursion inaugurated by the Union Company. Mr. Valentine will visit Tonga, Rarotonga, Samoa, and Tahiti, and other islands, for the purpose of taking the principal points of interest on the coastline and inland. He intends also illustrating, by a series of photographic views, the fruit industries of the Islands and the sugar industry, etc. It has been arranged to pass close to the volcanic island recently thrown up off Tonga, for the purpose of enabling Mr. Valentine to get a good photograph of it.[3]

Heading towards Tonga, or the 'Friendly Islands', the *Richmond*'s passengers could enjoy comfortable surrounds. On the main deck, a large social area under permanent awning, with piano for entertainment, formed 'a most roomy, cosy and pleasant apartment'.[4] Seeing to their guests' comfort were the ship's proprietors, Messrs Donald and Edenborough, who, having cornered a good portion of the expanding Pacific trade, carried on this passage some £4,000 worth of livestock and 'colonial goods'.[5] The presence of the newly appointed United States Consul to Samoa, H.M. Sewell, would have been especially interesting for Valentine, for Sewell had

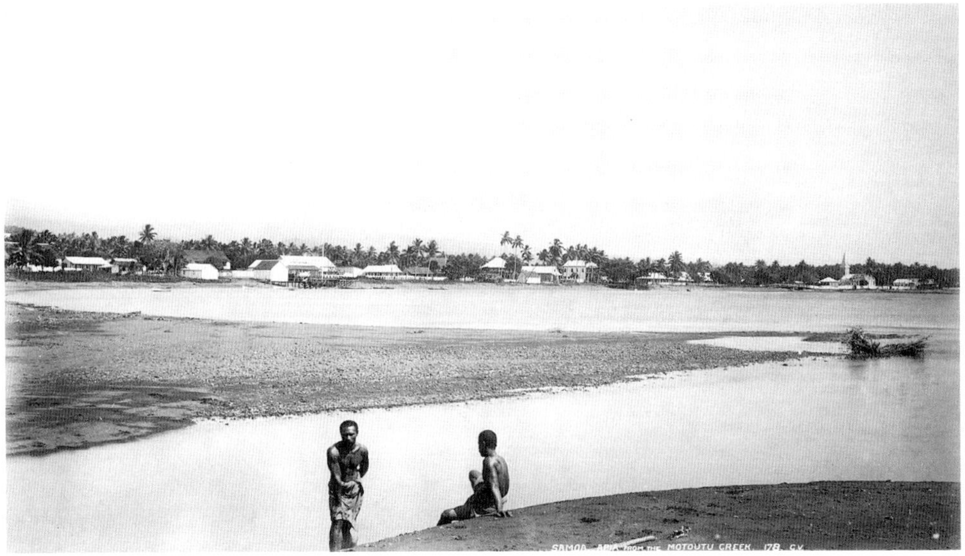

'Samoa. Apia from the Motoutu Creek', 1887

recently been to the Rotomahana district under the charge of Alfred Warbrick.[6]

After a 'very quick passage' of five days, the steamer reached Nuku'alofa, Tonga's capital on the principal island of Tongatapu, where cargo was unloaded and tropical produce taken on board.[7] George Valentine began his modest record of the two-day visit, beginning with a photograph of the palace and private chapel of Tonga's King Siaosi Tupou, or King George I, with harbour and islands in the distance. Another from the ship framed the town as a deceptively tranquil scene – for Tonga was at this time in the midst of its own peculiar eruption aftermath.[8]

An unhappy array of events in Tonga had been reported in New Zealand's papers for the previous six months, the major incident being an assassination attempt upon the elderly King's right-hand man, ex-missionary Premier the Rev Shirley Baker.[9] Before his conversion to Christianity, King Siaosi Tupou had brought Tonga's many spread-out islands together into a single kingdom. Later, the missionary Baker had found for himself a position of power, which he was now abusing in a campaign to convert all Wesleyan Church members over to his preferred independent Free Church. Some of those refusing to change had been imprisoned for months, and as the persecution had continued, a small group of escaped prisoners attempted an assassination. A tumult had followed, with the islands divided into religious factions. Armed and painted war parties arrived from the other main islands, and in their plundering of villages had created civil war. Six of the conspirators had been executed, many imprisoned and many more coerced over to Baker's Free Church. By the time of the S.S. *Richmond*'s visit, basic order had been restored, with the British Home Office extracting from the King the promise of religious freedom, though Wesleyan services and the Wesleyan College were still closed. Many thought Baker should be removed from his position of power, while in London's House of Commons it was suggested he 'be reported and tried for the recent religious disturbances'.[10] Meanwhile, it was 'openly stated among the natives of Tonga that the next attack on Mr. Baker will be made with clubs, as they will not trust firearms'.[11]

The *Richmond* left Tonga on 15 July; in two days the ship was at Apia, capital of Samoa, or the Navigator Group of islands. Apia was where Valentine's famous countryman and fellow consumptive, the author R.L. Stevenson, was soon to arrive 'only to grow old and die', finding it 'a fair place for the purpose'.[12] Here the *Richmond*'s arrival was hailed with a large social gathering thrown for passengers, including the new American Consul, by the principal English-speaking residents.[13] George Valentine was to produce five works from his two days in Apia: 'one from the sea, a second from Matafele, and a third from Motoutu. Among the landmarks in the latter are McArthur and Co.'s premises, the American Consulate, and the Roman Catholic Cathedral, with its lofty spire, built of coral. A fourth view gives a sketch of Samoan scenery, a group of native women washing clothes in native fashion by

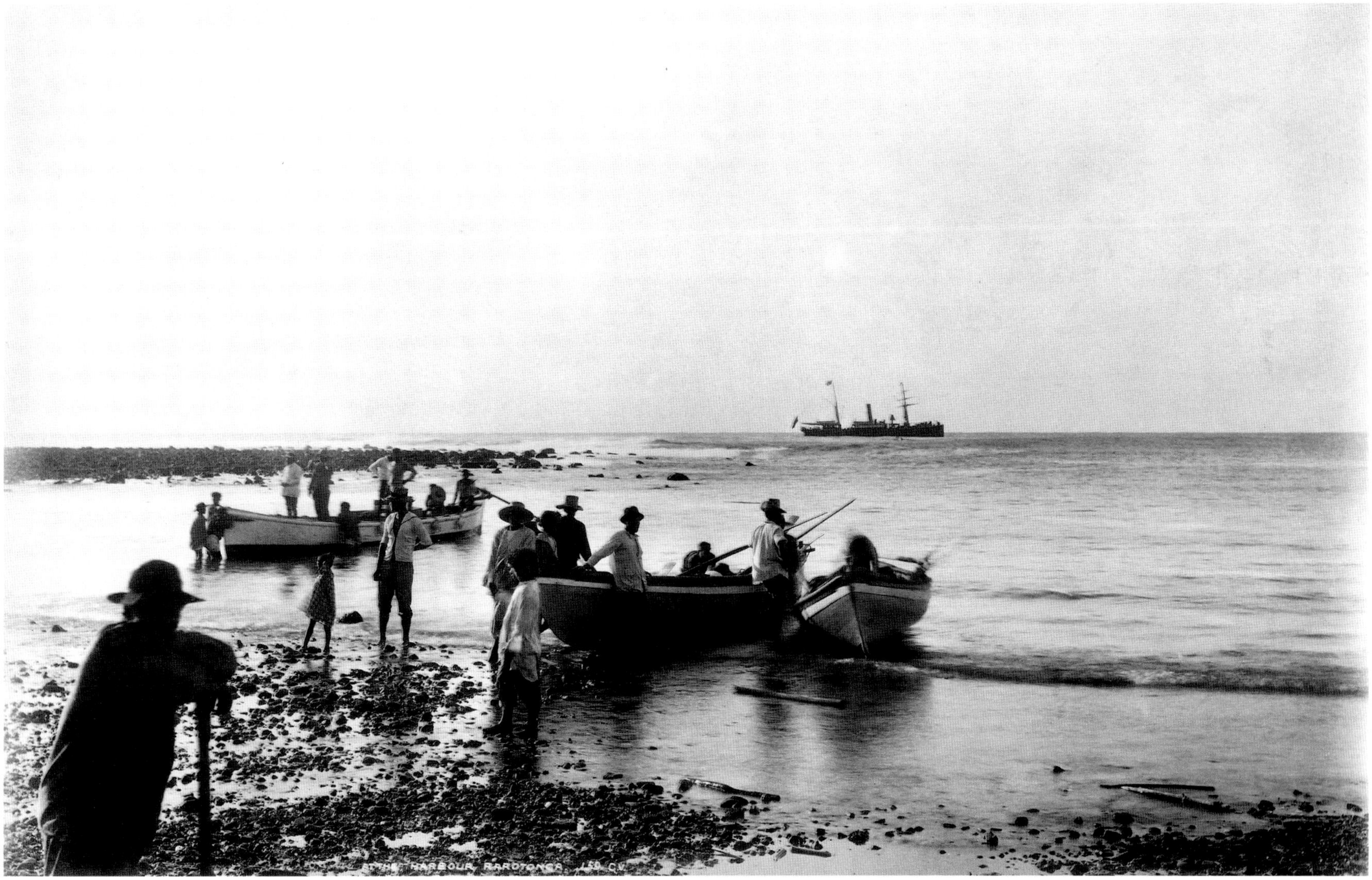

'At the Harbour. Rarotonga', 1887

beating on a stone, and of native outrigger canoes.'[14] As with photographs of Tonga, these few fragments of Samoan life and scenery betrayed little of the strain being felt in Samoa, or of the existing undertow of unease.

Since the earliest days of whaler and missionary contact, the destiny of these islands had been shaped by outsiders. Now the greatest influence over an almost fully literate Samoan population was through commerce and trade, with 200 or 300 mostly foreign-owned stores and residences in Apia, and nationalities represented including American, English, French and German. Each had its own consulate to protect trading interests, although the Germans with their ship-building yards, extensive coconut plantations and imported 'blackbird' labour were most numerous and in control of most of the trade.[15] Much land was also in foreign hands – over half of it was now in freehold to six foreign companies – with the largest proportion held by a New Zealand concern.[16]

For some time a German annexation of the islands had been feared, especially in the light of treaties between Germany and Samoa's highest chief, King Malieto'a, having been badly broken. In the previous year, flag-raising exercises had been made by both Germany and the United States, though the actions of the former had seemed more ominous, with the tearing down of the Samoan flag and the raising of the Imperial German one. The timing of the event had been especially threatening, with the arrival in Apia at the same time of the German-backed rival king Tamasese and his 700 armed followers. Following this, Malieto'a had sought help from Britain in a request for annexation or protectorate status, although Britain had shown reluctance to intervene.[17] Recently, by Malieto'a's invitation, the Hawaiian Government had sent the man-of-war *Kaimiloa*, which at the time of Valentine's visit had been in Samoa for a month. Samoa and Hawaii had made a treaty; soon the *Kaimiloa* would also head to Tonga to conclude a similar treaty.[18] Hawaii's aim was the formation of an alliance – a confederate Pacific kingdom – to preclude further intervention from the foreign powers. Not surprisingly, Germany had been 'highly indignant', and the *Kaimiloa*'s every movement was watched and followed by the German man-of-war *Adler*, with back-up gunboats also now heading this way.[19] Meanwhile, in Washington, a conference was being held to sort out the problems in Samoa, with Britain and Germany also represented.[20]

Two weeks after the *Richmond*'s visit (before its return to Auckland), Germany would declare war upon Malieto'a. Tamasese was declared chosen King, and the *Kaimiloa* was seen off by four German warships. A drunken brawl on the night of the German Emperor's birthday celebrations provided the spark for the action, with 1,300 troops and marines descending in a fury upon the islands and six large guns being placed in front of a ransacked Government House, with widespread looting and burning of villages to follow.[21]

The S.S. *Richmond* left Apia on 19 July for a week's voyage 1,500 miles to the east to the Society Islands. The first of these to be sighted from a distance was Bora Bora, then closer at hand Moorea, which Valentine managed to photograph with its fantastic volcanic outline. The ship's arrival at Tahiti and the capital, Papeete, would be 'quite an event for the Papeetians', judging by the welcome given its predecessor: 'The white faces, most diverse in shade and physiognomy, board us, then follow universal introductions and incessant hand-shaking. Meanwhile the aboriginals swarm the decks, and make themselves quite at home.'[22]

Tahiti's 'white faces' (including 500 Chinese) were by this time a tenth of the population, and the French by far in the majority.[23] Annexation to France was officially proclaimed in March 1881, although Tahiti had been a French protectorate since 1842. This status had lasted until 1880, when King Pomare V 'was persuaded to cede the nominal sovereignty in consideration of a life pension of twelve thousand dollars annually'.[24] The French colony was now the undisputed 'pearl of the Pacific', and Papeete a major centre for Pacific trade. It was also the place with which George Valentine would be especially enamoured. In this he differed little from the artist Paul Gauguin who, four years later, set there his idealised visions of 'unspoilt and primitive' Tahitian life.[25]

Three days in the capital gave plenty of time to soak up the French tropical flavour – the markets, cafés, wine bars and restaurants, and street names such as rue de Rivoli or rue de Paris. Regular evening performances by the French Admiral's brass band added to the atmosphere, attended by a host of dance-loving 'natives'. Beyond, amidst a fleet of merchant ships, lay the French Admiral's squadron, protecting French interests along with a garrison of 400 soldiers, a large staff of naval, military and civil officials, and a Governor of 'great local importance'.[26] The only non-photographic venture George Valentine is recorded as having undertaken on this journey was in Tahiti, where he purchased several vanilla beans for the purpose of attempting to grow them in Auckland. 'Who has not tasted vanilla chocolate, or vanilla ice-cream, or vanilla-flavoured custards, compounded with all the refinement of art and subtlety of manipulation in which Parisians pre-eminently excel?', a *Herald* reporter later wrote when Valentine's endeavour turned to failure.[27] More successful were his

> ... several capital views of Papeete, the capital of Tahiti. One is taken from the reef at the entrance of the harbour, showing the French warship Duquesne and other vessels of the French South Pacific squadron in port, as also numerous merchant vessels, and the town well nigh embowered in foliage, with its grand background, the Fataua ranges. A second view shows an extraordinary formation of hills, resembling those of Tarawera after the eruption, and giving the impression that they have been formed in a similar manner. The third view gives a graphic picture of the boat harbour, where at early morn come boats from the various islands laden with produce for Papeete market, and in the distance is to be seen the Roman Catholic Cathedral. A fourth view is from the ranges, showing the township and port from that point, the former scarcely visible, owing to the extensive use of shade trees on the thoroughfares. A sketch of Fataua gives an excellent idea of the general appearance of the shade trees, forming grand avenues for miles in length in the capital, and extending for 40 miles throughout the island.[28]

The *Richmond* left Papeete on 29 July for Papara and Vaieri, where a cargo of lime juice, oranges and coconuts was taken on board. Evidence of Tahiti's prolific orange-growing industry was recorded in a view of the long thatch-roofed sheds where the fruit was packed before transportation to

'Tahiti, Orange Loading at Viaroa', 1887

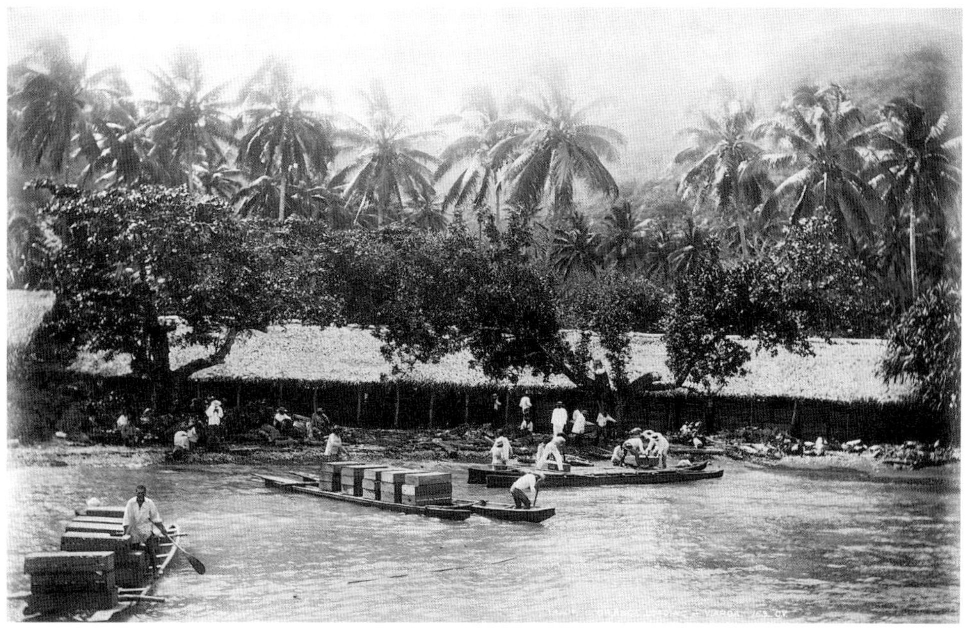

the steamer by outrigger canoe. After six days in the Society Islands, the steamer left on 1 August, heading southwest in the direction of New Zealand. It reached the Cook Islands Group and its principal island of Rarotonga in three days, and dropped anchor beyond the town of Avarua's reef and narrow harbour. Cotton, coffee and bananas were brought out by whale-boat, with passengers conveyed to the island for a one-day stop. Here Valentine took seven photographs, including a classic avenue of coconut palms; a palm-fringed lagoon with the distant Ikurangi peak; another of a small trading station; and an atmospheric scene of the whale-boat crews with the *Richmond* waiting in the distance.

Foreign control here was minimal in comparison with other parts of the Pacific, and a good proportion of trade was conducted by the islanders themselves. Of around 2,000 people on Rarotonga, 30 were Europeans (mostly from New Zealand) and a similar number Chinese. Continued rule by the ariki or traditional hierarchical chief system meant a measure of independence had been maintained, with missionary influence also playing a part. The sale and manufacture of alcoholic drinks was banned (with 'intoxication and excess' almost unknown); imported labour from other islands was also banned, meaning the islanders worked their own extensive plantations and cotton ginning-machines.[29] Such independence was perhaps the reason contemporary visitors judged the Rarotongans 'the most advanced of all the South Sea Islanders in European industrial civilization'. They were 'efficient artisans and mechanics' in the building of wagons and houses 'after the colonial type'.[30] They were also expert boat builders, and sought as crew members on foreign trading vessels. At the time of Valentine's visit, a threat to the independence of these islands had been seen in France's continued expansionist designs in the Pacific, leading Queen Makea – one of Rarotonga's three female ariki – to make a request for the islands to become a British protectorate, with their own Resident British Consul. The appeal would be granted in the following year.[31]

Strong southwesterly winds in the first four days after Rarotonga increased on the fifth day to a heavy gale and tremendous seas. Fearing his ship would be exhausted of coal before reaching Auckland, the captain altered his course to seek firewood fuel and shelter at Sunday Island, in the Kermadec Group – the island's sole inhabitants were known to supply firewood to occasional visiting whalers. On 11 August, after two long days, the *Richmond* arrived to spend the next few days attempting to load firewood against unabated weather and heavy surf. The island's residents – a 'South Seas Robinson Crusoe' family and its patriarch, Thomas Bell – informed the captain that in eight years of occupation they had not experienced such a heavy gale.[32]

Bell with his wife and eight children had lived here in virtual self-sufficiency until a British warship had landed in mid-1886 on the other side of the island to plant the flag and proclaim Her Majesty's sovereignty – apparently believing it to be uninhabited.[33] Before the *Richmond*'s departure from Sunday Island on 16 August, the New Zealand Government's S.S. *Stella* arrived 'upon official business' and was able to supply the Richmond with coal for the voyage home. On board was Assistant Surveyor-General Mr Percy Smith with a survey party to complete the (basically illegal) annexation. Smith would have had a chance to renew his acquaintance with Valentine, whose post-eruption photographs had so successfully illustrated his recently published book.[34] Thomas Bell, meanwhile, in the uncertainty of his own position, loaded 50 bales of wool aboard the *Stella* for the Auckland market.[35] His world was never to be the same.[36]

The *Richmond* reached Auckland 'after a very quick passage of 65 hours' on the morning of 19 August, with strong easterly winds and fine weather enjoyed all the way.[37] Valentine's return was noted by the press:

> By the s.s. Richmond yesterday Mr. G.D. Valentine returned from a photographic tour in the South Sea Islands, having taken a series of photographs of Tonga, Samoa, Tahiti, Morea and Rarotonga, which will be available to the public in a few days. The volcanic island thrown up, some time back, and which he went specially to photograph, is now scarcely visible above water. Mr. Valentine speaks in glowing terms of the scenery to be seen on this round island trip, especially that of Morea, Tahiti, and Rarotonga. Tourists will find the scenery of the Swiss Alps and that of the tropical islands combined; and if better known this would become one of the most popular routes for tourists to be found. The steamer now on the service, the Richmond, is a good seaboat, and her seagoing qualities were well tested in the late gale which she experienced.[38]

Just over a month later, results from the six-week voyage were available to the public, and described by a *Herald* reviewer as 'a series of some twenty-five ... executed with the taste and artistic finish which characterizes Mr. Valentine's work'. George Valentine was said to have been 'so enamoured with Tahiti and its beautiful scenery that he contemplates returning next season to complete his series, which limited time prevented his accomplishing on the present trip. Those relating to Samoa and Tonga are especially interesting in view of recent events, while the whole series embrace ground unfamiliar to the Auckland public, and therefore possessing the charm of novelty and freshness.'[39]

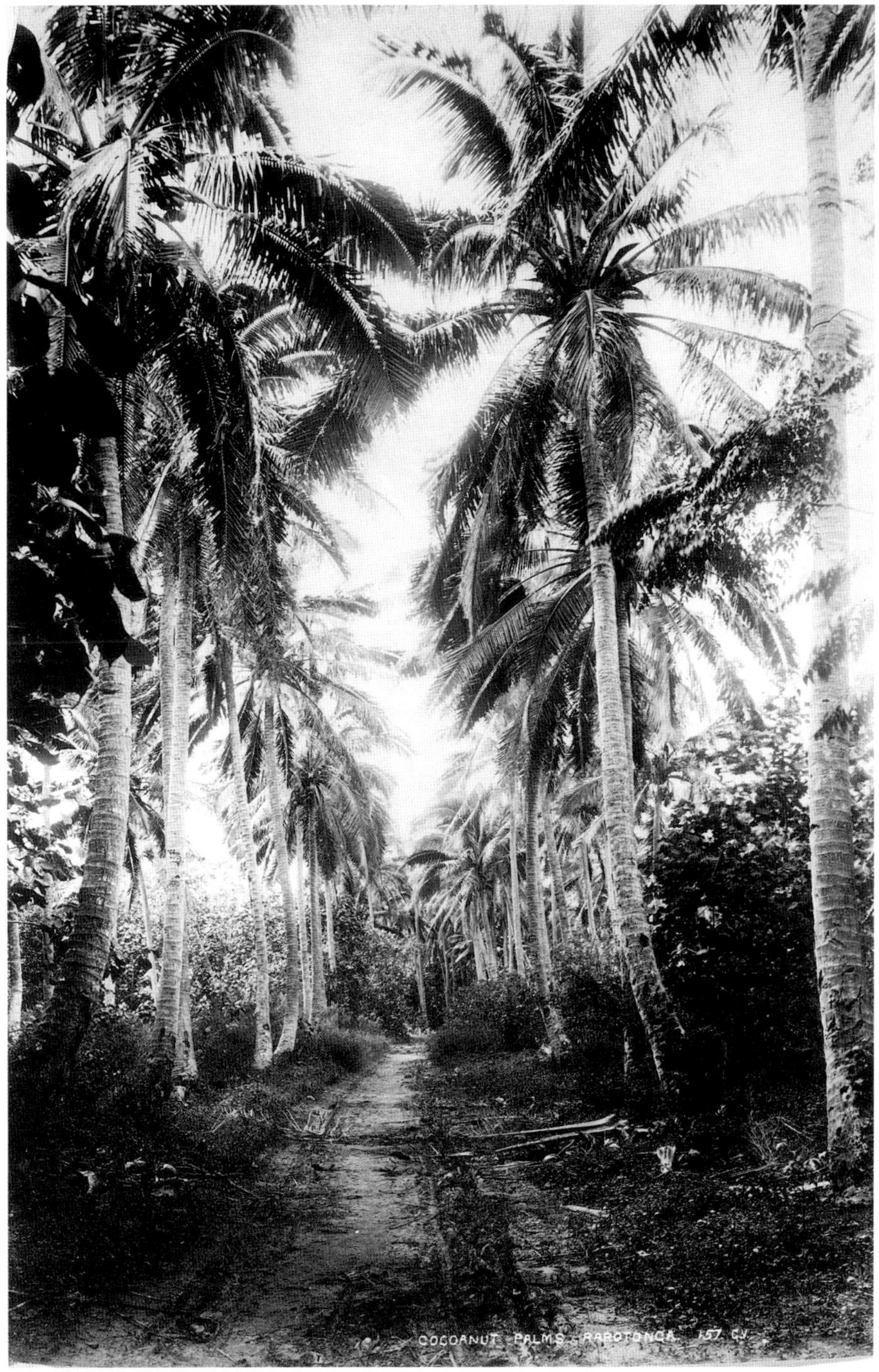

'Cocoanut Palms. Rarotonga', 1887

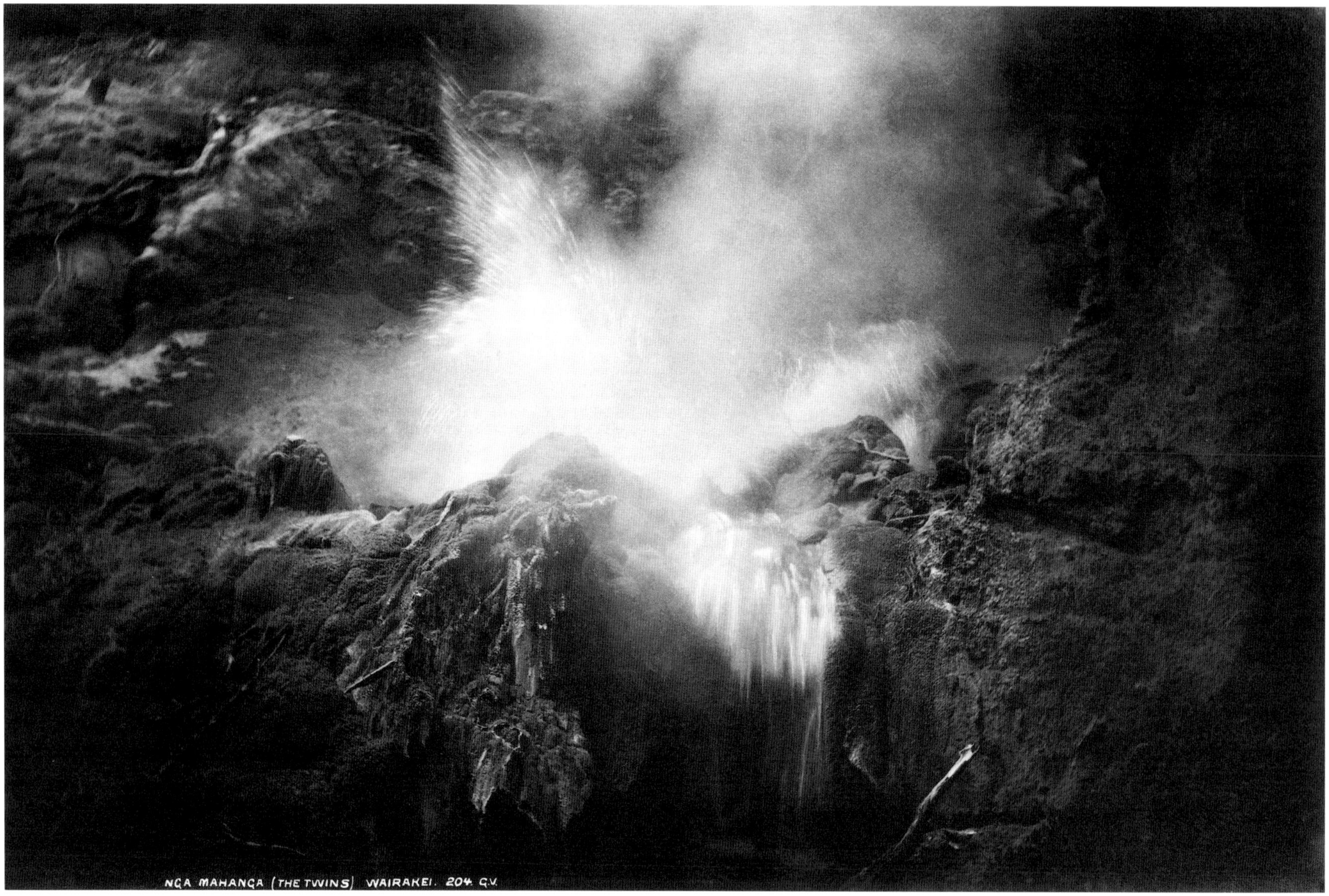

'Nga Mahanga (The Twins), Wairakei', 1887.

CHAPTER 10

THERMAL REGION

Despite his deteriorating health, Valentine continued to devote himself to the art which was both his passion and a creative distraction. The new drop-shutter photographic technique had already been tried with success, and he had published articles on his own inventive adaptations in the British *Yearbook of Photography and Photographic News Almanac.*[1] 'How to Make a Drop Shutter', the first of five articles, was published in 1888 and described his inventive use of a reconstructed cigar box (this at a time when a variety of sophisticated shutters were available on the British market). Another elaborated on the operation of his 'Instantaneous Shutter' ('For cloud effects, and also for seaside pictures and yachts, it can hardly be beaten ...'). This was the beginnings of 'instantaneous photography'– a significant advance that marked the threshold of a new era. At this time, much debate was occurring over the technique's usefulness for 'art photography'. If George Valentine's dramatic results had reached a wider audience, perhaps any such scepticism might have been dispelled.

At the end of 1887, a return to the Thermal Region offered generous possibilities for new work which would prove the value of this technique, this time from the locations of Tikitere, Wairākei, Taupō and Waiotapu, all of which were receiving greater public attention after the loss of the Terraces. All presented challenging and engaging subject matter, and from them would come some of Valentine's finest images.

The artist Charles Blomfield was one to vote the Wairākei geyser valley near Lake Taupō, 'a sight worth coming thousands of miles to see', its geysers 'far better than anything I have expected, and after Rotomahana ... the finest things I have seen yet'.[2] Thirty-five miles to the south of Ōhinemutu, the Wairākei estate had been purchased as a 4,000-acre block from Taupō Māori by Robert Graham in 1881.[3] Hosted now by Graham's widow, Valentine would make his way from a thatched-roof hotel along a creek in a green, enclosed valley towards the geyser circuit. Among the first to come into view were the Great Wairākei Geyser (a boiling pyramid of water 30 feet high) and Tūhuatahi, the Champagne Pool, with its miniature encrusted pink and white silica terrace formations reminiscent of Rotomahana. Valentine photographed both of these. To the west, past a simmering Blue Pool and nearby bathing pools, he captured the twin geysers Nga Māhanga using the drop-shutter technique, and dramatically stilled their geothermal force.

Beyond these and other thermal features nearby, Valentine photographed the Eagle's Nest, a geyser overlaid with layered sticks and brushwood, their petrified appearance the result of bubbling, silica-laden waters below. Again, his results would reveal his consummate skill and immaculate sense of composition. Again too, his timing was fortuitous, with the new road through the Wairākei block soon resulting in a deluge of visitors, whose presence would see this delicate formation destroyed within a year. Blomfield would later ruefully comment: 'Specimens which must have taken hundreds of years to form are now the prey of every passer-by. The curious Eagle's Nest is ruined, nearly all the encrusted sticks are gone, and a fire has made sad havoc among the graceful manuka; the lovely coralline filigree work of the red cascade is being smashed up, and what used to be a most beautiful glen has now a great ugly cutting extending all along its side.'[4]

In this same neighbourhood and within the Wairākei estate, Valentine photographed the Huka Falls from the new road before heading for another group of geothermal wonders a short distance to the south.[5] Stretched along the banks of the Waikato, a mile and a half from the lake, was another vast collection of steam holes, geysers, boiling cauldrons and mud volcanoes. The most famous of these was the Crow's Nest, an encrusted cone which every ten minutes issued forth clouds of steam, jets of spray and 'a beautiful column of boiling water, thrown up at an angle of about sixty degrees, and forming an arc between sixty and seventy feet high'.[6] A reviewer later considered Valentine as fortunate in getting 'the far-famed Crow's Nest geyser … in action, and securing a drop shutter photograph of this remarkable geyser, which at the time of his visit was shooting into the air to a height of 60 feet.'[7]

On this journey, Valentine was the first photographer to work at Waiotapu, a thermal valley some 15 miles to the south of Rotorua. The latest in a series of 'wonderlands' to open to the public, Waiotapu was another site virtually unknown before the Tarawera eruption. Two months after the eruption, a reporter exploring the valley described it as 'rich in the most marvellous creations of a mysterious nature. There are hundreds of fumaroles, hot springs, steam holes, lakes of the most lovely tints – from rich green to deep blue – natural baths clear as crystal and miniature terraces of great beauty although falling far short of the matchless charms of the Pink and White Terraces ... When properly opened out,' he concluded, 'with a good track through the valley ... the region will beyond question become the chief attraction of the Lake district.'[8]

Valentine had made a brief visit to Waiotapu during his second post-eruption journey, even taking upon himself the honour of naming some of the sights.[9] By the time of his second visit, the newly completed Taupō road offered easy access to Waiotapu by buggy, with a walking track cut through the valley to the various attractions.[10] While Valentine clearly enjoyed his visit, Waiotapu's features were not easily portrayed through photography, contributing perhaps to his also collecting written observations, evidently for publication:

> In some 'Notes on the Waiotapu Valley,' made during his photographic tour, Mr. G.D. Valentine gives some interesting particulars concerning its natural wonders, which are just being opened up for the benefit of tourists:- 'One curious feature of the Tohuringa mud volcano is that the liquid mud comes up in bubbles – an exact representation of the arum lily in shape – before bursting into the air. There is, on the way down the valley, after passing it, a beautiful miniature terrace of the shape of a fan coming out of the side of a bank of grey clay.
>
> Passing from there, the tourist goes over an enormous area of ground containing large pits, the walls of which are a perfect artists' or colourman's show board, every

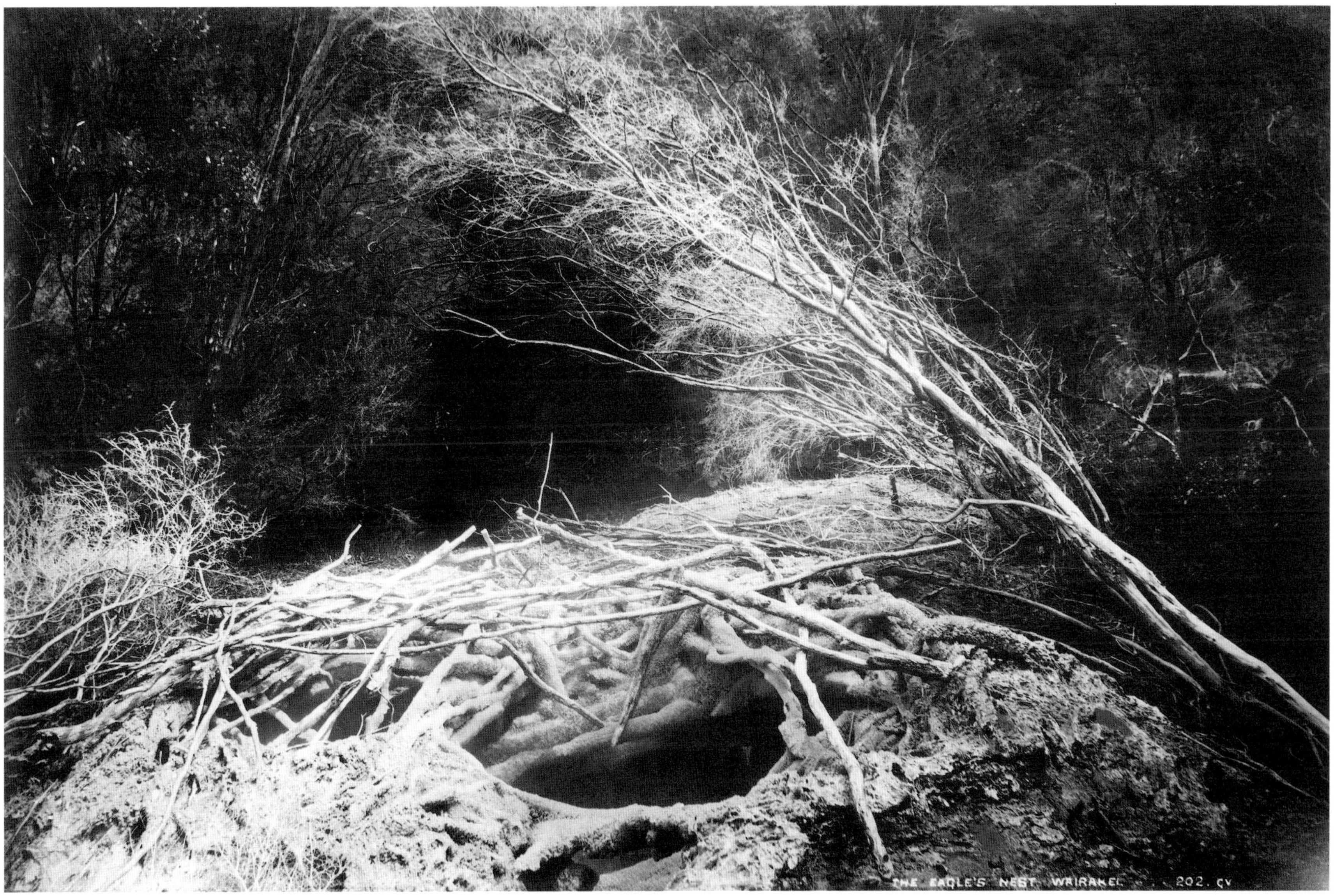

'The Eagle's Nest, Wairakei', 1887

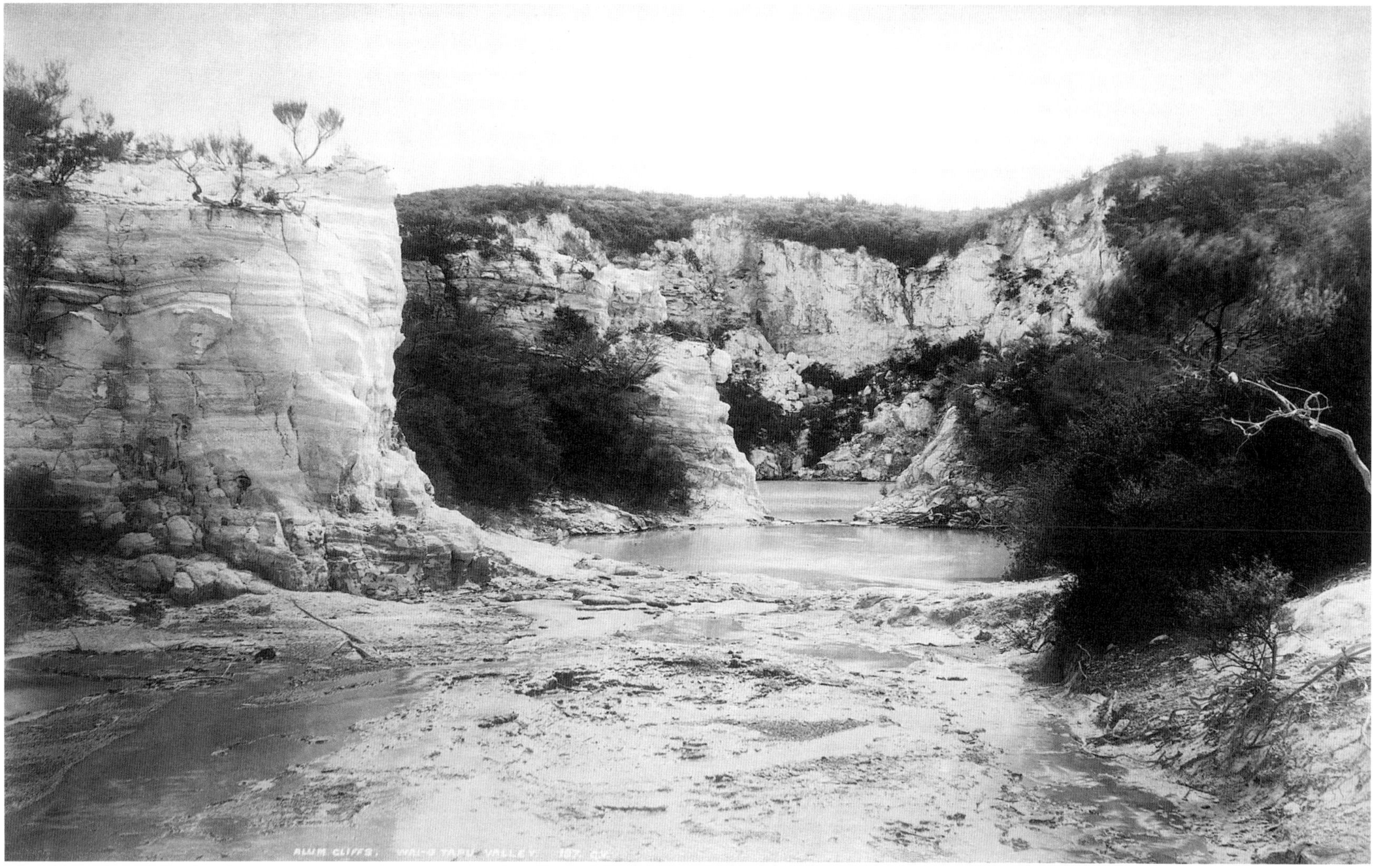

'Alum Cliffs, Wai-o-tapu Valley', 1887

conceivable colour – dark red, purples, and all shades of yellow. A remarkable feature is the sulphur caves in the sides of these pits, the fumes forming stalactites of sulphur, pendant from the mouth of the cave. These features are so delicate that at the slightest touch of the finger they crumble into dust. If these wonders of Nature are not protected by Government appointing a curator, the Vandalism of tourists will soon make them a thing of the past. As these natural beauties are all on Crown land the matter of their protection ought to be seen to.

The cauldron at Kotere-Kairamua is about an acre and a half in extent, and is full of boiling strongly acidulated water, the margin having beautifully scalloped edges. At one side of the terrace is a sulphurous spring, which from this point turns the whole of the overflow, and passing along a narrow race falls over a cliff of about 13 feet in height. The deposit forming on this is sulphur crystals, and gives a fall having the appearance of solid sulphur, and of exactly same formation as the staircase of the Pink Terrace. Standing at the foot of this fall, and looking to the left, one feels as if transported from a Valley of Horrors to Fairyland. Large cliffs of pure alum stand out in perspective like the side wings of a theatrical stage against a background of dark-red earth, in the centre of which are several of these sulphur caves, giving an exceeding variety of beauty and colour ...

The six views of the principal scenes of Waiotapu commence with a view of Maungakakaramea, Sentinel Rock Crater, at the foot of same famous mountain, and Tohuringa, a large mud volcano – in fact the largest mud volcano in the whole of the Lake district – measuring 18 feet in height, and 30 feet from lip to lip. Next is a terrace, the colour of which is a most delicate primrose. Its sole beauty being the delicate primrose colour, its reproduction by photography was an impossibility. Next comes Kotere-Kairamua – the new terrace formation, – although wanting in many of the striking features of the Rotomahana terraces, it may best be described as a reproduction of the trickling buttresses of the White Terraces. Another picture is the Sulphur Caves ... The Waiotapu series of photographs are the first given to the public of that famous valley, and will be, from their novelty and beauty, especially prized by tourists and lovers of nature.[11]

Valentine returned to Auckland in December, and in January 1888 the *Herald* reported on his results: 'Recently Mr. G.D. Valentine, the well-known photographer, made a photographic tour of the Lake Country and Taupo, and has returned to town. The whole series comprises Whakarewarewa, Tikitere, Wai-o-tapu Valley, Wairakei, and Taupo.'[12] The article noted his obtaining photographs of 'the four principal sights of the Wairakei Valley – the great Wairakei Geyser, Champagne Pool, Eagle's Nest, and the Twin Geysers', and commented that 'Some remarkable effects have been secured by the use of the instantaneous drop shutter.'[13]

Valentine copyright registered his new series and set to printing up works for sale. A letter he wrote shortly afterwards reveals his health to be worsening, with a tubercular cough that was now incessant. Probably this meant coughing blood, as well as fever, night sweats, further weight loss and shortness of breath. Despite such discomfort he seems to have maintained a reasonably positive frame of mind and continued to enjoy the intimacy of family life.[14]

Balgay, Parnell, Auckland 25/2/88
My dear Aunt Ellen,

I had your welcome letter, as Mina has told you, during her absence in Nelson and it was next best thing to a chat with you ... I think Mina has given you almost all the news if there is such an article here. The house is wonderfully quiet without Mary and no doubt I will grumble at the row she makes when she comes back. I find James very useful – you would scarcely believe it possible for a boy of seven to be able to feed the horse and clear out the stable, but he manages this and I think inherits his father's intense love for horses – you will no doubt remember how I used to go round with Mrs. Robertson's milk-cart for the pleasure of driving the horse. James is amply rewarded if on my return I get off the horse and let him ride round to the stable. I am trying to carry out the doctor's orders and ride every day, but sometimes I feel more inclined to sit and stare ... I am afraid my old friends would not recognize GDV in the confirmed loafer that now goes by that name. I am getting lazier every day and cost Mina many a sore battle to get me up in the mornings.

I think Mina has benefited by the change to Nelson – it

is very heartwarming to find so much real kindness shown to her by one and all of the old friends. Mrs. Webster has a very large heart that completely embraces our family and the only thing she seemed to fret about was that James and I were not with the others ...

Arnot has come back finding the world rather small for him and is 'bossing' us all round, very much to Ann Gin's vexation he completely ignores her ... she is very fond of him and was very 'lonesome' while he was away. Arnot has no fear and keeps me in hot water while he is out near the horse but the animal is very quiet and seems fond of the children. I found Arnot one day having a tea party under the horse's nose up in the stall, the horse looking on with evident interest. Our watch dog and he are great friends and many a thrashing he gives the 'puir bruit' who takes from the boy what none of us dare give him ...

Mistress says bed time has come so I must say good night and off to my barking which has to be gone through with tiresome regularity. Give my respect to all friends and with love.

I am your affectionate nephew,
George

While George Valentine produced little in the way of photography in this year, a survey of his articles written for *The Yearbook of Photography and Photographic News Almanac* at this time reveals his engagement with the technical aspects of his craft, together with a motivation to share such knowledge. Next to those on drop-shutter photography were brief illustrated articles on 'A Cheap and Easily Constructed Photographic Burnisher', 'Dark Slide Covers' and 'Economy in Lenses', which described 'a kind of interchangeable photographic lens'.[15] In these articles Valentine shows an inventive and resourceful disposition, knowledge of wood- and metal-working and an eye for economical construction.

Valentine did manage in 1888 to dispatch a selection of 20 works to the Melbourne Exhibition: 'Framed photographs of New Zealand and South Sea Island scenery', including one of each of the Terraces, three post-eruption images, four from his South Pacific series and six recent works from the Thermal Region.[16] He was also one of four New Zealand photographers to receive a '1st', with images of 'The Twins' and 'The Crow's Nest' singled out as 'illustrative of wildness and grandeur', and others, including that of Waitakere Falls, 'taken as exemplifying peace and repose'.[17]

Meanwhile, with his continued decline, proper provisions were made at the end of that year for Mina and the children to return to Scotland without him. On 20 November 1888, Valentine made his Last Will and Testament. 'I, George Dobson Valentine, late of Dundee in Scotland but at present in the City of Auckland in the Colony of New Zealand, Gentleman ...' began the writ. Proceeds from the sale of his New Zealand estate ('under the value of £3500') would cover funeral and legal expenses, and 'such further sums as shall be necessary for the comfortable maintenance of my said wife and children until they shall arrive at Dundee ...'[18]

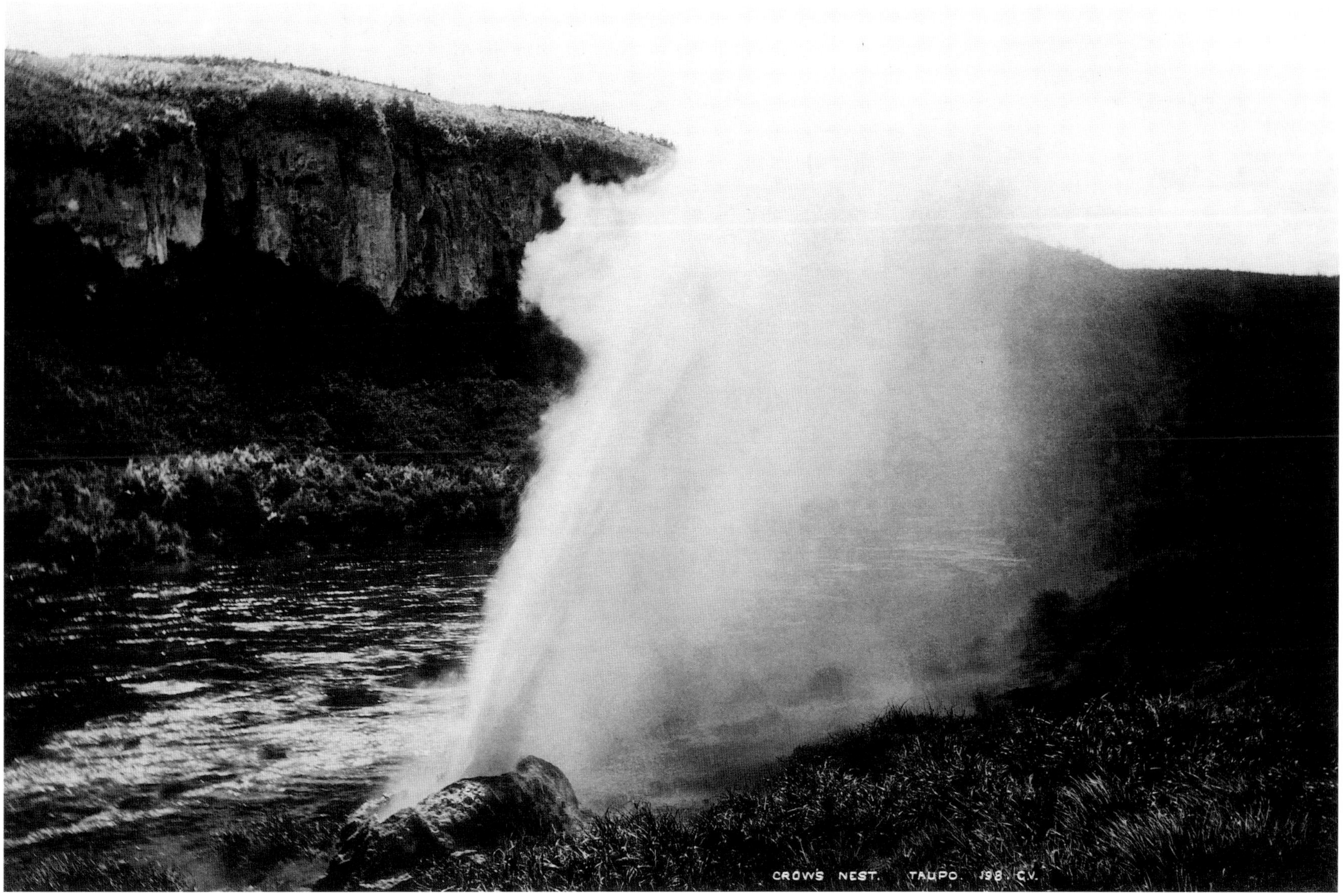

'Crow's Nest, Taupo', 1887

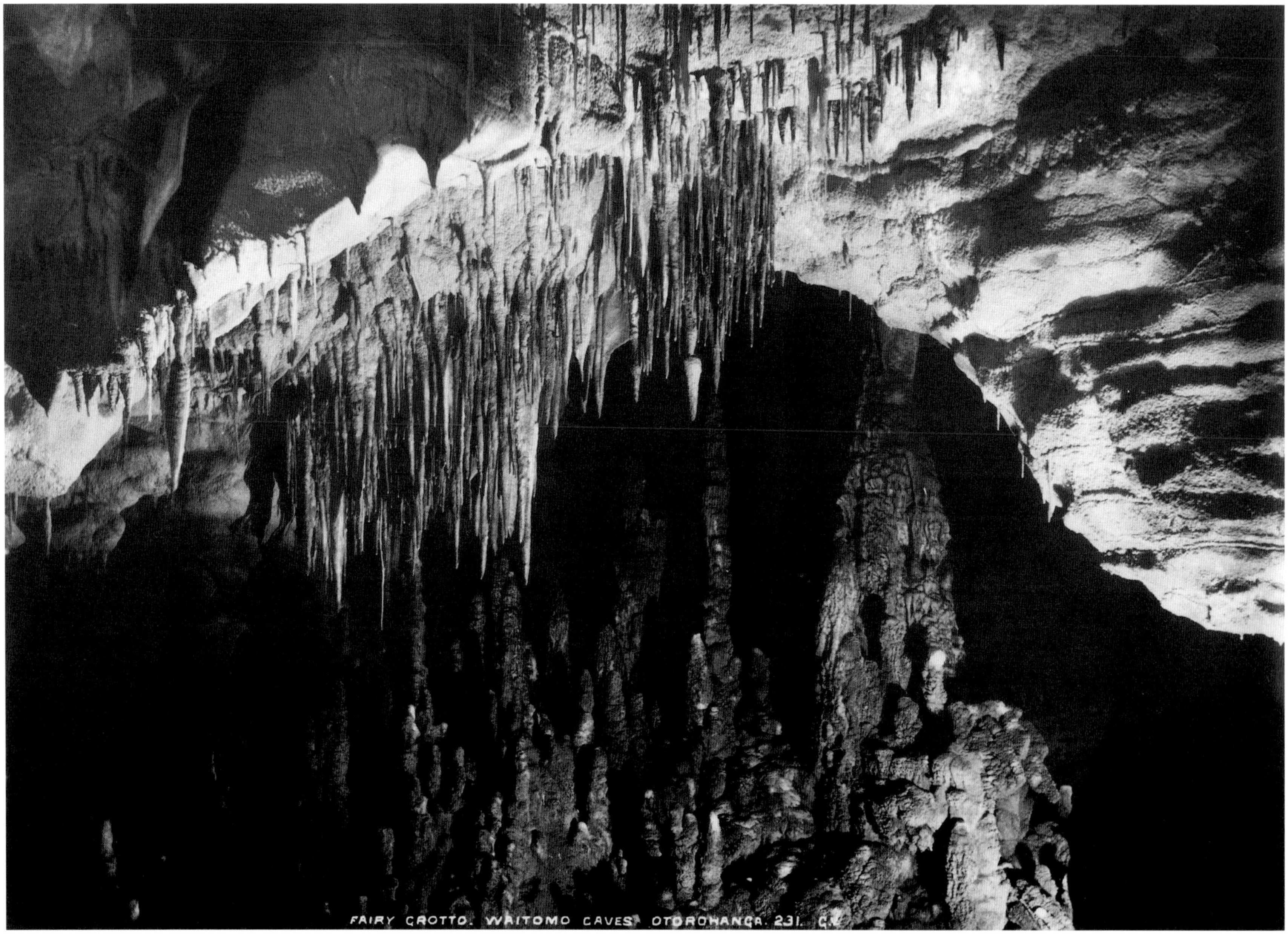

'Fairy Grotto, Waitomo Caves, Otorohanga', 1889

CHAPTER 11

WAITOMO

On a winter journey, in June 1889, George Valentine seems to have thrown concern for health aside in order to meet new challenge – this time through the opportunity to photograph the 'newly discovered' Waitomo Caves, 100 miles by rail south of Auckland.[1] Because of their location in the northern part of the Māori 'King Country', the Pākehā population had known little of these wonders; until recent years the region had been strictly out of bounds to Europeans.

Existing as an independent Māori state, the 'King Country' had encompassed some 7,000 square miles, or nearly one-sixth of the North Island.[2] Opposition to the settler policy of the colonial government had given birth to the King movement, with Potatau Te Wherowhero's election in 1858, and the royal seat inherited by his son Tawhiao upon his father's death in 1860. Following the invasion of the nearby Waikato by British forces in 1863, the mainly Ngāti Maniapoto inhabitants of the district had closed their borders and vowed not to sell land to Pākehā. For more than 20 years they had conducted their own affairs, sheltering fugitives from Pākehā justice, making and enforcing their own laws, and sometimes even killing Europeans who presumed to trespass across their borders.

The region's inhabitants had long known of the caves: sometimes their entrances had been used as refuges during times of war; certain dry caves had been used for burial; and others were a source for bones of the extinct moa, that were ground and used as pigment for moko (traditional tattoo). Waitomo means 'water entering a hole in the ground' – and parts of the stream running through the caves were prized as a fishing ground for the setting of eel-traps.[3]

The first European to record seeing caves in the region did so in 1849. Those who followed were mainly impressed by finds of moa bones and skulls.[4] With further exploration prevented by the region's closure, various attempts at reconciliation between Māori and Pākehā over the years had also failed. In 1881, however, a peace agreement between King Tawhiao and the Government marked the beginning of the end of this isolation. Permission for Pākehā to travel through the region was first granted in 1883.[5] Immediately afterwards, in 1884, surveyors were there to survey land and establish boundaries, build roads and a railway, and expedite the sale and lease of Māori land.[6] In 1886 a Māori Land Court was established at Ōtorohanga, a trading-post 12 miles to the north of Waitomo, which was also home to the timber and main-trunk railway workers.

Among the newcomers was London-born Fred Mace, who lived in Ōtorohanga as a farmer and surveyor's assistant. With another surveyor, Mace had been shown the entrance to the Waitomo cave in 1884, but a more investigative journey did not come until the end of 1887.[7] At this time, Mace's aim was a pleasant Christmas adventure, using a raft he had managed to construct from flax flower stalks, and he persuaded his somewhat hesitant friend Tāne Tinorau to accompany him on a journey through the caves.[8] Unbeknown to Mace, Tinorau had often travelled through the cave on fishing expeditions in the canoe *Te Pohara*.[9] Mace, however, interpreted his friend's reluctance to open up this prized fishing ground as his innate fear of taniwha and other such 'saurian monsters' inhabiting the forbidding recesses. On the makeshift raft, Mace and Tinorau floated down the spring-fed Waitomo Stream and into the cave's dark entrance. Immediately they had to lie down to avoid stalactites. With only two candles to light the way, they eventually found themselves under a shining grotto of spectacular glow-worm arches. Gaining little more than a glimpse, they poled their way back upstream, managing to drag the raft to the cave's entrance and daylight just before the candles were exhausted.

Two months later, Mace returned with his brother and two fellow surveyors from Ōtorohanga for a better exploration. Tinorau also joined the expedition, from which was to come more publicity and the start of Europeans entering the region in greater numbers. From this time Tāne Tinorau with his wife Huti began to run the caves as a private concern, with footbridges and ladders added to strategic places, many of the formations given names, and Huti acting as guide (for the modest charge of one candle per head). Land Department officials were slow to take action, but with the interest gathering Native Land Court Judge, Major W.G. Mair, made a visit in early 1889, and quickly saw the potential for tourist revenue. From this trip came plans for a secret official expedition to the caves for the purpose of mapping, photographing and making recommendations to Government.[10] Judge Mair returned in early June with a government survey party which included Auckland surveyor Thomas Humphries, an officer from the Department of Crown Lands; his assistant, Auckland engineer James Stewart (who had led the early post-eruption visit to Rotomahana to determine the fate of the Terraces); Auckland photographer J.R. Hanna and his assistant; and Native Land Court interpreter H.D. Johnson.

Headed by Humphries, and instructed to maintain strict secrecy about the mission, the party entered the cave by canoe on 1 June 1889. Led by Tinorau and his wife, the visitors were taken around the whole system of caves, with the help of climbing ladders 'about 25 feet long' and tracks laid with ponga logs. The Māori proprietors served a candle-lit banquet in one of the chambers, which was decorated with ferns, then brought out a visitors book, which the government party signed to the delight of their hosts. By the end of that week, the party was back in Auckland, and part of the secret evidently out, with details of the journey published in the *Herald*.[11] James Stewart declared the caves to be the finest things he had seen since the White Terrace.[12] Humphries confirmed also that they were of world importance: 'equal in splendour to the unique Pink and White Terraces of Rotorua'.[13] For fear of the caves being despoiled by visitors, Humphries recommended that 'if possible, the Government should either purchase the site of the cave or in some way, with the consent of the natives, assume control and management of them'.[14] Humphries' report to the Surveyor General gave Fred Mace especial credit for 'the service he has rendered to the tourist community'.[15]

Less than a month afterwards, despite the cold of winter, Valentine was at Waitomo. Auckland and Ōtorohanga had

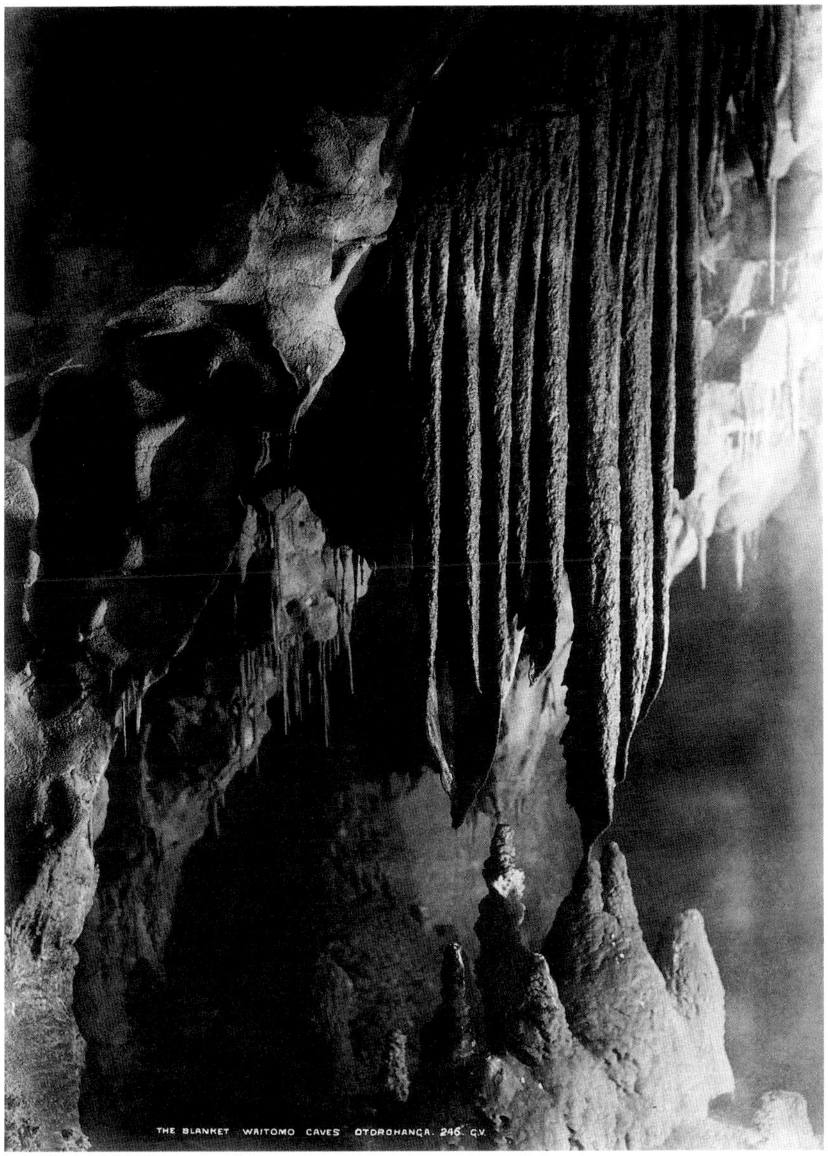

'The Blanket, Waitomo Caves, Otorohanga', 1889

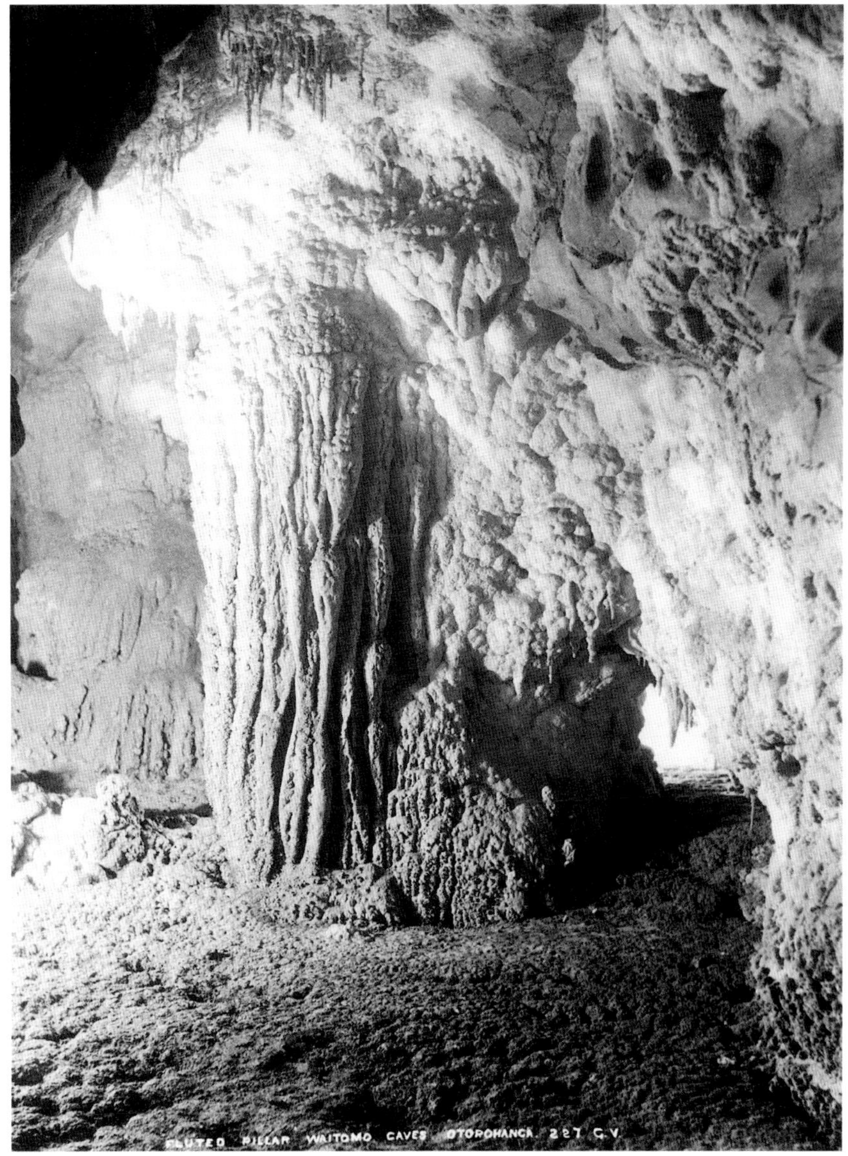

'Fluted Pillar, Waitomo Caves, Otorohanga', 1889

been connected by rail since 1887; from there to the caves an 11-mile bridle track was travelled on horseback. Valentine set up camp, met his guides and prepared himself for a new kind of challenge – climbing, discovering and searching out the subterranean depths. Inside the fantastic labyrinth he worked with characteristic assurance and outstanding technical skill. Cramped conditions and problems in lighting would increase the difficulty of capturing the various sites – 'The White Terrace', 'The Grand Organ', 'The Dungeons', 'Fairy Grotto' and 'The Blanket' among those to have been named. Of these, Valentine had some of his greatest success capturing 'The White Terrace'; the 20-by-30-foot 'Fairy Grotto' with its layered curtain of encrusted, crystallised and glass-like stalactites; and 'The Blanket which, with its translucent folds, creamy tint and reddish stripes, he later described as 'coloured exactly similar to the Maori shawl'.[16]

Visitors had been advised to use candles for travelling and to burn strips of magnesium ribbon for extended viewing.[17] Through their strategic placement and removal before exposure, candles would also be used by the photographer for focusing. Lighting a composition was achieved with magnesium – in effect, it was painting with light. While no published account was left of his time here, details from the previous month's survey journey clearly show the difficulty of the task: 'Nearly the whole of this time was taken up with the photographing, which was very tedious as we were greatly impeded by the smoke from the magnesium burning, which hung about so much. The whole party suffered more or less for some days afterwards through inhaling its fumes so continuously.'[18]

George Valentine's series of 27 Waitomo images was registered for copyright on 24 July 1889. It is not known whether these reached the public before J.R. Hanna's. Valentine's Waitomo series would, however, remain unsurpassed for at least the next 60 years.

The Government took action in October 1889 in support of Thomas Humphries' report, with Ōtorohanga resident J.L.R. Fraser appointed as caretaker of the Waitomo Caves, and instructions given to negotiate for their purchase, improve access and ensure protection from vandalism.[19] Shortly afterwards the Crown obtained a share in the block of land above the cave.[20] In 15 years they would own all the blocks around the mouth of the cave, with a Scenery Preservation Act passed in 1903 allowing them to dispossess the Māori owners of the remaining cave block. This happened in the following year, with the Government taking three years to award meagre compensation.[21] Later, the Waitomo Caves (including two other major caves nearby) would for a period of 45 years – between 1910 and 1955 – become the most lucrative tourist attractions in New Zealand.[22]

CHAPTER 12

LAST DAYS

At the end of 1889 George Valentine played a pivotal role in rejuvenating a failing Auckland Photographic Society. Formed in 1883, the society had at first flourished, but then waned almost to the point of extinction. Then on 29 October 1889 a small committee gathered and was 'instructed to frame by-laws, to be laid before a future meeting; to enquire for suitable rooms, and report as soon as possible'.[1] Rooms suitable for a darkroom and workroom were soon found in the Australian Mutual Provident Society's buildings in Queen Street, while newly drafted rules ensured that membership was 'open to all interested in the photographic art', including ladies.[2]

The committee also agreed for a public exhibition of work to be held each September and a private one in May. By the end of November everything was described as being 'in excellent order for photographic work, being fitted with all the necessary baths, drying tables, shades, etc., while a stock of materials for developing and other branches of the art has been supplied, and several valuable technical works donated'. With these, a rapidly expanding committee also decided 'to subscribe to the leading British and American journals on photography, and keep them for reference'.[3] At their next meeting on 11 December 'Mr. G.D. Valentine (of the eminent firm of photographers, Dundee) was unanimously elected president' and the society was 'congratulated on securing a president whose name is so well-known in photographic circles on both sides of the line'.[4]

Valentine continued to work and travel throughout this time, and made two summer journeys to the Thermal Region. The first of these (at the start of summer) was to Rotorua and Ōkoroire near Oxford (Tirau), at the extreme south of the Waikato on the Waihou River. The results of this journey were brought to the public in the *Auckland Weekly News*:

> The well-known photographer, Mr. G.D. Valentine, has recently made a trip to Rotorua and the Okoroire sanatorium with a view of photographing various points interest with which tourists are not so familiar. The Okoroire views are three in number – the first showing the Waihou river as it debouches from the waterfall with the bathing establishment and sanatorium; second, the natural bridge which forms one of the wonders of the sanatorium, and third, the Waihou above the falls. These will be quite new to the Auckland public. Of the Rotorua views there are four – one of

> 'Sodom and Gomorrah' [two large beds of sulphur near the mouth of the Puarenga stream] from the heights; second, of the Spout Pool as enlarged; third, the Pohutu Geyser, 70 feet high, with three distinct jets, known as 'the four o'clock geyser' by tourists owing to its generally playing up at that hour. This is an especially fine photograph, showing the geyser to advantage. A photograph of the site of the sunken pa at Ohinemutu point, illustrates very forcibly the lowered level at which Lake Rotorua now stands.[5]

Valentine left for his second summer journey immediately after his 11 December election as Auckland Photographic Society president. This time his purpose was a more thorough investigation of Whakarewarewa's geysers, all of which had shown a renewed vigour since the Tarawera eruption. Whakarewarewa, like Ōhinemutu, was a thermal village in the midst of steam, sulphur and boiling mud, leading to an American visitor's description of the pair as 'the most extraordinary of all the odd and curious towns I have seen in my travels in the four quarters of the globe'.[6] Following the eruption, many of the displaced inhabitants of Te Wairoa had settled at Whakarewarewa, including Sophia Hinerangi (known by now as 'the heroine of the eruption') who continued in her guiding role.[7] Valentine would have found a range of tourist accommodation with clearly established charges: food and lodgings were around £1 per week, and the charge to photographers from between £3 and £5.[8]

From these two journeys, Valentine captured all of the well-known Whakarewarewa geysers – Waikorohīhī, Waikite, Kereru, and Pōhutu – as well as the Oil Bath, a favourite spot for bathing and socialising in the village. One of the most memorable and poetic works made was of Pōhutu, the highest of whose three jets Valentine witnessed throwing hot water a distance of 200 feet from the centre.[9] Whatever the challenges faced by the photographer through the presence of hot water spray, even more must have been experienced by working on noisy, vibrating ground. Pōhutu's main jet was surrounded by a number of 'smaller geysers and steam funnels, and in periods of great activity several of these hot-water fountains play in concert with the large one ... Underfoot, in places, the ground trembles, and there is heard the whirr and shaking as of some immense subterranean machinery at work.'[10]

Valentine's photographic intentions were cut short on his second journey, evidently on account of his worsening physical condition. Back in Auckland, he found himself unable to preside over the 8 January 1890 Auckland Photographic Society meeting.[11] That day's *Herald*, however, published details of his latest excursion:

> The well-known photographer, Mr. G. Valentine, has recently returned from a photographic tour to the Lake Country. He has made a special study this visit of the Whakarewarewa geysers, which have been taken in all their varied aspects. Owing to their renewed activity they are attracting special attention. Every tourist makes a point of visiting the Korohihi, Kereru, Pohutu, and Waikite geysers. Some time ago Mr. Malfroy, C.E., started at Whakarewarewa the process of artificial terrace making. The experiment has been very successful, the silica depositing rapidly on the framework erected, and shortly (says Mr. Valentine) there will be a very respectable-looking terrace formation at Whakarewarewa. It was his intention to have gone on to Taupo and Tokaanu, but circumstances prevented. He states that the tourist traffic is very satisfactory, and quite up to expectations.[12]

This was Valentine's last publicised tour, for his health continued to decline. A family portrait taken in January shows the Valentines gathered together as if for the last

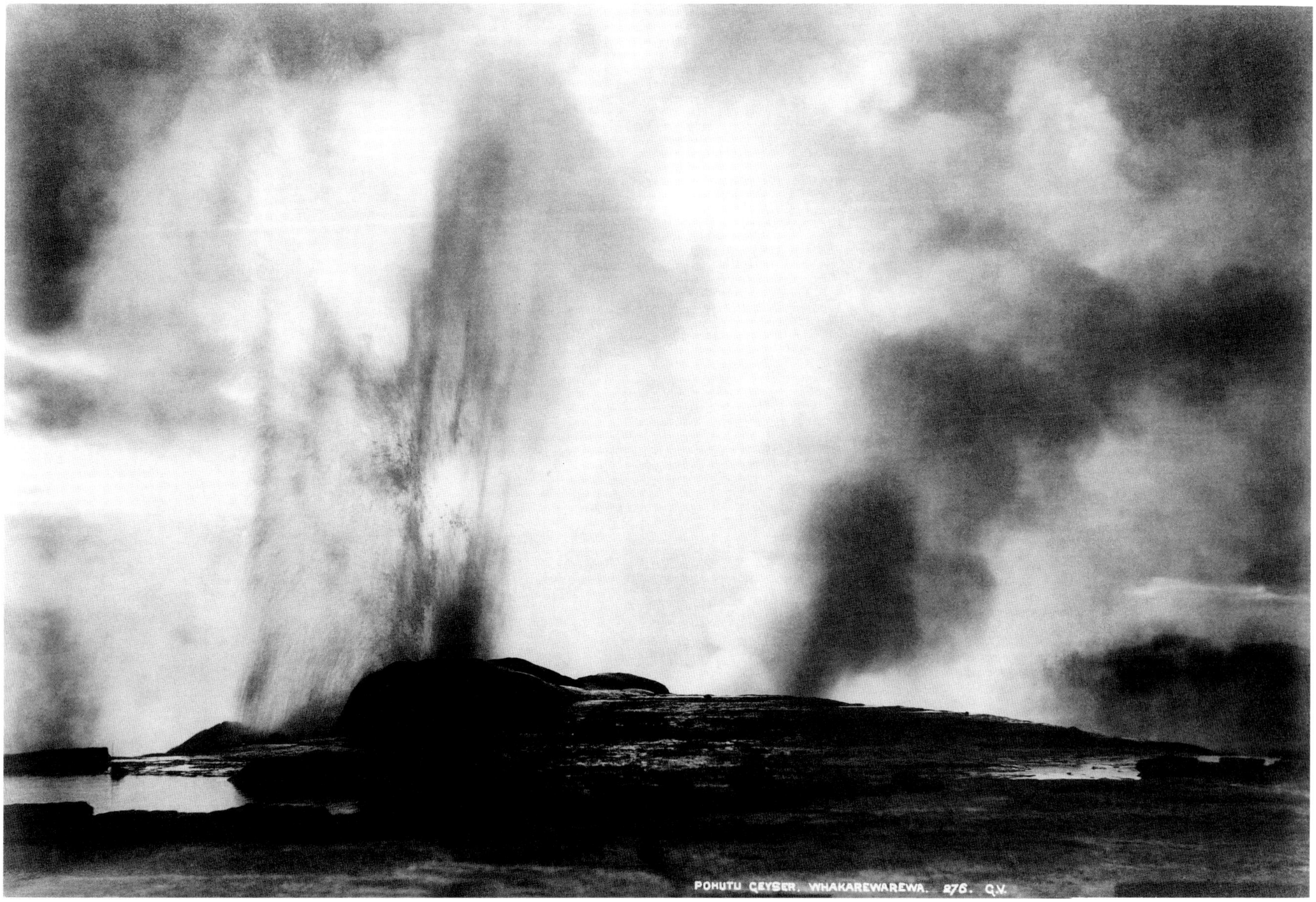

'Pohutu Geyser, Whakarewarewa', 1889

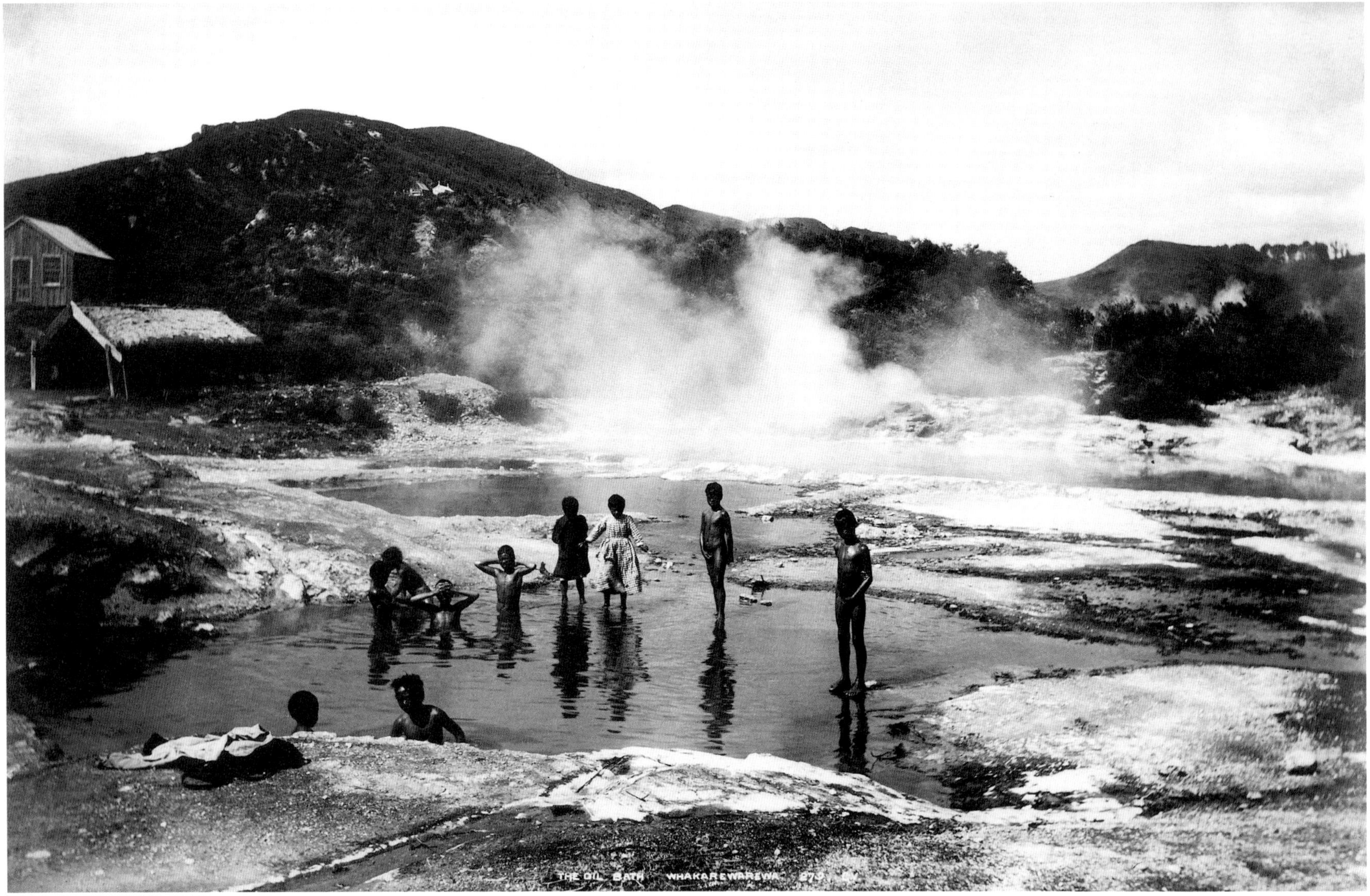

'The Oil Bath, Whakarewarewa', 1889

time – George himself appears gaunt and bleary. Despite this, he was at the end of January functioning in his role as president of the Auckland Photographic Society, and offering 'to provide the presentation prints for the next half-yearly distribution among the members'.[13] This was perhaps his goal in a final excursion to Auckland's Waitakere region, evidence of which exists in a single extant print of Nihotupu Upper Falls (the last to be numbered in his catalogue). 'The finest Falls in the North Island. 21 miles from Auckland' is the hand-written inscription he gave this superb image.[14] His artistic powers were clearly undiminished.

'It will be seen from our obituary column that Mr. G.D. Valentine, the well-known photographer, has passed away,' the *Herald* announcement began. At his Parnell residence, on 26 February 1890, tuberculosis claimed him at the tragically young age of 38. Treatment at home from the Auckland Surgeon General, Dr Edward Mackellar, had failed to halt his demise, 'although Dr. Mackellar did all that medical skill could accomplish for the patient'. Valentine's condition had deteriorated after the Rotorua visit, and it was supposed he had 'over-exerted himself in his delicate state of health'.

Outlining his career, the obituary noted Valentine as having been 'enthusiastic in the practice of his profession', with his 'views of the Rotomahana terraces, the Waitomo caves, etc... among the finest of their kind'. He was remembered also as 'a man of sterling qualities, and much respected and esteemed by those who had made his acquaintance'.[15] Shortly afterwards, Mina Valentine and the three young children left for the return voyage to Scotland.

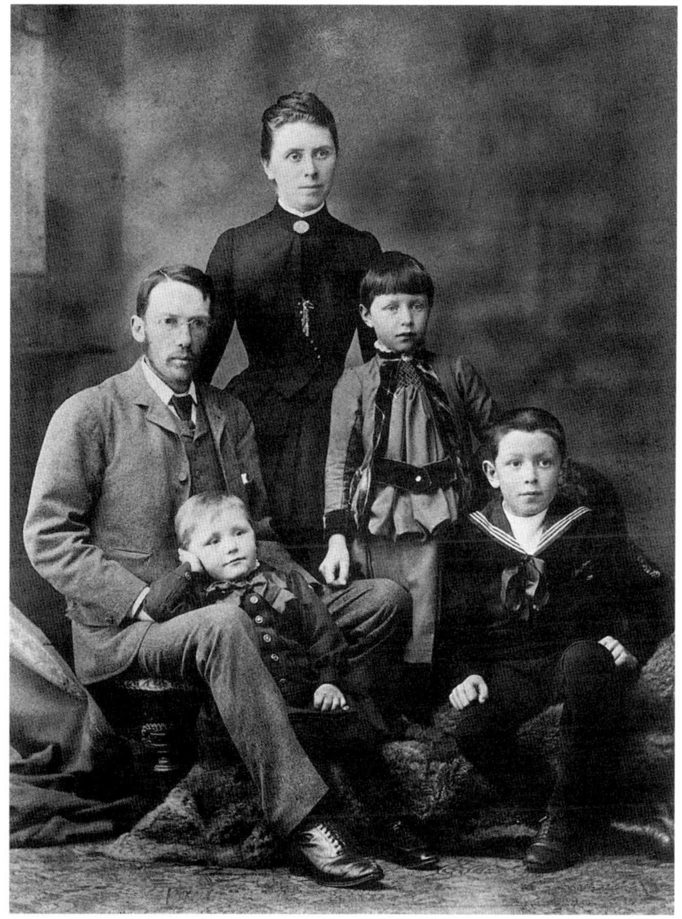

George and Mina Valentine with Mary, James and Arnot, by J.R. Hanna, January 1890

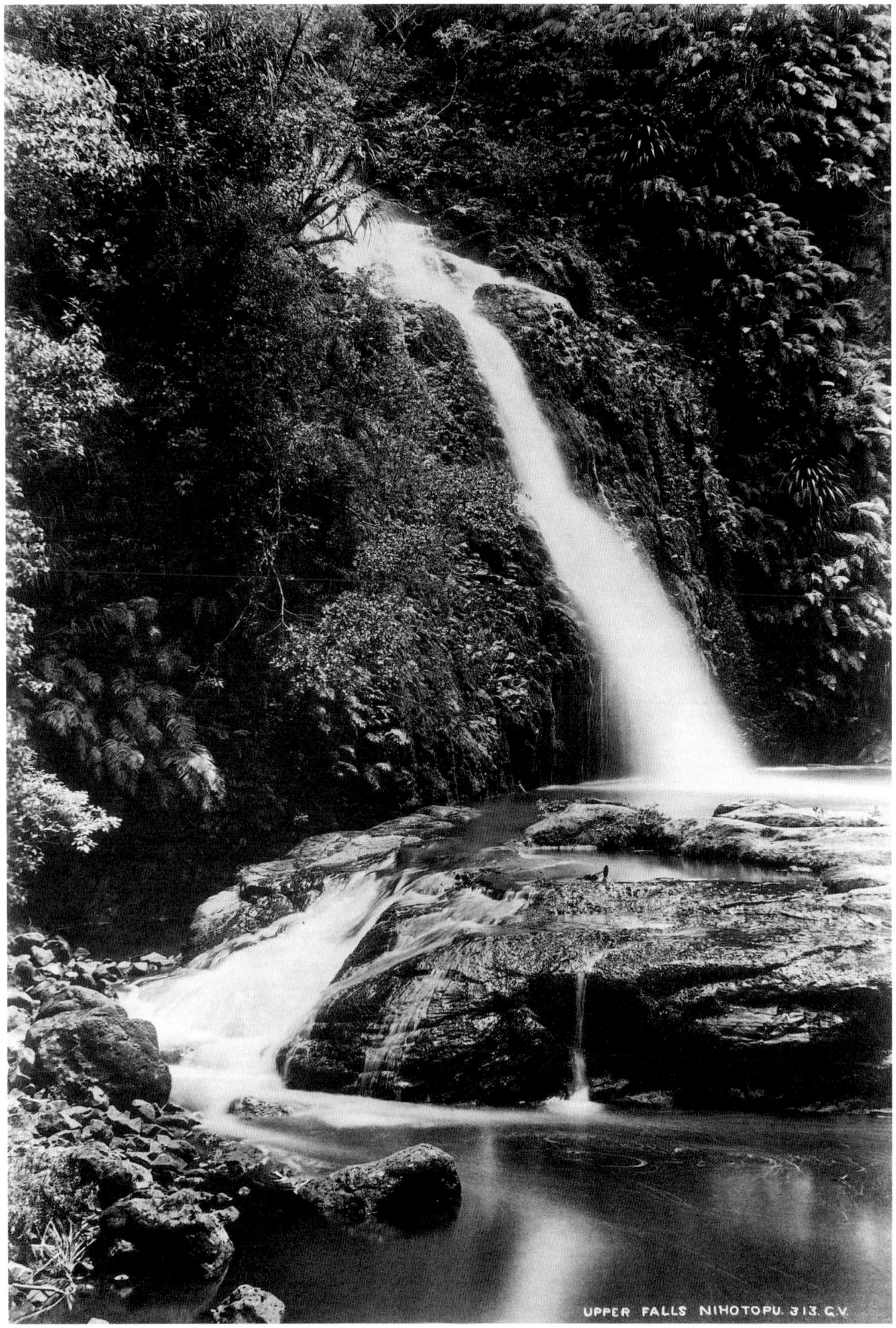

'Upper Falls, Nihotupu', c.1890

EPILOGUE

Present-day descendants of George Valentine knew little of their forebear or of his time in New Zealand. That he left Scotland owing to ill health, and that he had photographed the Pink and White Terraces in a timely way before their destruction, was about the sum total of what was known. Of his character and personality, there was little in the way of inherited memories, though one of his granddaughters had gained from his widow the recollection of 'a quiet, strong, retiring man' who operated 'freelance'.[1] One of his contemporaries, the photographer Josiah Martin, adds to this portrait by describing George Valentine as 'one of the best and kindest men that ever handled a camera'.[2]

THE VALENTINE FAMILY

Upon their return to Scotland, Mina Valentine and the children lived with (and kept house for) her bachelor brother James, a jute manufacturer in Dundee. A widow for 57 years, Mina was for the last 20 or so years of her life an invalid, having suffered from a stroke which left her paralysed on one side. She also became profoundly deaf, which made conversation difficult. Despite these infirmities, Mina is remembered kindly: she had 'a great sense of humour' and complained rarely.[3]

None of Mina Valentine's grandchildren recalls her mentioning her time in New Zealand; most recall no mention of their grandfather. Somewhat mystifying to descendants also is the fact of her remaining aloof from the other Valentines in Dundee, whose rapidly expanding business continued to go from strength to strength. Certainly no support came from this branch of the family – leading to the conclusion that there was a break in relations, after which time George and Mina had no further contact with them. Mina does, however, seem to have been well provided for.[4]

Mary, James and Arnot all attended Dundee High School, where their uncle Easton was Head of English. Mary never married, and for a time taught piano; later she devoted herself to the care of her deaf and paralysed mother.[5] A visitor to their home recalls the presence of a pair of paintings of the Pink and White Terraces, 'odd bits of Maori memorabilia as well; clubs, stone axes and the like'.[6]

Both sons left Dundee in due course, and their families were born and brought up in England. James Valentine became a schoolmaster, marrying the Norwegian Ragna Amundsen (a graduate of Oslo University), with whom he had two sons and three daughters. He died in 1920 at the age of 40.[7] Arnot Stirling Valentine had no memories of his New Zealand childhood to pass to his own children: 'The only mention my father made of his early life was the voyage

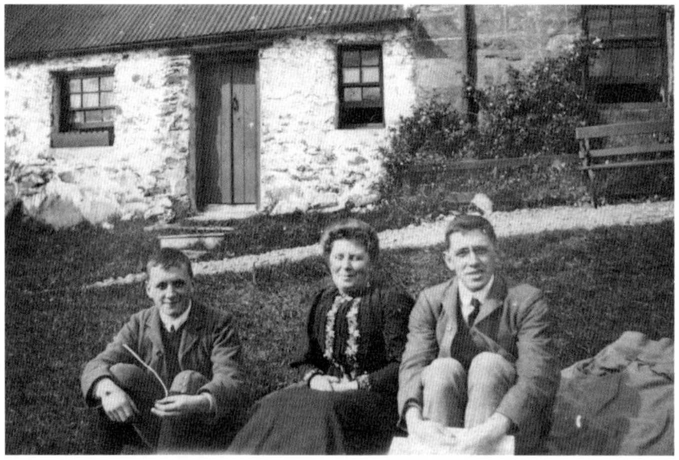

Arnot, Mina and James Valentine, on holiday in Perthshire, c.1901

home by sailing ship round the Cape Horn and being taken on deck to see the fires – he was about four years of age,' recalls his youngest daughter Ann.[8] Arnot Valentine became a leading civil engineer, married Violet Fairweather, with whom he also had two sons and three daughters, and died in 1973. 'George's son Arnot ... went on to get to the top of his profession as the managing director of Britain's premier firm of civil engineers, Balfour Beatty. As a young man he was involved in the greatest civil engineering project of the age, the digging of the tunnel under Ben Nevis to provide hydro-electric power for the British Aluminium Company, Fort William. In his maturer years Arnot built the Churchill Barriers in Orkney, causeways from island to island to protect the naval anchorage of Scapa Flow.'[9]

For the centenary of George Dobson Valentine's death in 1990, his eldest grandson, the late John Valentine, made plans from his home in the Channel Islands to visit New Zealand and the burial place of his grandfather. Sadly, through the loss of his wife and his own poor health, he was forced to cancel the journey. Through friends in Auckland, however, the grave was cleaned in time for the day, and a bouquet and note attached: 'In memory of George Dobson Valentine of Dundee, Scotland on the centenary of his death on 26th February 1890 from his 78 descendants currently living in Scotland, England, the Channel Islands, Canada, America, Italy and Hong Kong – 26th February 1990'.[10] At this present time, nearly 100 descendants are living in Scotland, England, Canada and the United States.

Valentine & Sons

Following George and Mina Valentine's departure to New Zealand, the family firm continued, not surprisingly, to expand at an astonishing rate. In 1892, two years after George's death, 'Valentine & Sons' was described by a Wellington newspaper as 'a famous firm employing 300 hands, and always hav[ing] eight operators in the field'.[11] One of these was Dundee photographer J.S. Powell, whose arrival in New Zealand to gather images for an ever-expanding catalogue was to cause some consternation among the country's own struggling landscape photographers.[12]

With the arrival of the scenic postcard at the turn of the century, 'Valentine & Sons', with their world-wide register of views, were easily able to take the lead in this new field. By 1904 they were employing around 700 people in Britain, with 'artists and photographers engaged in every part of the globe, even in the most out-of-the-way and little-known corners thereof'.[13] In 1906 the firm was recorded as producing 'between one and two tons of picture postcards daily'; in 1907 the company name was described as 'a household word from Australia to the West India Islands'.[14] By 1908 they were apparently responsible for 'the employment of over one thousand persons'; by mid-century, despite the difficult years following the war, the number of staff was at around 1,200, with an annual output of 45 million postcards.[15] Valentines of Dundee made their exit from the postcard market in the early 1970s, but continue today in the manufacture of greeting cards.[16]

The Region Valentine Photographed

In 1902, the question of the survival of the Pink and White Terraces became temporarily revived. Many thought that they still lay buried beneath tons of ash and mud, while others were convinced they had been completely blown to pieces. Two of George Valentine's photographs of Lake Rotomahana, from before and after the eruption, were published in the *Auckland Weekly News* of 6 March 1902.[17] Once again, any hopes were dispelled.

In the Thermal Region the memory of the Terraces remains, as may be experienced by a visit to the Rotorua Museum of Art and History. Graphic displays on the eruption co-exist with a fine collection of contemporary Māori and Pākehā art. At Ōhinemutu, Ngāti Whakaue perform lively concerts for visitors, and at Whakarewarewa, with its impressive geysers, young Māori learn the skills of their forebears at the New Zealand Māori Arts and Crafts Institute.

Te Wairoa now is 'The Buried Village', where archaeological excavations have revealed many prizes, including the remains of McRae's Rotomahana Hotel and what may possibly be the world's only 'petrified ham'. At places such as Tarawera and Waimangu, the descendants of eruption survivors from Tūhourangi and Ngāti Rangitihi guide tourists, with the summit of Tarawera reached by organised hikes or helicopter, the steaming panorama of coloured clays still a gaping wound. Lake Rotomahana is reached via the Waimangu Valley by bus trip or bush walk (covering part of the route of Valentine's second post-eruption survey). Here too is the small but recently formed multi-coloured Warbrick Terrace. On the lake itself, a boat cruise takes passengers to where the Terraces were situated. Continued thermal life may be seen around the lake edge, with an abundance of black swans and other bird life.

The Wairākei Valley is a somewhat disappointing circuit, its spectacular geyser field having long been utilised for a geothermal power station. However, a bold new tourist venture in the area deliberately invokes the memory of Rotomahana through the surprisingly successful artificial Wairākei Terrace, not far from the heli-pads of the foaming Huka Falls and accompanying exclusive luxury lodge.

Waiotapu Valley, which Valentine was the first to photograph, still offers unspoilt nature in open and vast surrounds, and the same formations may be seen, with an artist's palette of earth colours and glistening silica formations reminiscent of Rotomahana. Not a great distance away is Ōrākei-Kōrako, with its spectacular Terrace-like formations poised on the edge of an artificial lake. Here questions of land ownership and (surprisingly recent) misappropriation of land from the Māori owners also continue.[18]

Waitomo Caves, still drawing many thousands of tourists each year, have in recent years been returned to descendants of their original owners. Auckland's Waitakere Bush, the last place Valentine is known to have photographed, retains impressive stands of kauri, nikau and lush tropical vegetation, but the magnificent falls are gone, dammed to become part of Auckland's water supply.

George Valentine's Photography and Its Significance

George Valentine faced challenging circumstances with an apparent refusal to yield to inactivity or despair. Having left the demands and restraints of large-scale commercial production, he was in New Zealand able to devote himself completely to an expressive art for the first time. This he did with passion and sensibility, selecting his own subject matter and working as often as he could.

Valentine's landscapes display a clear appreciation for the variety and scale of nature, and often carry a timeless quality – they are images to lose oneself in. 'Coffee Cups, White Terrace. 19' is a fantastic and mystical image, a briefly glimpsed landscape from the world of dreams. 'Giant Buttress, White Terrace. 27' invites a similar sense of wonder through its combination of the monumental aspects of a landscape with delicate and sensitive detail. Valentine's intuitive, expressive approach is joined to an extraordinary technical facility: photography seems to be an extension of himself, a realm in which he has free rein. Consistently his works show a strong, natural sense of composition, underpinned by a structure of rhythms and shapes. This is done superbly in 'The Eagle's Nest, Wairākei. 202', with its multiple layers of light on dark and dark on light – a celebration of nature's infinite, subtle delicacy. Often his results approach abstraction. This sense of involvement is the quality separating him from his peers, whose works are more typically topographical.

Valentine's motivation seems more strongly balanced towards expressive aims than commercial ones – though clearly such results had commercial value. Tourism was the most obvious market for his work; the places which attracted him were those attracting tourists. This market (and his catalogue) would, however, remain small. While a moderate income from his photography is suggested through surviving records, it is impossible to guess at the extent of sales.[19] Evidently he arrived in New Zealand with capital and means: his family's livelihood was not dependent on commercial success.[20] It is interesting also to note that he described himself as 'gentleman' rather than 'photographer' in his will. (His New Zealand estate was worth up to £3,500, and his Scottish one 'not exceeding £1700' – no small fortune at this time.)[21] Valentine's photography, then, was at least partly a pursuit which filled the need for a useful and constructive activity, one which continued his sense of identity and purpose, and distracted him from real and pressing problems.

Valentine's work in most instances excludes any human presence, which adds to a sense of mystery and timelessness. Sometimes this is slightly frustrating – one would like to be able to determine the size or scale of what has been photographed, especially at Rotomahana. Occasionally groups of Māori are a distant feature in village settings as part of the landscape. Portraiture of Māori, however, is not a genre he chose to pursue. The pair of enigmatic unnamed portraits which do exist are surrounded by questions. Firstly, who are the sitters – the tattooed 'rangatira' with piercing eyes and his brooding female companion? Where and when did Valentine collect their likenesses? Can they have seen these photographs? Why were so few portraits taken, given that portraiture was his specialty in Scotland and such 'photogenic' subject matter was available? Can he have recognised in these sitters something of the pain and indignity of loss, or their discomfort at being made a spectacle?

Valentine's contribution to photography in New Zealand is significant. As his work becomes better known here, it also seems likely that his name will be placed on a world platform. Easily may he stand beside the most widely recognised 'names' from this era on both sides of the Atlantic – though he is most easily aligned with the celebrated early photographers of the American West. These include Timothy O'Sullivan, Carleton Watkins, Eadweard Muybridge and especially William Henry Jackson, whose work holds the most parallels with Valentine's – particularly in terms of subject matter.[22]

For George Dobson Valentine the opportunity to spend his days travelling and photographing was a gift. His photographic output in New Zealand and the Pacific was small, but the results left behind are likewise a remarkable gift. Until now, this taonga, or treasure, has been mostly hidden. With more than a third of his images still not found, there may yet be impressive works awaiting discovery.[23]

ENDNOTES

INTRODUCTION

1 Main, William, 'George Dobson Valentine in New Zealand', *History of Photography, An international quarterly,* October 1982, p.345.
2 Rockel, Ian, *Tarawera Eruption Centenary,* 1986, p.9.
3 Stevenson, Sara, *Light from the Dark Room, A Celebration of Scottish Photography,* 1995, p.11, p.123.
4 J.M. (Josiah Martin), 'Exposures', *Sharland's Trade Journal,* 7 May 1892, p.86, col.2.
5 Caldwell, Mark, *The Last Crusade. The War on Consumption. 1862–1954,* 1988, pp.17-20.

CHAPTER 1 A PHOTOGRAPHER'S JOURNEY

1 'Shipping', *Otago Daily Times,* 25 October 1882, p.3.
2 Main, W., 1982, p.347 (from *Guide to Dunedin,* 1883; the photographer whose work most impressed him at this meeting was J.C. Morris).
3 'Death of Mr. James Valentine, Photographer', *Dundee Advertiser,* 20 June 1879.
4 'Messrs. James Valentine and Sons at Dundee', *Photographic News,* 10 March 1882, p.115; 'Our Picture', *Philadelphia Photographer,* Vol.17, No.197, May 1880, p.10.
5 'Shipping', *New Zealand Herald,* 6 December 1882; 'Shipping', *Otago Daily Times,* 15 December 1882, 29 December 1882.
6 Annual Report, Dundee and East of Scotland Photographic Association, April 1883, care of J.B. Ramage, Dundee City Chief Librarian, 1993.

CHAPTER 2 GEORGE D. VALENTINE IN SCOTLAND

1 James Valentine and his first wife Christina Martin (d.1842) had Elizabeth (1840–1862), Mary (1841–1842) and John (1841–1867). James married Rachel Dobson in 1843 and they had seven children: William (b.1844), James (b.1846), Margaret (b.1848), Rachel (1850–1859), George (b. 3 June 1852), Helen (b.1854) and Easton (b.1858).
2 Valentine engraved a notice in 1849 advertising one of Burritt's meetings (photocopy held by St Andrew's University Library Collection). An 1851 letter by Burritt while in Edinburgh to the Rev Dick in Dundee mentions having dined with Valentine in Dundee. Cavendish Philatelic Auctions, Sale 619, 12 April 2002. Valentine also designed League of Universal Brotherhood pledges for Burritt.
3 Stowe was in Britain from 1853–56. The description of Rachel was by her granddaughter Rachel Webb. *A Family History, Bertram Gordon Valentine and Margaret Helen Japp, from Progenitors to Progeny,* Vol. 1, Gordon Alexander Valentine, 1994–1999.
4 James Valentine's new 'Uncle Tom' Anti-Slavery envelope was advertised in *The British Friend,* June 1854, p.164. The advertisement states that by this time 'nearly a million and a half' of his engraved 'Moral and Social Reform Envelopes' had been sold.
5 *British Journal of Photography,* 'Dry Plates in California: An Echo from the Far West', John Valentine, XI, No.227, 9 September 1864, pp.346-7; *British Journal of Photography,* 7 February 1868, p.62.
6 Smart, Robert N., '"Famous Throughout the World": Valentine & Sons Ltd., Dundee'. *Review of Scottish Culture,* Vol.4, 1988, p.77.
7 James Valentine's earliest travel souvenirs (from the early 1850s) were engraved 'picture cards' and depicted scenes of historical, scenic or architectural interest. Staff, Frank, *The Picture Postcard & its Origins,* 1966, p.38-9.
8 *Album, In Memoriam 1861 Glenmark to Fettercairn,* Royal Archives, Windsor; 'Second Great Expedition: To Invermark and Fettercairn' (20-21 September 1861), *Our Life in the Highlands,* pp.67-72; 'Our Editorial Table', *British Journal of Photography,* No.223, 12 August 1864, p.295. Having already given Valentine's portraiture an 'honourable mention', this latter article notes his 'turning his attention to landscapes also'.
9 James Valentine was the second in Scotland to receive the Royal Warrant (and the seventh of 47 in Britain and abroad to be thus honoured). Taylor, Roger, 'The Place and Quality of Photographer to Her Majesty in Scotland', *Happy and Glorious: Six Reigns of Royal Photography,* edited by Colin Ford, 1977, pp.47, 60-1; Dimond, Frances and Taylor, Roger, *Crown and Camera, The Royal Family and Photography, 1842–1910,* 1987, p.213.
10 James Valentine wrote in 1867, 'I have now used this carriage, & c., for upwards of three years.' *British Journal Photographic Almanac 1867,* 'A Substitute for a Dark Room in Field Operations', pp.100-01.
11 *Dundee Advertiser,* Obituary, 'Death of Mr. James Valentine, Photographer', 20 June 1879.
12 Letter on James Valentine's 1870s letterhead, written before August 1879, care of Mrs J. Williams, 18 October 1993.
13 Letter from G. Birnie to W. Main, September 1980.
14 1881 census, care of J.B. Ramage, Dundee City Chief Librarian, May 1993.
15 Margaret Rachel Valentine died aged nine months on 17 March 1879. George also lost his mother in August 1879.
16 Miss Frances Dimond, Royal Archives Photograph Collection Curator, is of the opinion that these were commissioned portraits. Correspondence to author, 13 November 1992.
17 Dundee and East of Scotland Photographic Association Rules, 1883; Secretary's Third Annual Report, 1883. J.B. Ramage, Dundee City Chief Librarian, 31 May 1993.
18 Annual Report, Dundee and East of Scotland Photographic Association, April 1883, p.7. J.B. Ramage, Dundee City Chief Librarian.
19 'Messrs. James Valentine and Sons at Dundee, *Photographic News,* March 10,

1882, pp.115-17. The company's output was so great that even today in auction sales of 19th-century photography, work attributed to James Valentine fills more catalogue space than for any other photographer.

20 Main, W., 1982, p.338.

21 Caldwell, M., 1988, p.9.

22 The death rate from the disease was less than Australia's, and less than half that of Britain's. *New Zealand Official Handbook 1883*, 1883.

23 'Notice to members of Dundee and East of Scotland Photographic Association', 19 November 1883, care of J.B. Ramage, Dundee City Chief Librarian, 1993. That Valentine travelled alone was stated in a letter from G. Birnie to W. Main, September 1980. The business partnership between George and William Valentine was dissolved 1 November 1883. Scottish Record Office, Edinburgh, SC70/1/288, pp.528-9.

CHAPTER 3 ANTIPODES

1 'Shipping', *New Zealand Herald*, 21 January 1884, p.4; 13 February 1884, p.4; 18 March 1884, p.4.

2 Batchelor, Brian, *Pioneers From Over the Sea, Cross Family Memories of Early Nelson*, 1992, pp.13-35. Captain Cross was said to have built the first house in Nelson. 'Walmer House' was built later, around 1854. The original address was Mary Ann Street, but is now 7 Richardson Street.

3 Ballara, Angela, *Proud to be White? A Survey of Pakeha Prejudice in New Zealand*, 1986, pp.58, 84-8. Māori had been outnumbered since the late 1850s, and were now at one of their lowest ebbs, at less than a quarter of the pre-European population. The highest rate of decrease recorded was in 1881; in 1886 the Māori population was 43,927 and still in decline. The Treaty of Waitangi was signed on 6 February 1840 between the British Crown and 'Chiefs of the Confederation of the United Tribes of New Zealand'.

4 The 1880s were to see almost a tenth of the populations of Great Britain and Ireland depart. See Ford, Colin and Harrison, Brian, *A Hundred Years Ago. Britain in the 1880s in Words and Photographs*, 1983, p.246.

5 Information from letters by George Valentine; details on Webster and Patties from Maurice Watson, Nelson Provincial Museum. There is also record of contact with local lawyer C.W. Fell, who later founded the Nelson Camera Club. Main, W., 1982, p.333.

6 A Valentine family album (St. Andrews University Library, Scotland) has several photographs of Tyree family members, including one of William Tyree in 1889. William established the portrait studio in 1878 and rebuilt it in late 1884, possibly with input and advice from Valentine.

7 A collection of 18 albumen prints belonging to a descendant of a Cross family relative includes work which is similar in composition and choice of subject matter to Valentine's earliest published works. It includes the image of 'Walmer House' with Mina, James and Mary identifiable in the foreground, and two images taken at the shore directly below the house. A copy of this set is held by the Alexander Turnbull Library.

8 Letter to Helen Dobson, George Valentine's mother's sister. Letter kindly forwarded by Mrs Jean Williams, 18 October 1993.

CHAPTER 4 HOT LAKES

1 Chapman, G.T., *Chapman's Traveller's Guide through the Lake District*, 1873; *Natural Wonders of New Zealand*, 1881.

2 Knox, Thomas W., *The Boy Travellers in Australasia*, 1889, p.228.

3 Cowan, Frank, *Fact and Fancy in New Zealand – The Terraces of Rotomahana: a poem*, 1885, p.38.

4 'Shipping', *New Zealand Herald*, 7 January 1885, p.4.

5 The intention to stay ten days was recorded by Blomfield in a letter to his wife on the day of their arrival, 13 January 1885. Williams, Muriel, *Charles Blomfield: His Life and Times*, 1979, pp.71-4.

6 ibid.

7 This route was becoming favoured over the alternative steamer and coach journey via Tauranga – Valentine's and Chapman's names are absent from 'Shipping' arrival lists to Tauranga from this time.

8 The camera Valentine used was probably a Meagher and the lens probably a Dallmeyer. Valentine & Sons were listed among famous photographers who used P. Meagher cameras in *Instruction in Photography*, Capt. W. De. W. Abney, London, 1882. Main, W., 1982, pp.334, 347.

9 Froude, J.A., *Oceana, or England and Her Colonies*, 1886, pp.224-9.

10 Kerry-Nicholls, J.H., 'The Wonders of the Lakes, No.1', *New Zealand Herald*, 24 February 1883, suppl. p.1, col.5.

11 Chapman, G.T., *Natural Wonders of New Zealand supplement*, 1881.

12 Williams, M., 1979, p.72.

13 Govt. Survey Dept., *The Sounds, Lakes and Rivers of New Zealand*, 1885, p.1; Chapman, G.T., *Natural Wonders of New Zealand supplement*, 1881, p.52.

14 Plots of land for Rotorua were first available for Europeans in 1881. The Pavilion Baths opened in 1882; in early 1885 the hospital, which was partly intended as a sanatorium for invalids at the baths, still awaited opening. 'Certain chronic potrinaires [TB sufferers]' were later said to pay 'periodical visits with advantage'. Those in advanced stages of the disease, however, were worsened by such treatment. *Report on the Statistics of New Zealand 1889*, 1891, p.219. Valentine's name is not found among those recorded as having used the baths.

15 The construction of the Anglican church more commonly known as 'St Faith's' was a bid from principal chiefs for a return to the faith embraced by a previous generation, before the devastations of the 1860s wars. The church was formally opened on 15 March 1885. Stafford, D.M., *The Founding Years in Rotorua, A History of Events to 1900*, 1986, pp.205-7.

16 *New Zealand Herald*, 11 June 1886, p.6.

17 Kerry-Nicholls, J.H., *New Zealand Herald*, 24 February 1883, suppl. p.1, col.4.

18 Differing accounts record Tiki as being carved c.1836 by a Ngāti Whakaue carver, or at an earlier unspecified date by Warauru of Ngāti Umukaria/Ngāti Wahiao. Ngāti Wahiao Tūhourangi occupied Pukeroa pā before Ngāti Whakaue in pre-European times. At Pukeroa Tiki was joined by two other kūwaha, or gateways, Pukaki and Panui-o-marama. Since 1889, the 16'5" (350cm) gateway has been entrusted to the care

of the Auckland Museum, and was an important feature of the Te Māori exhibition which travelled throughout the United States and New Zealand in 1984–85. Simmons, David, *Whakairo, Maori Tribal Art*, 1985, p.129; correspondence from Dr Roger Neich, Ethnologist, Auckland Museum and Institute, 23 August 1993, 10 April 1995; *New Zealand Herald*, 29 October 1889, p.4, col.8.

19 *New Zealand Herald*, 13 February 1885, p.6; Keam, R.F., *Tarawera: The Volcanic Eruption of 10th June 1886*, 1988, p.44.

20 *New Zealand Herald*, 13 February 1885, p.6.

21 *ibid.*, 11 June 1886, p.6, col.4. Disturbances at Rotokākahi were recorded in April 1881 and October 1883. Keam, R.F., 1988, p.79.

22 Alfred, Duke of Edinburgh, visited in 1870 and Anthony Trollope in 1872. Some have claimed a figure of 5,000 visitors was reached in the early 1880s, but a safer, more conservative estimate is reached through a combination of sources, including Charles Blomfield (Williams, M., 1979, p.74) and Ginders' record of Te Wairoa's annual income through tourism (Keam, R.F., 1988, p.57).

23 Wilson, Alex (Union Steamship Company), *Maoriland*, 1884, pp.262-3.

24 Talbot, Thorpe, *The New Guide to the Lakes and Hot Springs*, 1882, p.43; also Froude, J.A., 1886, p.244. At the time of Valentine's visit, the efforts of temperance crusaders such as the young American William Snow and the Rev. Alfred Fairbrother had done much to adjust the situation, with inhabitants said to be showing 'great signs of improvement, and many are holding firmly to their temperance pledges'. *New Zealand Herald*, 13 February 1885, p.6. Fairbrother was present in Te Wairoa in January 1885. Williams, M., 1979, p.71.

25 *New Zealand Herald*, 22 March 1886, p.6. Sophia is also known as Te Paea Hinerangi, and Kate as Keita Rangitukia Middlemass. Ion, Lois, *Keita Rangitukia Middlemass*, 2002.

26 Hunter, Norman M., Ms-1053, Alexander Turnbull Library, 29 September 1882.

27 Williams, M., 1979, p.73.

28 ibid., p.72.

CHAPTER 5 THE PINK AND WHITE TERRACES

1 Williams, M., 1979, p.71.

2 Wilson, A. (Union Steamship Company), 1884, p.275.

3 Talbot, T., 1882, pp.4-6.

4 Brett, H., *Brett's Auckland Almanac*, 1879, p.118. According to certain traditions, Tarawera was also home to the North Island's last moa. *New Zealand Herald*, 11 June 1886, p.6, col.4.

5 Brett, H., 1879, p.118; Chapman, G.T., 1881, p.84.

6 Traditionally the Kaiwaka was a valued food source for its abundant bird life. A rigid rāhui kept the stream out of bounds for most of the year, protecting the resource during breeding season until the young birds were fledged. The restriction was lifted after 1878; at the time of Valentine's visit, tourists were being charged 2s 6d 'to come back in the canoe down the creek' after seeing Rotomahana. Warbrick, A., *Adventures in Geyserland*, 1934, p.34; Stafford, D.M., 1986, p.94; Williams, M., 1979, p.70.

7 Kerry-Nicholls, J.H., *New Zealand Herald*, 14 April 1883, suppl. p.1, col.2.

8 Chapman, G.T., 1881, p.98; Talbot, T., 1882, p.48.

9 Williams, M., 1979, p.71. Later Blomfield records tourists as usually reaching the White Terrace at about 11 a.m., p.74.

10 Those leaving signatures included Sir George Grey and Alfred, Duke of Edinburgh.

11 Williams, M., 1979, pp.71-5.

12 ibid., p.74.

13 ibid., pp.74-5

14 Valentine had published only ten photographs in New Zealand prior to his stay at Rotomahana.

15 Valentine and Chapman stayed at Wairākei on 20 January 1885. *New Zealand Herald*, 16 February 1885, p.5.

16 According to a descendant, Arnot Stirling Valentine was born at Mary Ann Street 'at a time when diptheria was rife'. G. Birnie to W. Main, September 1980.

CHAPTER 6 ACCLAIM

1 *New Zealand Herald*, 'The Exhibition at Wellington', 3 August 1885, p.5, cols.3-6.

2 ibid., 2, 23, 28, 30 September; 1, 10, 12 October 1885.

3 *Nelson Evening Mail*, 29 June 1885.

4 *New Zealand Herald*, 10 October 1885, p.5; Main, W., 1982, p.334.

5 'Shipping', *New Zealand Herald*, 27 September 1885.

6 *New Zealand Herald*, 17 October 1885, p.5.

7 Letters to Helen Dobson, George Valentine's mother's sister, found and kindly forwarded by Mrs Jean Williams, 18 October 1993.

9 Letter by George Valentine to Helen Dobson, 25 February 1888.

10 Auckland Congregational Church District Report, 1890. The Congregational Church's first service in Parnell was at the Oddfellows Hall, 18 October 1885; the church formed February 1886. Rev Dr J.B. Chambers to author, 24 March 1993 and 15 April 1993.

11 *New Zealand Herald*, 27 Feb 1885, p.6, cols.3-4.

12 The photograph of Queen Street was used in 1889 by the artist Jacques Carabain as a direct basis for a painting now in the collection of the Auckland City Art Gallery (purchased in London in 1986 for £50,000).

13 The 'Colonial & Indian Exhibition' was opened by Queen Victoria on 4 May 1886 and ran until November. The New Zealand section included entries by photographers Josiah Martin and Alfred Burton, and painters Charles Blomfield, Gottfried Lindauer, Kennett Watkins and Eugene von Guérard.

14 Froude, J.A., 1886, p.213.

15 ibid., p.240.

16 This claim was made by Charles Blomfield. Williams, M., 1979, p.77.

17 Stafford, D.M., 1986, p.96; *Bay of Plenty Times*, 10 August 1878.
18 Andrews, P., *Tarawera and the Terraces*, 1986, p.26.
19 *Bay of Plenty Times*, 10 August 1878; 28 December 1878.
20 *New Zealand Herald*, 22 March 1886, p.6, col.3.
21 ibid., 15 June 1886, p.5, col.4; Keam, R.F., 1988, pp.81-4.
22 Keam, R.F., 1988, p.83.
23 *New Zealand Herald*, 10 June 1886.

CHAPTER 7 ERUPTION

1 Darlington, T., *Memoir of Edwin Bainbridge*, 1887, pp.88-9.
2 ibid., pp.82, 87.
3 Minett, A., *New Zealand Herald*, 15 June 1886, p.6.
4 Roche, H., 'Tarawera Eruption: June 10, 1886', *NZ Science Review*, 20 October 1948, pp.77-8.
5 McRae, J., *New Zealand Herald*, 22 June 1886, p.5.
6 Bird, W., *Rotorua Morning Post*, 13 June 1942.
7 Minett, *New Zealand Herald*, 15 June 1886, p.6.
8 Mair, W.G., 'Notes on the Eruption of Tarawera Mountain and Rotomahana, 10th June, 1886, as seen from Taheke, Lake Rotoiti', *Transactions of the New Zealand Institute*, Vol.19, 1887.
9 Dansey, R.D., in [Story, Edith May], *Our Fathers have Told Us, Typescripts of Reminiscences*, qMS STO, Alexander Turnbull Library, pp.637-8.
10 Minett, A., *New Zealand Herald*, 15 June 1886, p.6.
11 McRae, J., *New Zealand Herald*, 22 June 1885, p.5.
12 Bird, W., *Rotorua Morning Post*, 13 June 1942.
13 Humphreys, Mrs., *New Zealand Herald*, 22 June 1886, p.6.
14 Haszard, Clara, *New Zealand Herald*, 14 June 1886, p.5; *Auckland Evening Star*, 14 June 1886, p.2.
15 Hobbs, Ina (née Haszard), 'The Tarawera Eruption 1886 – An Eye-Witness Story', *Whakatane and District Historical Review*, Vol.18, No.2, pp.80-2.
16 Hinerangi, Sophia, 'Sophia's Story', *Tarawera Eruption Centennial, 1886–1986*, 1986, p.131.
17 Mair, W.G., 'Notes on the Eruption of Tarawera Mountain', *Transactions of the New Zealand Institute*, Vol.19, 1887.
18 Humphreys, Mrs., *New Zealand Herald*, 22 June 1886, p.6.
19 Minett, A., *New Zealand Herald*, 15 June 1886, p.6.
20 McRae, J., in Keam, R.F., *Tarawera Eruption*, 1958, p.20.
21 Minett, A., *New Zealand Herald*, 22 June 1886, p.6.
22 Roche, H., MS (typescript) account of Tarawera eruption, copy in R.F. Keam's possession (Keam, R.F., 1988, p.116).
23 Humphreys, Mrs., *New Zealand Herald*, 22 June 1886, p.6.
24 Humphreys, C., *Evening Post*, 9 July 1886, p.2.
25 *New Zealand Herald*, 12 June, p.5, col.6.
26 McRae, J., in Keam, R.F., 1958, p.20.
27 Bird, W., 'Eruption of Mount Tarawera', in Pedlar, Olive P., *The Eruption of Mount Tarawera*, Typescript, Rotorua Public Library (Andrews, P., 1986, p.32).
28 McArthur, J.P. in a letter to Bainbridge's grandfather, 22 June 1886, in Darlington, T., 1887, pp.88-9.
29 Minett, J., *New Zealand Herald*, 15 June 1886, p.6; McArthur, J.P., in Darlington, T., 1887, pp.111-12.
30 McRae, J., in Keam, R.F., 1958, p.20.
31 Humphreys, Mrs., *New Zealand Herald*, 22 June 1886, p.6.
32 Bird, W., in Pedlar, O., Typescript, Rotorua Public Library (Andrews, P., 1986, p.32).
33 Minett, A., *New Zealand Herald*, 15 June 1886, p.6.
34 Blythe, J.C., in Thomas, A.P.W., 1886 field book, University of Auckland, Geology Department, pp.77-8.
35 Blythe, J.C., Evidence at inquest into deaths of Haszard family members, 12 June 1886, J86/1256 (Coroner), National Archives, Wellington.
36 McRae, J., in Keam, R.F., 1958, p.20.
37 McRae, J., evidence at inquest into death of E.A. Bainbridge, 12 June 1886, J86/1257 (Coroner), National Archives, Wellington, pp.3-4.
38 ibid.
39 ibid.
40 McRae, J., *Auckland Evening Star*, 12 June 1886, p.2.
41 McRae, J., *New Zealand Herald*, 12 June 1886, p.5.
42 Massy, E.I., *The Tarawera Eruption*, 1886, p.18.
43 ibid., p.21.

CHAPTER 8 AFTERMATH

1 Tensions between England and Russia (over Afghanistan), together with conflicting reports over the ship's track and destination, had already caused some public concern.
2 *New Zealand Herald*, 11 June 1886, p.9, col.6.
3 *Auckland Evening Star*, 10 June 1886, p.2, col.8; *New Zealand Herald*, 11 June 1886, p.5, col.7.
4 *New Zealand Herald*, 11 June 1886, p.9, col.6.
5 *Auckland Evening Star*, 10 June 1886, p.2, col.7.
6 *New Zealand Herald*, 11 June 1886, p.6, col.1.
7 ibid., p.5, col.7.
8 ibid., p.6, col.2.
9 ibid., p.6, col.2.
10 ibid., p.6, cols.3-4.
11 ibid., p.6, cols.2-3. What was described here as 'lava' was in fact almost entirely mud.
12 ibid., p.4, col.7.
13 ibid., 12 June 1886, p.5, col.2.
14 This estimation was made by R.F. Keam in personal correspondence with author, 2 March 1996. See also Keam, R.F., 1988, pp.389-90, for the list of those whose names are recorded.
15 *New Zealand Herald*, 15 June 1886, p.5, cols.4-5.
16 ibid., 11 June 1886, p.4, col.6.
17 ibid., 12 June 1886, p.5, cols.2,3.
18 *Auckland Evening Star*, 12 June 1886, p.2, col.8.

19 *New Zealand Herald,* 12 June 1886, p.5, col.6.
20 The party included brothers Joseph and Arthur Warbrick, in search of their Ngāti Rangitihi kin. *Bay of Plenty Times,* 17 June 1886, p.2, col.4-5.
21 *New Zealand Herald,* 14 June 1886, p.5, col.5.
22 ibid., p.5, col.6-7.
23 Leys, Thomson W., *The Volcanic Eruption at Tarawera,* 1886, pp.36-9.
24 *New Zealand Herald,* 15 June 1886, p.5, col.4-5.
25 ibid., col.6.
26 This was A.L. Hawkins from the Sydney-based 'Tuttle & Co'. Tauranga photographer Charles Spencer joined the Government Survey party of 14 June, and was first to photograph the still active craters. Keam, R.F., 1988, pp.300-02. Spencer was also responsible for the first overseas photographs on the Valentine & Sons' catalogue, which were of the Terraces, and published shortly after the eruption. They had printed some of these for Spencer in 1883, in the form of brass-framed, oval 'medallion photographs', to be later sold through G.T. Chapman's. *Bay of Plenty Times,* 6 December 1883, p.2. Evidently George Valentine chose to work independently from the firm.
27 Two of Valentine's photographs of the Terraces were reproduced as engravings in the *Auckland Weekly News Pictorial Supplement,* 26 June 1886. Keam, R.F., 1988, p.313.
28 *Otago Daily Times,* 16 June 1886, p.5, col.6-7; *Evening Star* (Dunedin), 21 June 1886, p.3.
29 *Otago Daily Times,* 26 June 1886, p.2.
30 See Keam, R.F., 1988, p.65; pp.70-1. He also has an ingenious possible explanation of the 'phantom canoe', p.374 (Appendix E).
31 *New Zealand Herald,* 15 June 1886, p.5, col.6. Some also believed Tuhoto Ariki to be responsible for recent deaths in the region by his powers of mākutu, or witchcraft. He was to die in hospital two weeks later. Keam, R.F., 1988, pp. 66, 89, 208. See also Warbrick, A., 1934, pp.63-4; and Binney, Judith, *Redemption Songs: A Life of Te Kooti Arikirangi Te Turuki,* Auckland, 1995, pp.347-51.
32 *New Zealand Herald,* 28 September 1886, p.5, col.1.
33 ibid., 'Photographing the New Wonderland', 13 October 1886, p.5, col.2.
34 ibid., 8 December 1886, p.4, col.7.
35 *Auckland Weekly News,* 'Meanderings in Wonderland', 15 January 1887, pp.7-8.
36 *New Zealand Herald,* 8 December 1886, p.4, col.7.
37 ibid.; Smith, S. Percy, *The Eruption of Tarawera, New Zealand,* 1887.
38 Correspondence with Mark Strange, Museum of New Zealand Te Papa Tongarewa, 8 March 1989.
39 Meeting 3 February 1887, *Dundee Courier,* 5 February 1887.
40 *New Zealand Herald,* 25 Jan 1887, p.5, col.2; 28 Jan 1887, p.5, col.3.
41 ibid., 9 May 1887, p.5, col.4.

CHAPTER 9 THE SOUTH SEA ISLANDS

1 *New Zealand Herald,* 22 January 1887, suppl. p.1, col.5.
2 ibid., 20 August 1887, p.4, col.1.
3 ibid., 9 July 1887, p.4, col.8.
4 ibid., 21 May 1887, p.4, col.2.
5 Goods included timber, joinery and preserved meats. Ibid., 21 May 1887, p.4, cols.2,6; 12 May 1887, p.5, col.2.
6 ibid., 8 July 1887, p.5, col.1.
7 ibid., 20 August 1887, p.4, col.7.
8 Photographs from this series in Kirk Album, Alexander Turnbull Library, and Valentine Album 40, Auckland Institute and Museum.
9 *New Zealand Herald,* 2 October 1886; 8–9, 11–12, 14–19, 21, 23–24 February; 16, 18, 20, 29 March; 4, 6, 18, 26 April; 16, 18–19, 30–31 May 1887.
10 ibid., 19 May 1887, p.5, col.6.
11 ibid., 30 May 1887, p.5, col.6; Baker was deported from the island in 1890, and prevented from returning for two years. Rutherford, Noel, *Shirley Baker and the King of Tonga,* c.1996, p.169.
12 R.L. Stevenson's South Sea sojourn began with six months in Hawaii from June 1888. He arrived with his family in Apia at the end of 1889. 'Two Samoas, Still Coming of Age', *National Geographic,* Vol.168, No.4, October 1985, p.472.
13 *New Zealand Herald,* 23 October 1886, p.5, col.6; 20 August 1887, p.6, col.4.
14 ibid., 24 September 1887.
15 Knox, T.W., 1889, pp.102,124.
16 *New Zealand Herald,* 30 October 1886, suppl. p.1, cols.3-4; 23 October 1886, suppl. p.1, cols.6. The New Zealand company was McArthur & Co. See *New Zealand Herald,* 9 September 1886, 'The Great Samoan Land Case'.
17 ibid., 9 October 1886, suppl. p.1, col.5.
18 ibid., 18 May 1887, p.5, col.7; 13 July 1887, p.5, col.4.
19 ibid., 23 July 1887, p.5, col.6.
20 ibid., 31 May 1887, p.5, col.4; Rutherford, N., c.1996, p.155.
21 *New Zealand Herald,* 9 September 1887, p.5, col.3. Samoa was about to pass into the hands of the Germans, with Malieto'a to be taken on board a German warship and carried into exile in New Guinea, while the new king, Tamasese, was maintained on the throne by a German garrison at Apia. Later Samoa would be annexed and divided, with Germany to take the western side and United States the eastern.
22 ibid., 4 December 1886, suppl. p.5.
23 ibid.
24 Knox, T.W., 1889, p.82; *New Zealand Herald,* 13 Nov 1886, suppl. p.1.
25 Paul Gaugin's first stay of two years began in 1891, his second visit in 1895.
26 Knox, T.W., 1889, p.81.
27 *New Zealand Herald,* 1 September 1887, p.4, col.7.
28 ibid., 24 September 1887.

29 ibid., 24 December 1886, suppl. p.1.

30 ibid.

31 ibid., 1 June 1887, p.5, col.6. This request was first issued in the 1860s, but politely refused by Britain. This time, however, with the encouragement of mainly New Zealand traders, it was to be granted late in 1888.

32 ibid., 20 August 1887, p.4, col.1. See also Morton, Elsie K., *Crusoes of Sunday Island,* 1964, pp.11,18. Bell's introduction to the Pacific had been as a British soldier in New Zealand; later he lost a flax mill in the Hawke's Bay from a Hauhau uprising; at attempt to start a Pacific trading station in Samoa had also failed.

33 The ship arrived 31 July 1886. *New Zealand Herald* suppl., 8 January 1887, p.1; suppl. 18 September 1886, p.1, col.7; Morton, E.K., 1964, pp.173, 180.

34 *New Zealand Herald,* 9 May 1887, p.5, col.4.

35 ibid., 31 August 1887, p.5, col.5; 11 September 1886, p.1, col.7; 31 December 1886, suppl. p.2.

36 Bell was guaranteed almost a quart of the island's farming land by the Surveyor General, but this promise was to be badly broken. Morton, Elsie K., *Crusoes of Sunday Island,* 1964, pp.175-6; *New Zealand Herald,* 16 August 1887, p.5, col.2; 31 August 1887, p.5, cols 4-5. Sunday Island is now Raoul Island.

37 *New Zealand Herald,* 20 August 1887, p.4, col.7.

38 ibid., col.8.

39 ibid., 24 September 1887. For further information on the events in Samoa, see *New Zealand Herald,* 19 September 1887, p.5, col.5; 21 September 1887, p.5, col.4. There had also been news of German designs upon New Zealand, the Prince Bismarck having shown an interest in the cessation of New Zealand. Some feared that as Britain was losing so much money on the colony, little would be done if Germany were to make such a move.

CHAPTER 10 THERMAL REGION

1 These articles were evidently submitted as a group and published in consecutive years. Valentine, George W. [sic], *The Yearbook of Photography and Photographic News Almanac,* 'How to Make a Drop Shutter', 1888, pp.61-2; 'A Cheap and Easily Constructed Photographic Burnisher', 1889, pp.43-4; 'Instantaneous Shutter', 1890, pp.78-9; 'Dark Slide Covers', 1891, p.111; 'Economy in Lenses', 1892, p.116. [The 'W' in the author's signature is best explained by his handwritten 'D' in some instances resembling this letter.]

2 Williams, M., 1979, p.103, letter from Charles Blomfield to his wife Ellen, 13 October 1886.

3 Graham's purchase occurred six months before the passing of a Thermal Springs Act which prevented Europeans from acquiring private land in the region.

4 Williams, M., 1979, pp.157,158 (written by Blomfield c.1888?)

5 The new road formed part of the proposed new route from Rotorua via Waiotapu Valley, Ōrākei-Kōrako to Wairākei and Taupō. *New Zealand Herald,* 16 January 1888, p.5, col.2; *Auckland Weekly News,* 28 January 1888, p.7, cols.3-4.

6 Alpers, O.T.J., *Three in a Coach,* 1891, pp.17-18.

7 *New Zealand Herald,* 16 January 1888, p.5, col.2; *Auckland Weekly News,* 28 January 1888, p.7, cols.3-4.

8 *New Zealand Herald,* 14 August 1886.

9 *Auckland Weekly News,* 'Meanderings in Wonderland', 15 January 1887, pp.7-8.

10 Waiotapu lacked accommodation until the end of 1888.

11 *Auckland Weekly News,* 28 January 1888, p.7, cols.3-4.

12 *New Zealand Herald,* 16 January 1888, p.5, col.2. Copyright forms were applied for 22 December 1887, and the series was registered 9 January 1888. National Archives, Wellington.

13 *New Zealand Herald,* 16 January 1888, p.5, col.2; *Auckland Weekly News,* 28 January 1888, p.7, cols.3-4. The few Whakarewarewa works in this series were taken during his first post-eruption survey in October 1886.

14 Letter to Helen Dobson, George Valentine's mother's sister, kindly forwarded by Mrs Jean Williams, 18 October 1993.

15 See ref. 1.

16 *1888 Melbourne Exhibition, New Zealand Court Catalogue,* courtesy of W. Main, 12 March 1994.

17 *Centennial International Exhibition at Melbourne 1888,* New Zealand, 1889, pp.9, 17. Other 1sts went to Burton Bros., Dunedin; F.A. Coxhead, Dunedin; Helen Stuart, Auckland.

18 National Archives, Auckland.

CHAPTER 11 WAITOMO

1 The Waitomo series was copyright registered 24 July 1889, National Archives.

2 Survey in 1884, Foster, B.J. 'King Country', *Encyclopaedia of N.Z.,* Vol.2, pp.233-4; Belich, James, *The New Zealand Wars, and the Victorian Interpretation of Racial Conflict,* 1988, p.306.

3 Morgan, Vaughan, *A History of Waitomo; Maori and Pakeha Side by Side,* 1983, p.76.

4 Arrell, Robert, *Waitomo Caves, A Century of Tourism,* 1984, p.2.

5 ibid., p.3.

6 Also in 1884, Tawhiao was in England with a petition to Queen Victoria, requesting that the Treaty of Waitangi be honoured – a request which failed to reach attentive ears. Mahuta, R.T., *The Dictionary of New Zealand Biography, Vol.2, 1870–1900,* 1993, pp.509-10.

7 Arrell, R., 1984, p.5.

8 Born and raised in Kawhia, Tāne Tinorau had married Te Nekehanga Tutawa, the daughter of an important local elder. Te Nekehanga had been unable to bear children, so had vacated the marriage bed to Whariki Huti. In 1887 Te Nekehanga became Fred Mace's wife. ibid., p.9.

9 *Te Pohara* is remembered in oral history, Morgan, V., 1983.

10 Arrell, R., 1984, pp.10-11.

11 *New Zealand Herald*, 7 June 1889; ref.4, p.13.
12 Morgan, V., 1983, p.77.
13 Wills, A.D., *N.Z. Illustrated*, 1889.
14 Humphries Report, 21/6/89, Land & Survey Dept. Corresp. Files, Vols.1-2.
15 Morgan, V., 1983, p.78.
16 The inscription is in a privately owned album, which was a gift to its first owner from Valentine.
17 Morgan, V., 1983, p.80.
18 Humphries Report, 21/6/89, Lands & Surveys Dept. Corresp. Files, Vols.1-2.
19 Arrell, R., 1984, p.17.
20 ibid., p.18.
21 This block was purchased 31 August 1904 for £625, which was paid three years later, ref.4, p.21.
22 Shadbolt, Maurice, *Reader's Digest Guide to New Zealand*, 1990, p.125. Of the caves in the region (including the major ones of Waitomo, Ruakurī and Aranui), so far about 100km of underground passages have been explored. Probably twice as much again remains unexplored.

CHAPTER 12 LAST DAYS

1 *New Zealand Herald*, 29 October 1889, p.4, col.8.The committee was formed under J.P.E. Francis, a well-known Master at Auckland Grammar School. T. Hodges, *A history of the Auckland Photographic Society from 1883–1985*, 13 January 1985, p.2.
2 Members were given 'the privilege of introducing one lady friend each', and rooms were to be 'reserved for the use of lady members on Tuesdays and Thursdays from 2 to 5 p.m.' *New Zealand Herald*, 7 November 1889, p.4, col.8; 27 November 1889, p.5, col.2.
3 ibid., 28 November 1889, p.4, col.8.
4 ibid., 12 December 1889, p.5, col.3.
5 *Auckland Weekly News*, 30 November 1889, p.17, col.5.
6 Cowan, F., 1885, p.56.
7 Whakarewarewa traditionally belonged to Ngāti Whakaue of Ōhinemutu. Since the late 1870s, a number of Ngāti Wahiao Tūhourangi also lived in the village; following the eruption they were joined by some of their Te Wairoa kin. Kate Middlemass had settled here following her marriage in 1885, but increasing deafness meant she no longer guided tourists. *New Zealand Herald*, 25 June 1886, p.6, col.3.
8 Brett, H., 1879, p.117.
9 From an inscription in a privately owned album which was a gift to its first owner from Valentine.
10 Brett, H., 1879, pp.116-17.
11 *New Zealand Herald*, 9 January 1890, p.6, col.1.
12 ibid., 8 January 1890, p.5, col.6; 'Mr Valentine in New Zealand', *Photography*, Vol.2, No.73, 3 April 1890, London, p.217. J.M. Camille Malfroy was appointed engineer-in-charge at Rotorua immediately after the eruption. His work and research into geothermal phenomena would contribute greatly to the growing tourist industry.
13 *New Zealand Herald*, 23 January 1890, p.5, col.1.
14 From an inscription in a privately owned album which was a gift to its first owner from Valentine.
15 *New Zealand Herald*, 27 February 1890, p.4, col.7; *Photography*, Vol.2, No.76, 24 April 1890, London, p.261. Edward D.M. Mackellar's MD and MS qualifications were received in Glasgow, 1881. There is no record of George Valentine's name under hospital admissions of 1885–90.

EPILOGUE

1 Mrs E.I. Birnie, c/- G. Birnie to W. Main, September 1980 ('This is entirely in character and such independence continues as a trait in the Valentine family').
2 J.M. (Josiah Martin), *Sharland's Trade Journal*, 1892, p.86, col.2 (W. Main, 1982, p.347).
3 (Mrs H.) Ann Patterson to author, 11 February 1995; Williamina Valentine died in 1947.
4 J.R.M. Valentine to author, November 1992, 11 February 1995. At the time of George's death, he was owed £2,000 by his brother William, as the balance of his share and interest from his father's estate. £500 of this was sent from Scotland on 1 February 1890. The balance (at least legally) went to Mina. Scottish Record Office, Edinburgh, SC 70/1/288, pp.528-9.
5 Sydney Scroggie to author, 3 November 1992; Mary Valentine died in 1968.
6 ibid., 16 October 1992. The paintings were by Auckland artist Thomas Ball in 1887, and are based on photographs by George Valentine. They were gifted to the Alexander Turnbull Library in 1973 from the estate of Arnot S. Valentine.
7 Margaret Fraser (Wolverhampton, England) to author, 29 March 1993.
8 (Mrs H.) Ann Patterson to author, 20 November 1992.
9 ref.5, 3 November 1992.
10 J.R.M. Valentine to author, 31 October 1992. George Valentine is buried in Pūrewa cemetery, Auckland.
11 *New Zealand Mail*, 6 May 1892, p.14, cols.1-2.
12 *Sharland's Trade Journal*, Letters to the Editor, 'A Practical Photographer', 7 November 1892. Powell arrived in New Zealand with an intended stay of one year, taking his camera the length and breadth of the country. His work has at times been wrongly attributed to George Valentine, but may be distinguished by its numbering in the 'J.V.' 17000 and 18000 series. The negatives for these are recorded as having been destroyed in Dundee in 1961. George Valentine's New Zealand photographs were never used by the Valentine company.
13 'The Dundee Works of Messrs. Valentine and Sons, Dundee', *British Journal of Photography*, 16 September 1904, pp.808-809.
14 The Watchman, 'Words from the Watchtower', *American Amateur Photographer*, Vol.17, 4 April 1906, p.162; 'Death of Mr W.D. Valentine. Well-known

Business Man', *Dundee Advertiser*, 7 November 1907.

15 *Amateur Photographer and Photographic News*, 3 November 1908, p.434; Gernsheim, Helmut, 'Through Five Generations ... Valentine & Sons Ltd Dundee', *Functional Photography*, London, 1952, pp.19-21.

16 Hannavy, John, 'Valentine of Dundee', *Photo Technique*, Arizona State University, September 1978. The company is now owned by Hallmark Cards Inc., with no direct family link. Their Dundee factory closed in 1994.

17 *Auckland Weekly News*, 6 March 1902, p.11.

18 In 1961 the location of the traditional Ngāti Tahu settlement at Ōrākei-Kōrako – with two-thirds of the active geothermal area – was lost under the Public Works Act for hydro power generation. Part of Ōrākei-Kōrako is managed as a privately-owned tourist attraction, while some of the geothermal area remains in Ngāti Tahu ownership.

19 Legal records show that at the time of his death he was owed £40 by G.T. Chapman's and £50 by Rotorua storekeeper R.H. Griffiths, presumably for photographs in stock. Scottish Record Office, Edinburgh, SC70/1/288, 1 October 1890, p.531.

20 Valentine was the manager of a thriving portrait studio, and as a partner in the Valentine & Sons business had also received part of his father's inheritance.

21 National Archives, Auckland. While cashflow problems had been experienced following the move to Auckland, but this was a time full of expenses and before major sales of his work could have occurred.

22 Valentine's Rotomahana and Whakarewarewa geyser works recall Jackson's work, both at Yellowstone and on his later visit to New Zealand.

23 Two major gaps exist in the cataloguing, the first (182–196) from the second half of 1887, and the second (252–275) from July to November 1889 (from which three Auckland photographs are known).

MĀORI GLOSSARY

MĀORI WORDS FOUND IN TEXT

haka — war dance; act of defiance
kai — food
kōura — crayfish
kūwaha — doorway, gateway to pā, waharoa
mana — power, prestige, status
mānuka — tea-tree (also 'Ti-tree') *Leptospernum scoparium*
moa — an extinct giant, flightless bird
ngāwhā — hot spring, boiling spring
nikau — palm *Rhopalostylis sapida*
pā — fortified village, (loosely) village
pōhutukawa — tree *Metrosideros excelsa*, NZ Christmas tree
ponga — silver tree fern
puia — steam vent, fumarole, geyser
rangatira — chief
taipo — devil, goblin, ghost
tangi — cry, weep; mourning ceremony
taniwha — a fabulous monster supposed to reside in deep water
tapu — sacred, under religious restriction
tohunga — traditional priest, religious expert
wahine — woman, wife
whare — house, building
whare puni — meeting house, main house of village

MĀORI PLACE NAMES AND THEIR MEANINGS*

*These cannot be translated literally. Often they were given to commemorate specific incidents, whereas literal translations can mean something quite different.

Hinemihi — meeting house of Ngāti Hinemihi
Huka — snow, foam or hoar frost
Kaiwaka — destroyer of canoes
Kapiti — cleft, crevice
Karapiti — put or fasten together, side by side
Kōingo — grieve, yearn, sorrow (from sighing sound)
Maungakakaramea — red ochre mountain
Mokoia — tattooed
Mourā — an archaic name, brought from the ancestral homeland of Hawaiki
Ngā Māhanga — the twins
Ngāwanga — a cave which had served as the birthplace for eight generations of chiefs (Talbot: 1882)
Nihotupu — new teeth
Ōhinemutu — place of 'the girl cut off'; the name was given by the great chief Ihenga after his wife Hine-te-kakara was murdered in a boiling mud pool; a memorial stone was erected at this place
Ōkoroire — the place of koroire, an extinct duck
Ōrākei-Kōrako — white adorning place (ōrākei: the place of adorning, kōrako: white sinter)
Ōtorohanga — food eked out for a journey
Ōtūkapuarangi — cloud of the heavens, cloudy atmosphere; fountain of the clouded sky
Pākaraka — village of the karaka tree
Pōhutu — explosion of water
Puarenga — flowers of sulphur; turbid, muddy
Pukeroa — long hill
Rotokākahi — lake of freshwater shellfish
Rotomahana — warm lake
Rotomakariri — cold lake
Rotorua — number two lake (by tradition, the second lake discovered by Ihenga)
Rotowherowhero — reddish lake
Ruawāhia — the split or cloven hole or cave
Tamatekapua — son of the clouds (ancestral meeting house at Ōhinemutu, named after the captain of the *Arawa* canoe)
Tarawera — the skin scorched with heat, the burnt cliff or peaks
Taupō — Taupō-nui-a-Tia, the great cloak of Tia
Tauranga — sheltered anchorage, landing place for canoes
Te Ariki — the high chief
Te Tarata — tattooed rock
Te Wairoa — long stream, or high waterfall
Te Whare Karakia o te Whakapono tapu — house of prayer of the sacred faith
Te Whatapohu — pain in the stomach
Tikitapu — the sacred image, referring to an incident when a young woman lost a precious tiki, or greenstone pendant while bathing in the lake
Tikitere — a contraction of Taku tiki, i tere ne, 'my youngest has floated away', the cry of a mother whose daughter jumped into a boiling mud pool
Tokaanu — cold stone
Tūhuatahi — from tūhua, hard obsidian rock
Wāhanga — bursting open
Waihou — new river
Waikānapanapa — bright shining water
Waikato — full flowing river

Waikite	water seen (wai: water, kite: to see. This geyser was once clearly seen from Rotorua)
Waikorohihī	water spurting up
Waimangu	black water, after a famous extinct geyser
Waiotapu	sacred waters
Waipā	river by a pā
Wairākei	adorning waters
Waitakere	poss. cascading waters; prob. from a chief who was murdered at the mouth of the stream
Waitomo	water entering a hole in the ground
Whakarewarewa	from Te-Whakarewarewatanga-o-te-ope-taua-a-Wahiao, the uprising of a war dance performed before battle, the warriors of Wahiao
Whakataratara	making points, as sharpening stakes or darts

PEOPLE

Ngāti Hinemihi	a section of the Tūhourangi hapū of Te Arawa, Te Wairoa
Ngāti Rangitihi	hapū of Te Arawa at Moura and Waingongongo (now based largely at Matata)
Ngāti Taoi	a small section of the Tūhourangi hapū of Te Arawa, Te Ariki
Ngāti Wahiao	Tūhourangi hapū of Te Arawa, resident at Whakarewarewa and Horohoro
Ngāti Whakaue	hapū of Te Arawa, resident at Ōhinemutu
Pākehā	a European or non-Māori
Te Arawa	the iwi or tribe descended from Te Arawa canoe voyagers
Tūhourangi	hapū of Te Arawa, resident at Te Wairoa

BIBLIOGRAPHY

BOOKS

Alpers, O.T.J. *Three in a Coach*, Christchurch Press Co., 1891.

Andrews, Philip. *Tarawera and the Terraces*, Wilson & Horton, Auckland, 1986.

Arrell, Robert. *Waitomo Caves, A Century of Tourism*, Waitomo Caves Museum Soc. Inc., Waitomo, 1984.

Ballara, Angela. *Proud to be White? A Survey of Pakeha Prejudice in New Zealand*, Heinemann, Auckland, 1986.

Batchelor, Brian. *Pioneers From Over the Sea, Cross Family Memories of Early Nelson*, Reunion Committee of the Cross Family, Nelson, 1992.

Beale, G.A. (editor) *Te Tarata; The Tattooed Rock. Contemporary Accounts of the Thermal Terraces at Rotomahana*, G.A. Beale, London, 1971.

Belich, James. *The New Zealand Wars, and the Victorian Interpretation of Racial Conflict*, Penguin Books, 1988 (first pub. Auckland University Books, 1986).

Brett, H. *Brett's Auckland Almanac*, 1879.

Buckland, Elfreda. 'An Outline of Postcard History', Appendix to *The World of Donald McGill*, Elfreda Buckland, Blandford Press, Dorset, 1984.

Caldwell, Mark. *The Last Crusade. The War on Consumption. 1862–1954*, Atheneum, New York, 1988.

Chapman, George T. *Chapman's Traveller's Guide through the Lake District. The Boiling Lakes and Springs, the Intermitting Fountains, the Burning Mountain, and the Mud Volcanoes in the Province of Auckland, New Zealand*, G.T. Chapman, Auckland, *c.*1873.

Chapman, George T. (editor). *Natural Wonders of New Zealand: the Wonderland of the Pacific: Its Boiling Lakes, Steam Holes, Mud Volcanoes; Sulphur Baths, Medicinal Springs and Burning Mountains*, G.T. Chapman, Auckland, 1881(2nd edition).

Conly, Geoff. *The Destruction of the Pink And White Terraces*, Grantham House Publishing, Wellington, 1985.

Cowan, Frank. *Fact and Fancy in New Zealand – The Terraces of Rotomahana: a poem*, Josiah Martin (publisher), Auckland, 1885.

Darlington, T., *Memoir of Edwin Bainbridge, 1887*, Morgan & Scott, London, 1887.

Department of Internal Affairs, *Dictionary of New Zealand Biography, Vol.2, 1870–1900*, Bridget Williams Books, Wellington, 1993.

Dimond, Frances and Taylor, Roger. *Crown and Camera, The Royal Family and Photography, 1842–1910*, Viking, London, 1987.

Ford, Colin (editor). *Happy and Glorious: Six Reigns of Royal Photography*, Angus & Robertson, London, 1977.

Ford, Colin and Brian Harrison, *A Hundred Years Ago. Britain in the 1880s in Words and Photographs*, Allen Lane/Penguin Books, London, 1983.

Froude, James Anthony. *Oceana, or England and Her Colonies*, Longmans, London, 1886.

Grayland, Eugene and Valerie. *Tarawera*, Hodder & Stoughton, Auckland, 1971.

Ion, Lois. *Keita Rangitukia Middlemass*, published by author, Rotorua, 2002.

Keam, R.F. *Tarawera Eruption*, published by author, Auckland, 1958.

Keam, R.F. *Tarawera: The Volcanic Eruption of 10 June 1886*, published by author, Physics Department, Auckland University, Auckland, 1988.

Kerry-Nicholls, J.H. *The King Country, or Explorations in New Zealand*, Sampson Low, etc., London, 1884; Reprint, Capper Press, Christchurch, 1974.

Knight, Hardwicke. *Photography in New Zealand. A Social and Technical History*, John

McIndoe, Dunedin, 1971.
Knight, Hardwicke. *New Zealand Photographers – A Selection,* Allied Press, Dunedin, 1981.
Knox, Thomas W. *The Boy Travellers in Australasia,* Harper & Brothers, New York, 1889; Reprint, Paul Flesch, Sydney, 1971.
Leys, Thomson W. *The Volcanic Eruption at Tarawera,* H. Brett, Auckland, 1886.
Main, William and John B. Turner, *New Zealand Photography from the 1840s to the present,* Photoforum, Auckland, 1993.
Massy, E.I., *The Tarawera Eruption 1886 and Some Maori Legends,* Reprinted from The Empire Review, 2nd edn. *c.*1906.
Meade, Lt. The Hon Herbert. *A Ride Through The Disturbed Districts Of New Zealand; together with some account of the South Sea Islands,* John Murray, London, 1870; Reprint, Capper Press, Christchurch, 1984.
Moore, Dr J.M. *New Zealand for the Emigrant, Invalid, and Tourist,* Samson Low, 1890.
Morgan, Vaughan. *A History of Waitomo; Maori and Pakeha Side by Side,* Outrigger Publishers, New Zealand, 1983.
Morton, Elsie K. *Crusoes of Sunday Island,* A.H. & A.W. Reed, Wellington, Auckland, 1964.
Mundy, D.L. *Rotomahana and the Boiling Springs of New Zealand, with Descriptive Notes by Ferdinand von Hochstetter,* London, 1875.
New Zealand Survey Department (Publishers). *The Sounds, Lakes and Rivers of New Zealand,* Wellington, 1885.
Pritchard, H. Baden. *The Photographic Studios of Europe,* Piper & Carter, London, 1882.
Rotorua District Council (Publishers), *Tarawera Eruption Centennial Exhibition 1886–1986,* 1986.
Rutherford, Noel. *Shirley Baker and the King of Tonga,* Pasifika Press, Auckland, c.1996 (1st edn. Melbourne 1971).
Simmons, David R., *Whakairo: Maori Tribal Art,* Oxford University Press, Auckland, 1994 (1st edn. Auckland, New York, 1985).
Smith, S. Percy. *The Eruption of Tarawera, New Zealand,* Government Printer, Wellington, 1887.
Staff, Frank. *The Picture Postcard & Its Origins,* Lutterworth Press, London, 1966.
Stafford, D.M. *Te Arawa, A History of the Arawa People,* A.H. & A.W. Reed, Wellington, 1967.
Stafford, D.M. *The Founding Years in Rotorua, A History of Events to 1900,* Ray Richards Publisher and Rotorua District Council, Rotorua, 1986.
Stanford, Edward (Publisher). *New Zealand Official Handbook 1883,* London, 1883.
Stevenson, Sara. *Light from the Dark Room, A Celebration of Scottish Photography,* National Galleries of Scotland, Edinburgh, 1995.
Talbot, Thorpe. *The New Guide to the Lakes and Hot Springs (and a Month in Hot Water),* Wilsons & Horton, Auckland, 1882.
Trollope, Anthony. *Australia and New Zealand,* Chapman and Hall (in two volumes), 1873, Reprint edited by A.H. Reed, *With Anthony Trollope in New Zealand, 1872,* A.H. & A.W. Reed, Wellington, 1969.
Union Steam Ship Company. *Maoriland* (written by A. Wilson, R. Waddell, T.W. Whitson), George Robertson & Co., Melbourne, 1884.
Valentine, Gordon Alexander. *A Family History, Bertram Gordon Valentine and Margaret Helen Japp, from Progenitors to Progeny, Vol. 1,* published by author, Denver, Colorado, 1994–1999.
von Hochstetter, Dr Ferdinand. *New Zealand: Its Physical Geography, Geology and Natural History,* translation by E. Sauter, J.G. Cotta, Stuttgart, 1867.
Warbrick, Alfred. *Adventures in Geyserland,* A.H. & A.W. Reed, Dunedin, 1934.
Williams, Muriel. *Charles Blomfield: His Life and Times,* Hodder & Stoughton, Auckland, 1979.
Willis, A.D. (Publisher). *N.Z. Illustrated,* 1889.

ARTICLES IN JOURNALS

Amateur Photographer and Photographic News, 3 November 1908, p.434.
American Amateur Photographer, 'Words from the Watch Tower, "The Watchman"', XVII, 4 April 1906, pp.162-3.
Anthony's Photographic Bulletin, 'Warming the Studio', Vol.9, No.7, July 1878, pp.209-11.
British Journal of Photography, 'Our Editorial Table', Vol.11, No.223, 12 August 1864, p.295.
British Journal of Photography, 'Dry Plates in California: An Echo from the Far West', John Valentine, XI, No.227, 9 September 1864, pp.346-7.
British Journal Photographic Almanac 1867, 'A Substitute for a Dark Room in Field Operations', James Valentine, 1867, pp.100-01.
British Journal of Photography, 7 February 1868, p.62.
British Journal of Photography, Notice of James Valentine's appointment as 'Photographer to the Queen', 4 December 1868, p.583.
British Journal of Photography, 'The Dundee Works of Messrs. Valentine and Sons, Dundee', 16 September 1904, p.809.
Functional Photography, 'Through Five Generations...Valentine & Sons Ltd Dundee', Helmut Gernsheim, 1952, pp.18-21.
History of Photography, An international quarterly, 'George Dobson Valentine in New Zealand', William Main, October 1982.
Image (Journal of Photography and Motion Pictures of the George Eastman House), 'Messrs. James Valentine and Sons, Dundee', Robert A. Sobieszek, Vol.14, No.2, March 1971, pp.6-8; 'A Further Note on Messrs. James Valentine and Sons, Dundee', Robert A. Sobieszek, Vol.14, No.3, June 1971, p.18.
League Journal, 'Obituary, The Late James Valentine, Dundee', 19 July 1879, Vol.18, No.916, Glasgow, p.226.
N.Z. Science Review, 'Tarawera Eruption: June 10, 1886', H. Roche, 20 October 1948, pp.77-8.
Philadelphia Photographer, 'Our Picture', Vol.17, No.197, May 1880, pp.133-4.
Photo Technique, 'Valentine of Dundee', John Hannavy, Arizona State University, September 1978.

Photographic News, 'Messrs. James Valentine and Sons at Dundee', 10 March 1882, pp.115-17.

Photographic News, 'At Messrs. Valentine and Sons, Dundee', Vol.35, No.1732, 13 November 1891, p.778.

Photography, 'Mr. Valentine in New Zealand', Vol.2, No.73, 3 April 1890, London, p.217; Vol.2, No.76, 24 April 1890, p.261.

Quarterly Journal of the Geological Society, 'The Terraces of Rotomahana, N.Z.', Josiah Martin, Vol.43, 1887.

Review of Scottish Culture, '"Famous Throughout the World": Valentine & Sons Ltd., Dundee', Robert N. Smart, Vol.4, 1988, pp.75-87.

Sharland's Trade Journal, 'Exposures', J.M. (Josiah Martin), 7 May 1892, p.86, col.2.

Sharland's Trade Journal, Letters to the Editor, 'A Practical Photographer', 7 November 1892.

Transactions of the New Zealand Institute, 'Notes on the Volcanoes and Geysers of New Zealand', William Collie, Vol.12, 1879.

Transactions of the New Zealand Institute, 'Notes on the Influence of Atmospheric Changes on the Hot Springs and Geysers in the Rotorua District', Captain Gilbert Mair, Vol.9, 1876.

Transactions of the New Zealand Institute, 'Notes on the Eruption of Tarawera Mountain and Rotomahana, 10th June, 1886, as seen from Taheke, Lake Rotoiti', W.G. Mair, Vol.19, 1887.

Whakatane and District Historical Review, Vol.18, No.2, 'The Tarawera Eruption 1886 – An Eye-Witness Story', Ina Hobbs (née Haszard), pp.80-2.

Yearbook of Photography and Photographic News Almanac, Piper & Carter, London, articles by George W. [sic] Valentine, 'How to Make a Drop Shutter', 1888, pp.61-2; 'A Cheap and Easily Constructed Photographic Burnisher', 1889, pp.43-4; 'Instantaneous Shutter', 1890, pp.78-9; 'Dark Slide Covers', 1891, p.111; 'Economy in Lenses', 1892, p.116.

NEWSPAPERS

Auckland Evening Star, 1886.

Auckland Weekly News, 1886-1902.

Bay of Plenty Times, 10 August 1878; 28 December 1878; 17 June 1886.

Dundee Advertiser, 'Death of Mr. James Valentine, Photographer', 20 June 1879.

Dundee Advertiser, 'Death of Mr. W.D. Valentine', 7 November 1907.

Dundee Courier, 5 February 1887.

Evening Post, 9 July 1886.

Evening Star (Dunedin), 21 June 1886.

Nelson Evening Mail, 29 June 1885.

The New Zealander, 'Notes from a Journal', Dr John Johnson, late 1847 (Beale, p.9-10).

New Zealand Herald, Auckland, 1882-1890.

New Zealand Mail, 6 May 1892, p.14, cols.1-2.

Otago Daily Times, 'Shipping' columns, 1882.

Rotorua Morning Post, 13 June 1942.

MANUSCRIPTS AND REPORTS

Auckland Congregational Church District Report, 1890.

Bird, W., 'Eruption of Mount Tarawera', in Pedlar, Olive P., *The Eruption of Mount Tarawera*, Typescript, Rotorua Public Library.

Dansey, R.D., in [Story, Edith May], *Our Fathers Have Told Us*, Typescripts of Reminiscences, qMS STO, Alexander Turnbull Library, pp.637-8.

Dundee and East of Scotland Photographic Association, Annual Report, April 1883.

Dundee and East of Scotland Photographic Association Rules, 1883.

Hunter, Norman M. Ms-1053 (diary, 1882–1883), 29 September 1882, Alexander Turnbull Library.

Report on the Statistics of New Zealand 1889, Government Printer, Wellington, 1891.

CATALOGUE OF PHOTOGRAPHS BY GEORGE D. VALENTINE

This list records the numbered New Zealand and Pacific works by Valentine located in public and private collections. Gaps signify those that remain unknown. Works that share titles mostly indicate half-plate copies.

1884

2. Nelson Harbour
4. S.S. Wanaka
5. In Nelson Harbour
9. New Zealand Bush Track
10. Nikau Palms, N.Z.

JANUARY 1885

11. Cauldron, White Terrace
12. Cold Water Basins, White Terrace
13. The Stairs, Pink Terrace
15. White Terrace and Lake Rotomahana
16. Koingo, L. Rotomahana
17. Umbrella Buttress, Pink Terrace
18. Cold Water Basins, White Terrace
19. Coffee Cups, White Terrace
20. Hot Bath, White Terrace
21. Boar's Head, White Terrace
22. Trickling Buttress, White Terrace
23. White Terrace, Lake Rotomahana
24. White Terrace, L. Rotomahana
25. Trickling Buttresses, White Terrace
26. Cold Water Basins, White Terrace
27. Giant Buttress, White Terrace
28. White Terrace, L. Rotomahana
29. Pink Terrace, L. Rotomahana
30. The Porridge Pot, L. Rotomahana
31. Whio, L. Rotomahana
32. Whakataratara, L. Rotomahana
33. Whatapoho, L. Rotomahana
35. Hot Baths, Pink Terrace
36. Carved House, Ohinemutu
37. Tarawera Lake and Mountain
38. Rotomahana Hotel, Te Wairoa
39. Lake Rotokakahi
40. Lake Tiki Tapu
41. In the Tiki Tapu Bush
42. Lake Rotomahana
43. Auckland from Upper Queen Street
44. Auckland, Albert Park and Harbour, from Upper Queen Street
45. On the Waikato at Ateamure [sic]
48. Carved House, Ohinemutu
49. Rotomahana Hotel, Te Wairoa
51. Pink Terrace, Lake Rotomahana
52. Giant Buttress, White Terrace
53. White Terrace, L. Rotomahana
55. Pink Terrace, L. Rotomahana
59. Giant Buttress, White Terrace
63. Trickling Buttresses, White Terrace
65. Hot Baths, Pink Terrace
67. Lake Rotomahana
70. Entrance Nelson Harbour
72. On the Waikato at Ateamure [sic]
76. Tarawera Lake and Mountain
77. ['Guide Kate', Kate Middlemass, Te Wairoa]
78. ['Guide Sophia', Sophia Hinerangi at Te Tarata]
79. New Zealand Bush Scenery
80. New Zealand Bush Scenery
84. Pink Terrace, Lake Rotomahana

LATE 1885 – EARLY 1886

85. Auckland Harbour from St. Georges Bay
87. Auckland Harbour, North Shore and Rangitoto
88. Auckland Harbour, North Shore and Rangitoto
89. Waitakeri [sic] Falls
91. New Zealand Kauri Trees
92. On the Waitakeri [sic] Creek
93. In the Waitakeri [sic] Bush
94. Waitakeri [sic] Falls
96. Auckland Harbour, Queen Street Wharf
99. Auckland from Mnt. Eden
100. Auckland Harbour from Mnt. Eden
101. Queen Street, Auckland
102. Auckland from North Shore

OCTOBER 1886

109. Whakarewarewa
110. Whakarewarewa
111. Waikite Geyser, Whakarewarewa
113. Lake Rotorua and Mokoia
114. Lake Rotorua and Mokoia
115. Ohinemutu, Lake Rotorua
116. Ohinemutu, Lake Rotorua
117. Tiki, Gate of Te Pukeroa Pah [sic], Ohinemutu

119. Tiki-Tapu Bush, after Eruption
121. Old Mill, Te Wairoa
123. Te Wairoa, McRae's Hotel
124. Whakarewarewa
125. Te Wairoa, McRae's Hotel, Sophia's Whare and Terrace Hotel
126. Te Wairoa, after Eruption
127. Wahanga and Tarawera Mnts. from Lake Tarawera
128. Wahanga and Tarawera Mnts. from Lake Tarawera
129. Mnts. Tarawera and Ruawahia from Te Ariki
131. Mnt. Tarawera from Lake Rotomakiriri showing Rent
132. Mnt. Tarawera from Lake Rotomakiriri showing Rent
133. Rotomahana looking to Site of Pink Terrace
134. Whakarewarewa
135. Rotomahana, showing Site of White Terrace
136. Waikite Geyser, Whakarewarewa

LATE NOVEMBER – DECEMBER 1886

138. The Rent in Rotomahana from the Black Crater
139. The Rent in Rotomahana from Black Crater
140. Echo Lake and Hole in the Wall Crater
141. Echo Lake and Hole in the Wall Crater, Rotomahana
142. South Crater, the Termination of Rotomahana Rent
143. South Crater, the Termination of Rotomahana Rent
144. Fumarole Peaks, Rotomahana
145. The Pinnacle
146. Rotomahana from Hape O'Toroa
147. Fumarole Peaks and Site of White Terrace, Rotomahana

LATE 1886 – MID 1887

149. Rangatira Maori and Wahine
151. Rangatira Maori

13 JULY – 4 AUGUST 1887

156. Samoa, Apia from the Sea
157. Cocoanut [sic] Palms, Rarotonga
158. The Wharf, Papeete, Tahiti
159. At the Harbour, Rarotonga
160. Tahiti, Papeete from the Motu
162. Fataua Avenue, Tahiti
163. Orange Loading at Viaroa, Tahiti
164. "A Bit", Rarotonga
165. Ihurangi Peak, Rarotonga
166. Nukualofa, Tonga
169. Tahiti, Papeete from the Fort
170. Morea from the Sea
172. Nukualofa, Tonga
174. Papeete, Tahiti
175. Samoa, Apia from Matafele
178. Samoa, Apia from the Motoutu Creek
179. Washing Day, Motoutu Creek, Apia, Samoa
180. Trading Station, Rarotonga

LATE 1887

181. Inferno Crater
197. Alum Cliffs, Wai-o-tapu Valley
198. Crow's Nest, Taupo
199. Te Huinga, Wai-o-tapu Valley
200. The Great Wairakei Geyser
201. Huka Falls, Taupo
202. The Eagle's Nest, Wairakei
203. Maungakakaramea, Wai-o-tapu Valley
204. Nga Mahanga (The Twins), Wairakei
205. Tuhuatahi (Champagne Pool), Wairakei
206. Sentinel Rock Crater, Wai-o-tapu Valley
207. Primrose Falls, Wai-o-tapu Valley
208. The Spa, Taupo
210. Kotere-Karamua, Wai-o-tapu Valley
211. Tikitere
212. Primrose Falls, Wai-o-tapu Valley
213. Kotere-Kairamua, Wai-o-tapu Valley
215. The Great Wairakei Geyser
217. Tikitere, Rotorua
218. Alum Cliffs, Wai-o-tapu Valley
220. Sentinel Rock Crater, Wai-o-tapu Valley
222. Te Huinga, Wai-o-tapu Valley

MID 1889

224. Entrance Waitomo Caves, Otorohanga
226. Grand Organ, Waitomo Caves, Otorohanga
227. Fluted Pillar, Waitomo Caves, Otorohanga
228. The Dungeons, Waitomo Caves, Otorohanga
229. Stalactites, Waitomo Caves, Otorohanga
230. In the Waitomo Caves, Otorohanga
231. Fairy Grotto, Waitomo Caves, Otorohanga
232. Gallery in the Waitomo Caves, Otorohanga
233. In the Waitomo Caves, Otorohanga
234. The Blanket, Waitomo Caves, Otorohanga
235. Fairy Grotto, Waitomo Caves, Otorohanga
236. Entrance to Organ Loft, Waitomo Caves
237. The Terrace, Waitomo Caves, Otorohanga
238. The Blanket, Waitomo Caves, Otorohanga
239. The Blanket, Waitomo Caves, Otorohanga
240. In the Waitomo Caves, Otorohanga
241. Entrance to Organ Loft, Waitomo Caves
242. Entrance Waitomo Caves, Otorohanga

243. Fairy Grotto, Waitomo Caves, Otorohanga
244. Stalactites, Waitomo Caves, Otorohanga
245. The Blanket, Waitomo Caves, Otorohanga
246. The Blanket, Waitomo Caves, Otorohanga
247. Lower Chamber, Waitomo Caves, Otorohanga
248. The Terrace, Waitomo Caves, Otorohanga
249. Fairy Grotto, Waitomo Caves, Otorohanga
250. The Dungeons, Waitomo Caves, Otorohanga
251. The Blanket, Chamber, Waitomo Caves, Otorohanga

MID – LATE 1889

259. Auckland Hospital
263. Auckland Hospital
273. In the Albert Park, Auckland

NOVEMBER 1889

276. Pohutu Geyser, Whakarewarewa
278. Turikore and Lake Rotorua
279. The Oil Bath, Whakarewarewa
282. The Sunken Pah [sic], Ohinemutu
283. Sunken Pah [sic], Ohinemutu
285. Turikore and Lake Rotorua
286. Whakarewarewa
291. The Wahou River at Okoroire
292. Okoroire Sanatorium

DECEMBER 1889 – JANUARY 1890

295. On the Puarenga River, Whakarewarewa
297. Kereru and Pohutu Geysers, Whakarewarewa
299. Korohihi Geyser, Whakarewarewa
301. Te Wairoa Geyser, Whakarewarewa
302. Te Wairoa Geyser, Whakarewarewa
303. Pohutu Geyser, Whakarewarewa
305. Kereru and Pohutu Geysers, Whakarewarewa
308. On the Puarenga River, Whakarewarewa
313. Upper Falls, Nihotopu [sic]

OTHER PHOTOGRAPHS IN WHICH NUMBERS ARE ILLEGIBLE

Hot Baths, Pink Terrace
Rotomahana, Echo Lake & Hole in the Wall Crater

PHOTOGRAPH AND ILLUSTRATION SOURCES

Originals, unless otherwise specified, are albumen prints.

Cover
COFFEE CUPS, WHITE TERRACE. 19 G.V.
18.8 x 29.1 cm
Alexander Turnbull Library, PA1:q:212, Saxby Album 1, p.20

Frontispiece Photographs
Page 6 RANGATIRA MAORI AND WAHINE. 149 G.V.
29 x 19 cm
Alexander Turnbull Library, PA1:q:138, Kirk Album, p.33

Page 9 RANGATIRA MAORI. 151 G.V.
16.1 x 10.4 cm
Alexander Turnbull Library, PA1:q:260, Webster II Album, p.52

George D. Valentine – A Photographer's Journey
Page 13 George Valentine, by Tyree Bros., c.1884–85
16.3 x 12 cm
Tasman Bays Heritage Trust/Nelson Provincial Museum, Tyree Studio Collection, 29671/3

Scotland
Page 14 James Valentine, by Thomas Rodger (attrib.), c.1854
16.9 x 13.5 cm
St. Andrews University Library

Page 14 George Valentine, by James Valentine, c.1856
7.2 x 5.3 cm
Lorraine Cameron Collection, Canada

Page 14 'Uncle Tom' Anti-Slavery envelope, by James Valentine, 1854
7.9 x 12.4 cm
J. Bohn Collection, England

Page 16 Falls of Unich, by James Valentine, 1864
17.8 x 22.8 cm
Royal Archives ©, Her Majesty Queen Elizabeth II, Album: In Memoriam, 1861, Glenmark to Fettercairn, p.7

Page 18 George and Margaret Rachel Valentine, James Valentine & Sons, c.1878
10 x 5.9 cm
St. Andrews University Library, Patterson Album #3, p.26

Page 18 Williamina Arnot Stirling Smith, by James Valentine, Dundee, c.1876
9.5 x 5.9 cm
Alexander Turnbull Library, PA Coll. 2850, Ken Hall Collection

Page 18 Mary Smith Valentine, c.1882–83
9.4 x 5.7 cm
St. Andrews University Library, Patterson Album #1, p.2

Page 18 James Valentine, c.1882–83
9.4 x 5.7 cm
St. Andrew's University Library, Patterson Album #1, p.6

Page 19 REFORM STREET, DUNDEE. 1040 J.V., c.1875–78
18.2 x 23.9 cm
St. Andrews University Library, glass-plate negative

Antipodes
Page 20 IN NELSON HARBOUR, N.Z. 5 G.V.
13.6 x 21 cm
Alexander Turnbull Library, PA1:q:138, Kirk Album, p.28

Page 22 House of G.D. Valentine in New Zealand, 'Walmer House', Mary Ann Street, Nelson, c.1884–85
15 x 20.2 cm
Alexander Turnbull Library, Barbara Smith Collection, PA Coll. 4848

Page 23 ENTRANCE NELSON HARBOUR. 70 G.V.
13.6 x 21 cm
Alexander Turnbull Library, PA1:q:138, Kirk Album, p.24

Hot Lakes
Page 24 AUCKLAND HARBOUR, QUEEN STREET WHARF. 96 G.V.
18.9 x 29 cm
Alexander Turnbull Library, PA7-54-17

Page 26 Map of North Island and Thermal District
Canterbury Times Illustrated Supplement, 18 June 1886
Canterbury Museum, Pictorial Archives

Page 27 CARVED HOUSE, OHINEMUTU. 36 G.V.
19.1 x 29 cm
Auckland War Memorial Museum, Sparrow Album #1, p.60

Page 28 LAKE ROTORUA AND MOKOIA. 113 G.V.
19.2 x 29.4 cm
Private Collection

Page 29 THE SUNKEN PAH, OHINEMUTU. 282 G.V.
19 x 29.2 cm
Private Collection

Page 30 TIKI, GATE OF TE PUKEROA PAH, OHINEMUTU. 117 G.V.
29 x 18.8 cm
Alexander Turnbull Library, Ken Hall Collection (original with St. Andrews University Library)

Page 32 IN THE TIKI TAPU BUSH. 41 G.V.
28.8 x 19 cm
Alexander Turnbull Library, PA7-54-24

Page 33 ROTOMAHANA HOTEL, TE WAIROA. 38 G.V.
19 x 29.1 cm
Alexander Turnbull Library, PA7-60-02

Page 35 GUIDE KATE. 77 G.V.
20.3 x 13 cm
R.F. Keam Collection, G.D. Valentine Album #1, p.9

The Pink and White Terraces
Page 36 WHITE TERRACE, L. ROTOMAHANA. 24 G.V.
19.3 x 29.5 cm
Private Collection

Page 38 WHITE TERRACE, L. ROTOMAHANA. 28 G.V.
11.8 x 16.4 cm
Canterbury Museum, Neg. 1118/$^1/_2$

Page 39 GUIDE SOPHIA, 1885. 78 G.V.
13.5 x 21 cm
Alexander Turnbull Library, PA1:q:138, Kirk Album, p.21

Page 40 GIANT BUTTRESS, WHITE TERRACE. 27 G.V.
19.4 x 29.4 cm
Private Collection

Page 41 COFFEE CUPS, WHITE TERRACE. 19 G.V.
18.8 x 29.1 cm
Alexander Turnbull Library, PA1:q:212, Saxby Album 1, p.20

Page 42 PINK TERRACE, L. ROTOMAHANA. 29 G.V.
19.3 x 29.2 cm
Private Collection

Page 43 PINK TERRACE, L. ROTOMAHANA. 34 G.V.
18.8 x 29.1 cm
Alexander Turnbull Library, PA1:q:138, Kirk Album, p.11

Page 44 CAULDRON, WHITE TERRACE. 11 G.V.
19 x 29.1 cm
Alexander Turnbull Library, PA1:q:212, Saxby Album 1, p.33

Page 44 KOINGO, L. ROTOMAHANA. 16 G.V.
11.9 x 16.4 cm
Canterbury Museum, Neg. 1110/$^1/_2$

Page 47 HOT BATHS, PINK TERRACE. 35 G.V.
19.2 x 29.3 cm
Auckland War Memorial Museum, G.D. Valentine Album #1, p.17

Acclaim
Page 48 NEW ZEALAND KAURI TREES. 91 G.V.
29.2 x 19.1 cm
Auckland War Memorial Museum, G.D. Valentine Album #1, p.31

Page 50 AUCKLAND HARBOUR FROM ST. GEORGES BAY. 85 G.V.
19.1 x 29.2 cm
Private Collection

Page 51 George Valentine, by J.R. Hanna, Auckland
14.6 x 10.2 cm
St. Andrew's University Library, Patterson Album #3, p.2

Page 51 Mina Valentine, by J.R. Hanna, Auckland
14.6 x 10.2 cm
St. Andrews University Library, Patterson Album #2, p.27

Page 52 'Balgay', Cleveland Road, Parnell, c.1885–86
13.8 x 24 cm
Alexander Turnbull Library, Ken Hall Collection

Page 53 IN THE WAITAKERI BUSH. 93 G.V.
29.2 x 19.4 cm
Private Collection

Page 55 WAITAKERI FALLS. 89 G.V.
29.3 x 19.3 cm
Private Collection

Page 56 QUEEN STREET, AUCKLAND. 101 G.V.
19.1 x 29.2 cm
Auckland War Memorial Museum, G.D. Valentine Album #1, p.32

Aftermath
Page 65 TIKI-TAPU BUSH. AFTER ERUPTION. 119 G.V.
29.1 x 18.8 cm
Alexander Turnbull Library, PA7:54:03

Page 67 ROTOMAHANA, LOOKING TO SITE OF PINK TERRACE.
133 G.V.
19.3 x 29.3 cm
Private Collection

Page 69 TE WAIROA, MCRAE'S HOTEL, SOPHIA'S WHARE AND TERRACE HOTEL. 125 G.V.
19.1 x 29 cm
Hocken Library, loose print

Page 70 TE WAIROA, MCRAE'S HOTEL. 123 G.V.
13.9 x 21.4 cm
Auckland War Memorial Museum, Sparrow Album #11, p.7

Page 73 MNTS. TARAWERA AND RUAWHIA FROM TE ARIKI. 129 G.V.
18.7 x 28.9 cm
Alexander Turnbull Library, PA7:54:01

Page 75 MT. TARAWERA FROM LAKE ROTOMAKIRIRI, SHOWING RENT. 131 G.V.
19.4 x 29.5 cm
Private Collection

Page 76 THE RENT IN ROTOMAHANA FROM THE BLACK CRATER. 138 G.V.
18.8 x 29.1 cm
Alexander Turnbull Library, PA1:q:138, Kirk Album, p.6

Page 77 SOUTH CRATER, THE TERMINATION OF ROTOMAHANA RENT. 142 G.V.
18.7 x 29 cm
Alexander Turnbull Library, PA7:60:01

Page 79 ROTOMAHANA FROM HAPE O'TOROA. 146 G.V.
18.9 x 29.1 cm
Alexander Turnbull Library, PA1:q:138, Kirk Album, p.5

The South Sea Islands
Page 82 THE WHARF. PAPEETE, TAHITI. 158 G.V.
19 x 29.1 cm
Alexander Turnbull Library, PA1:q:138, Kirk Album, p.83

Page 84 SAMOA. APIA FROM THE MOTOUTU CREEK. 178 G.V.
19 x 29.1 cm
Alexander Turnbull Library, PA1:q:138, Kirk Album, p.84

Page 85 AT THE HARBOUR. RAROTONGA. 159 G.V.
19 x 29 cm
Alexander Turnbull Library, PA1:q:138, Kirk Album, p.73

Page 87 TAHITI, ORANGE LOADING AT VIAROA. 163 G.V.
18.8 x 29.2 cm
Alexander Turnbull Library, PA1:q:138, Kirk Album, p.78

Page 89 COCOANUT PALMS. RAROTONGA. 157 G.V.
29.4 x 19 cm
Alexander Turnbull Library, PA1:q:138, Kirk Album, p.75

Thermal Region
Page 90 NGA MAHANGA (THE TWINS), WAIRAKEI. 204 G.V.
19.3 x 29.4 cm
Private Collection

Page 93 THE EAGLE'S NEST, WAIRAKEI. 202 G.V.
19.4 x 29.5 cm
Private Collection

Page 94 ALUM CLIFFS, WAI-O-TAPU VALLEY. 197 G.V.
18.8 x 28.8 cm
Alexander Turnbull Library, PA1:q:138, Kirk Album, p.2

Page 97 CROW'S NEST, TAUPO. 198 G.V.
19.3 x 29.3 cm
Private Collection

Waitomo
Page 98 FAIRY GROTTO, WAITOMO CAVES, OTOROHANGA. 231 G.V.
15.2 x 20.5 cm
Alexander Turnbull Library, PA1:q:138, Kirk Album, p.43

Page 101 THE BLANKET, WAITOMO CAVES, OTOROHANGA. 246 G.V.
29.4 x 19.2 cm
Private Collection

Page 101 FLUTED PILLAR, WAITOMO CAVES, OTOROHANGA. 227 G.V.
20.5 x 14.9 cm
Alexander Turnbull Library, PA1:q:138, Kirk Album, p.61

Last Days
Page 105 POHUTU GEYSER, WHAKAREWAREWA. 276 G.V.
19.5 x 29.5 cm
Private Collection

Page 106 THE OIL BATH, WHAKAREWAREWA. 279 G.V.
19 x 29 cm (approx.)
Shatford Collection, Canterbury Museum

Page 107 George and Mina Valentine with Mary, James and Arnot, Auckland, January 1890
14.4 x 10.1 cm
St. Andrews University Library, Patterson Album #3, p.2

Epilogue
Page 108 UPPER FALLS, NIHOTOPU. 313 G.V.
29.4 x 19.3 cm
Private Collection

Page 110 Arnot, Mina and James Valentine on holiday in Perthshire, c.1901
5.6 x 8.1 cm
Mrs E.I. Birnie Collection, Scotland

INDEX

A
Adler (*see also* Hawaii, aim for confederate Pacific kingdom; *Kaimiloa*), 86
Alfred, Duke of Edinburgh, 34
***'Alum Cliffs, Wai-o-tapu Valley'*, 94**
Apia (Samoa), 84, **84**, 86
***'At the Harbour. Rarotonga'*, 85**
Auckland, 12, 21, 22, **24**, 25, 27, 46, **50**, 50–52, 54, **56**, 57, 63, 89, 99, 100, 103, 111
Auckland Evening Star, 68
***'Auckland Harbour from St. Georges Bay'*, 50**
***'Auckland Harbour, Queen Street Wharf'*, 24**
Auckland Photographic Society, 103, 104, 107
Auckland Weekly News, 103, 111

B
Bainbridge, Edwin, 58, 60–62, 64, 66
Balgay (Valentine family N.Z. residence), 50–51, **52**, 54, 95, 107
Baker, Rev. Shirley (Premier), 84
Ballance, Hon. John (Minister of Native Affairs), 31, 80–81
Bell, Thomas (*see also* Sunday Island annexation), 88
Berry, William, 68
Bird, William, 62
***'The Blanket, Waitomo Caves, Otorohanga'*, 101**, 102
Blomfield, Charles, 25–26, 34, 45, 91–92
Blomfield, Mary, 25–26, 45–46
Blue Lake (*see* Lake Tikitapu), 31
Bora Bora, 86
Blythe, Jane, 72, 78
Blythe, John (Government surveyor), 57, 64, 66, 72, 78
Burton, Alfred, 9, 49, 71

C
Cambridge, 27
***'Carved House, Ohinemutu' [Tamatekapua]*, 27**
***'Cauldron, White Terrace'*, 44**
Champagne Pool (Tūhuatahi), 91, 95
Chapman, Charles R., 22, 25–27, 31, 39, 45–46, 50–51, 71
Chapman, George T., 25, 27, 44, 54
charging of photographers and artists, 25–26
***'Cocoanut Palms. Rarotonga'*, 89**
***'Coffee Cups, White Terrace'*,** (cover), **41**, 46, 50, 111–112
Collie, William, 9
Colonial Government of New Zealand, 49, 54, 57, 66, 72, 99
  and Waitomo caves, 100, 102
  desire to purchase Rotomahana region, 57
  need to protect Waiotapu, 94
  tourism, 56–57, 91, 100, 102
Colonial Governments
  France in the Pacific, 86–88
  Germany in Samoa, 86
  Great Britain in New Zealand, 99
  Great Britain in the Pacific, 86, 88
  New Zealand in Samoa, 86
  United States in Samoa, 83, 86
Cook Islands, 88
Congregational church, 15, 21, 54
Cross, Captain James, 21
***'Crow's Nest, Taupo'*, 97**
Crows Nest geyser, 92, 96, 97

D
Dansey, Roger, 59, 63
Dobson, Helen (aunt in Scotland), 22–23, 51–52
'drop-shutter' photography, 91
'dry-plate' photography, 27, 45–46
Dundee, 9, 12, 15–19, 19, 96, 109, 110
Dundee and East of Scotland Photographic Association, 17, 80
Dunedin, 12, 71
Dunedin Photographic Society, 12

E
Eagle's Nest, 92, **93**, 95
***'The Eagle's Nest, Wairakei'*, 93**, 112
***'Entrance Nelson Harbour'*, 23**
The Eruption of Tarawera, New Zealand, 80
Exhibitions
  Colonial & Indian, London (1886), 54
  Light from the Dark Room (1995), 9
  Melbourne (1888), 96
  New Zealand Industrial Exhibition (1885), 49
    G.V. receives second prize in, 49–50

F
***'Fairy Grotto, Waitomo Caves, Otorohanga'*, 98**, 102
***'Falls of Unich'*, 16**
***'Fluted Pillar, Waitomo Caves, Otorohanga'*, 101**
Fox, William (Premier), 57
Fraser, J.L.R., 102
Froude, James, 27, 54

G
Gauguin, Paul, 87
George Valentine, by William Tyree, **13**
***'Giant Buttress, White Terrace.'* 40**, 46, 112
Graham, Mrs., 91
Graham, Robert, 27, 34, 91
Green Lake (*see* Rotokākahi)
Guide Kate (*see* Middlemass, Kate)
Guide Sophia (*see* Hinerangi, Sophia)

H
Hanna, J.R., 51, 100, 102, 107
Haszard, Amelia, 63, 64, 66
Haszard, Charles, 26, 59, 61, 63–64, 66
Haszard, Clara, 26, 61, 63–64, 66
Haszard, Ina, 59, 66
Hawaii
  aims for confederate Pacific kingdom, 86
Hector, Dr. James, 80
Hinemihi, 34, 62
Hinerangi, Sophia (Te Paea), 33–34, **33**, 37, 39, **39**, 45, 54, 59, 61, 62, 64, 71, 81, 104
***'Hot Baths, Pink Terrace'*, 47**
***'House of G.D. Valentine in New Zealand'*, 22**
Huka Falls, 92, 111
Humphreys, Charles, 57–62
Humphreys, Mrs., 59, 61–62, 64
Humphries, Thomas (Government surveyor), 100, 102

I
***'In Nelson Harbour'*, 20**
***'In the Tiki Tapu Bush'*, 32**
***'In the Waitakere Bush'*, 53**

J
Jackson, William Henry, 112
James Valentine & Sons, 12, 15–18, 50, 110
Jervois, Sir William F. D. (Governor-General), 49

K
Kaimiloa, 86
Kaiteriria, 72
Kaiwaka Stream, 37, 39, 72
King Country, 49, 99
***'Koingo, L. Rotomahana'*, 44**
Kotere-Kairamua, 94–95

L
***'Lake Rotorua and Mokoia'*, 28**
Leys, Thomson, 68
'Light from the Dark Room' exhibition (1995), 9
Lundius, Harry, 61, 66

M
McRae's Hotel (*see* Rotomohana Hotel)
McRae, Joseph, 10, **33**, 34, 58–66, **69**, **70**, 71
Mace, Fred, 100
Main, William, 9–10
Makea, Queen of Rarotonga, 88
Malieto'a, King of Samoa, 86
Māori
  and land and colonisation issues, 27, 31, 57, 68, 99–100, 102
  population in 1884, 21
  uses of thermal areas, 25, 31
Martin, Josiah, 9, 109
Maungakakaramea, 72, 74, 95
Middlemass, Kate, 34, 35, 54, 119
Minett, Alfred, 57–60
Moorea (Tahiti), 86, 89
***'Mt. Tarawera from Lake Rotomakariri, showing Rent'*, 75**
***'Mnts. Tarawera and Ruawahia from Te Ariki'*,** 10, 71, **73**
Moura, 37, 62, 64, 66
Mundy, Daniel, 9
Muruika pā, **29**, 31
Muybridge, Eadweard, 17, 112

N
National Galleries of Scotland, 9
Nelson, **20**, 21–23, **22**, **23**, 25, 46, 49, 52
Nelson Evening Mail, 49
New Zealand Herald, 34, 50, 57, 63, 68, 72, 87, 89, 95, 100, 104, 107
  post-eruption article, 72, 74, 78, 80
***'New Zealand Kauri Trees'*, 48**
New Zealand Maori Arts and Crafts Institute, 111
New Zealand, population in 1884, 21, 114
Ngā Mahanga (geyser), **90**, 91, 96
***'Nga Mahanga (The Twins), Wairakei'*, 90**
Ngahuia, Lake, 74
Ngāti Hinemihi, 34
Ngāti Maniapoto, 99
Ngati Rangitihi, 37, 57, 111
Ngāti Taoi Tuhourangi, 37
Ngāti Tu, 72
Ngāti Whakaue, 31

O
Ōhinemutu, **27**, **28**, **29**, **30**, 27–31, 66, 71, 91, 104, 111
***'The Oil Bath, Whakarewarewa'*,** 104, **106**
Okaro, Lake, 74
Ōkoroire, 103
Ōrākei-Korako, 111
O'Sullivan, Timothy, 112
Ōtorohanga, 99–100
Ōtukapuarangi (see Pink Terrace)
Oxford (Tirau), 27, 103

P
Papeete, 86–87
Pareheru, 72, 78, 80
Parnell Congregational Church, 54
photographic techniques (see also Valentine, George D. and subject matter), 9–10
Pink and White Terraces (Ōtukapuarangi and

- Te Tarata), 9, 11, 25, 31, 36–47, 54, 57, 64, 66, 68, 71, 92, 95, 100, 107, 109, 111
  - charging of tourists, 37
- Pink Terrace (Ōtukapuarangi), 37, 39, **42**, **43**, 45, **47**, 57, 58, **67**, 81, 95
  - site of, **67**, 68, 72, 78, 81
- ***'Pink Terrace, L. Rotomahana'*** **(G.V. 29), 42**
- ***'Pink Terrace, L. Rotomahana'*** **(G.V. 34), 43**
- Pohutu Geyser, 104, **105**
- ***'Pohutu Geyser, Whakarewarewa'*, 105**
- Pomare V, King of Tahiti, 86–87
- Pulman, Charles, 9
- Pukeroa pā, 31

Q
- ***'Queen Street, Auckland'*, 56**

R
- ***'Rangatira Maori'*, 8**
- ***'Rangatira Maori and Wahine'*, 6**
- Rarotonga, 83, **85**, 88, 89, **89**
- ***'The Rent in Rotomahana from the Black Crater'*, 76**
- ***'Reform Street, Dundee'*, 19**
- *Richmond* (S.S.), 83–84, 85, 86–89
- Rotokākahi (Green Lake), 31
- Rotomahana, 9, 11, 25, 39, 45–46, 54, 57–58, 64, 66, **67**, 71–72, 78, **79**, 80, 91, 95, 112
  - Black Crater, 78, 80
  - Koho Lake, 78
- ***'Rotomahana from Hape O'Toroa'*, 79**
- Rotomahana Hotel (McRae's Hotel), 10, **33**, 34, 58–64, 66, **69**, **70**, 71, 111
- ***'Rotomahana Hotel, Te Wairoa'*, 33**
- Rotomahana, Lake, 9, 11, 25, 39, **42**, 60, 64, 66, 68, **76**, **79**, 80, 111
  - charging of photographers and artists, 25–26
- ***'Rotomahana, looking to site of Pink Terrace'*, 67**
- Rotomakariri, 72, **75**, **76**
- Rotorua, 31, 63, 64, 66, 72, 103, 107
- Rotorua, Lake, 27, 28, 29, 31, 104
- Rotorua Museum of Art and History Te Whare Taonga o Te Arawa, 111
- Ruawāhia, 37, 73, 78

S
- Samoa, 83–84, **84**, 86, 89
- ***'Samoa. Apia from the Motoutu Creek'*, 84**
- Sewell, H.M. (US Consul to Samoa), 83–84
- Siaosi Tupou, King of Tonga, 84
- Smith, S. Percy (Assistant Surveyor-General), 72, 80–81, 88
- ***'South Crater, the Termination of Rotomahana Rent'*, 77**
- South Seas voyage, 83–89
- Spencer, Charles, 9
- Spencer, Seymour, 34
- Stevenson, Robert Louis, 84
- Stewart, James, 66, 100
- Stowe, Harriet Beecher, 15
- Stubbs, Charles, 58–59
- Sunday Island annexation, 88
- ***'The Sunken Pah, Ohinemutu'*, 29**

T
- Tahiti (Society Islands), **82**, 83, 86–87, **87**, 89
- ***'Tahiti, Orange Loading at Viaroa'*, 87**
- Tamasese, 86
- Tamatekapua, **27**, 31, 66
- Tarawera, Lake, 31, 37, 39, 59, 63, 71
  - phantom canoe, 71
- Tarawera, Mount, 10, 27, 37, 63–64, 68, 72, **73**, **75**, **76**, **77**, **79**, 80, 111
  - eruption of, 10, 57–62, 71
  - aftermath, 63–71
  - loss of lives, 63–64, 66
  - loss of Terraces, 64, 66, 68
- Taupo, 63, 91, 92, 95, **97**
- Te Arawa, 31, 37
- Te Ariki, 10, 37, 62, 64, 66, 71, 78
- Te Keu, Tamihana (Thompson), 26, 34, 39, 45, 64
- *Te Pohara*, 100
- Te Rangipuawhe, Wi Keepa, 26, 34, 57
- Te Takapo, 39
- Te Tarata (*see* Pink and White Terraces)
- Te Wairoa, 10, 26, 31, 31, **33**, 34, 54, 57, 59, 63–64, 66, 68, **69**, **70**, 71–72, 104, 111
- ***'Te Wairoa, McRae's Hotel'*, 70**
- ***'Te Wairoa, McRae's Hotel, Sophia's Whare and Terrace Hotel'*, 69**
- Te Whare Karakia o te Whakapono Tapu (St. Faith's), **28**, 31
- Te Wharekaniwha, Aporo, 10, **33**
- Te Whatapohu, 45
- Te Wherowhero, Potatau (King), 99
- Te Wherowhero, Tawhiao (King), 99
- Terrace Hotel, 34, 57–59, **69**, 71
- Terraces (see Pink Terrace; White Terrace; Pink and White Terraces)
- thermal region, 9, 25–27, **26**, 91–92, 94–96, 103, 111
- Tiawihio (Sophia Hinerangi's husband), 59, 62
- ***'Tiki, Gate of Te Pukeroa Pah, Ohinemutu'*, 30**, 31, 115
- Tikitapu, Lake (Blue Lake), 31, 68
- Tikitapu Bush, 31, **32**, 64, **65**, 71
- ***'Tiki-Tapu Bush, after Eruption'*, 65**
- Tikitere, 31, 91, 95
- Tinorau, Huti, 100
- Tinorau, Tāne, 100
- Tohuringa, 92, 95
- Tonga, 83–84, 86, 89
- Totarariki, 64
- tourism in New Zealand, 25, 27, 54, 57, 104, 111–112
- Trollope, Anthony, 34
- Tūhourangi, 25–26, 37, 57, 64, 66, 71, 111
- Tuhuto, 71
- Tyree, William, 13, 21, 46, 49

U
- 'Uncle Tom' Anti-Slavery envelope, by James Valentine **14**, 15, 113
- Uncle Tom's Cabin, 15
- ***'Upper Falls, Nihotupu'*, 108**, 111

V
- Valentine, Arnot Stirling Valentine, 46, 96, **107**, 109–110, **110**
- Valentine, Easton, 16, 51, 109
- Valentine, George Dobson (1852–1890), 9–18, **13**, **14**, **17**, 21–23, 25, 27, 31, 34, 37, 39, 45–46, **51**, 64, 71–72, 74, 80, 95–96, 99–100, 102–104, **107**, 107, 109, 111–112
  - birth of, 15
  - contribution to New Zealand photography, 112
  - death of, 107, 110
  - correspondence with family, 22–23, 51–52
  - descendants of, 109–110
  - emigrates to New Zealand, 13, 18, 21
  - and health problems, 10, 12, 18, 51–52, 54, 71, 95, 104, 109
  - joins family firm, 16
  - landscape photography in Scotland, 16–18
  - marriage and family life, 12, 16, 95–96
  - moves to Auckland, 49–51
  - and other thermal region photographers, 9
  - photographs as engravings in *Oceana, or England and Her Colonies*, 54
  - photography, commercial aspects, 16–18, 54
  - photography, portraiture, 6, **8**, 16, **17**, 18, 34, **35**, **39**, 112
  - photography, for Queen Victoria, 16–17
  - photography, technical aspects, 9–11, 27, 45–46, 80, 91–92, 95, 102–103, 111–112
  - post-eruption visits to thermal region, 10, 71–72, 74, 78, 80, 91–92, 94–95
  - reputation, 12, 17–18
  - returns to Scotland, 12
  - as Scottish photographer, 9, 12
  - South Seas voyage and photography, 83–84, 86–89
  - visits New Zealand for health, 12, 18
  - visits the Pink and White Terraces, 37
  - visits thermal district, 25–27, 31, 34, 103, 104
  - visits Waitomo caves, 99–102
- Valentine, James (1815–1879, *G.V.'s father*), **14**, 14–16, 113
  - Burritt, Elihu, 15
  - commemorative album for Queen Victoria, 15
  - develops portable darkroom, 16
  - landscape by, **16**
  - opens 'Photographic Portrait Rooms', 15
  - photographer of Royal family, 15–16
  - photography, commercial aspects, 15–16
  - social reformer, 14–15
- Valentine, James (*G.V.'s son*), 16–17, **17**, 21 95–96, **107**, 109, **110**
- Valentine, John, 15, 113
- Valentine, Margaret Rachel, 16–17, **17**
- Valentine, Mary Smith, 16–17, 17, 21, 95, 107, 109
- Valentine, Rachel, 15
- Valentine, William, 15–18
- Valentine, Williamina Arnot Stirling ('Mina', née Smith), 16–17, **17**, 21, **51**, 51–52, 95, 96, **107**, 107, 109, **110**
- Victoria, Queen of England, 15–17
- Vogel, Sir Julius (Premier of New Zealand) 49

W
- Wāhanga, 37, 68
- Waihou River, 103
- Waikānapanapa, 39, 45
- Waikato, 92, 99, 103
- Waiotapu, 74, 91–92, **94**, 94–95, 111
- Wairākei, **90**, 91–92, **93**, 95, 111
- Wairākei Geyser, 95
- Wairākei Terrace, 111
- Wairoa Falls, 34
- Wairoa Valley, 31
- Waitakere, **53**, 54, **55**, 96, 107, **108**, 111
- ***'Waitakere Falls'*, 55**
- Waitomo Caves, 10, **98**, 98–102, **101**, 107, 111
  - European discovery of, 10, 99–100
  - Government obtains for tourism, 102
  - Māori traditional use of, 99–100
- Walmer House, 21–22, **22**
- Warbrick, Alfred, 10, 71, 81, 84
- Warbrick Terrace, 111
- Watkins, Carleton, 112
- Whakarewarewa, 31, 95, 104, **105**, **106**, 111
- Whakataratara, 45
- ***'The Wharf. Papeete, Tahiti'*, 82**
- White Terrace (Te Tarata), **36**, **38**, 39, **39**, **40**, **41**, **44**, 45–46, 68, 81, 95, 100, 111–112
  - site of, 72, 80–81
- ***White Terrace, L. Rotomahana (G.V. 24)*, 36**, 46
- ***'White Terrace, L. Rotomahana' (G.V. 28)*, 38**

Y
- *Yearbook of Photography and Photographic News Almanac*, 91, 96